Economic Imperialism in Theory and Practice

Economic Imperialism in Theory and Practice

The Case of South African Gold Mining Finance 1886–1914

Robert V. Kubicek

Number 45 in a series published for the
Duke University Center for Commonwealth and Comparative Studies
Duke University Press, Durham, N.C.
1979

L.C.C. card no. 78–52488
I.S.B.N. 0–8223–0409–0

Printed in the United States of
America by Kingsport Press, Inc.

For Mila and Brett

Acknowledgments

This book has been in the making for more than a decade. In the interval I have received many forms of selfless assistance and encouragement, though the book's completion necessitated many impositions.

My benefactors include: officials and staffs of companies descended from firms featured in the book, particularly of Barlow Rand Limited, Consolidated Gold Fields of South Africa, and Chartered Consolidated Services Limited; the staffs of the Long Room of the Public Record Office and the Register of Companies; special collections, the Library of the University of British Columbia, particularly Anne Yandle; the Institute of Commonwealth Studies especially the late Trevor Reese; many colleagues at UBC among whom I would especially like to mention Ted Hill, Harvey Mitchell, John Norris, Don Paterson, Margaret Prang and Jim Winter; the Canada Council; the research administration, UBC; and, of course, the Center for Commonwealth and Comparative Studies, Duke University.

I have also received valued advice or criticism from Roger T. Anstey, A. P. Cartwright, John W. Cell, Noel G. Garson, A. S. Kanya-Forstner, Simon Katzenellenbogen, and Shula Marks. Alan Jeeves on more than one occasion has been most generous in sharing his findings and insights. Reynolds Smith has been a most cordial and efficient editor.

I like to think the work was prolonged not only because the criticism of fellow historians required more research and many drafts (they of course bear no responsibility for its errors and omissions), but because I did not entirely neglect obligations to my family, students, and university. But authorship is a selfish act. To all from whom I have received and to all who have allowed me to impose my grateful thanks.

Vancouver, July 1978

R. V. K.

Contents

Maps, Charts, Tables

Economic Imperialism in Theory and Practice

• 1 •

Interpretative Trends and Methodological Problems

This work probes the financial history of South Africa's gold mines with the object of testing various economic theories advanced to explain the great expansion of Europe in the three decades before 1914. The theories selected for examination are: J. A. Hobson's theory of imperialism, the neo-Marxist exposition of capitalist imperialism, and the notion, elaborated by R. Robinson and J. Gallagher and widely applied by D. K. Fieldhouse, of peripheral imperialism. Records left behind by the mines' controllers are the principal evidence used to examine these theories. Although much of this evidence defies systematic analysis, it is sometimes possible, through laborious reworking, to extract from it revealing conclusions. The issues animating the debate on economic imperialism and the nature of the evidence available preclude a sophisticated economic history. Nevertheless, they permit a study of wider and less parochial questions than are usually found in descriptive company history.

A. G. Hopkins provides a notable rationale for and a useful approach to our subject. "There is," he writes, "no lack of opinion . . . about the expatriate firms operating in Africa during the colonial era. These opinions . . . share one dominant trait: they are almost certainly based on inadequate evidence, not merely on matters of detail, but on central and controversial issues." The expatriate companies of the late nineteenth and early twentieth centuries examined here have been scrutinized more than most, and yet they too suffer from the kinds of neglect to which Hopkins alludes. Little attention has been given to such "matters of detail" as "the business strategy of the firms, the structural and administrative changes they experienced, their efficiency in relation to resources employed, their profitability."[1]

It is certainly true, however, that such "central and controversial issues" as the role these companies had "in developing or underdeveloping" South Africa have not been as neglected as the foregoing "matters of detail." Beginning with Hobson's seminal study and continuing with a host of followers, Marxist adapters, and their critics, an immense body of literature on economic imperialism has emerged,[2] in which South Africa's gold mines are prominently featured. But, curiously enough, it has been the political activity and economic impact of the mines' controllers *in* South Africa which has been most studied and for which considerable evidence has been unearthed. As Hopkins points out, such a basic relationship as that "between mineral discoveries and imperial policy has scarcely been explored, despite the long-standing controversy over Hobson's 'surplus' capital thesis."[3] Even more fundamental, the activity of the mines' controllers as a function of European industrialization and capital formation has been very little researched. This oversight seems extraordinary. If imperialism was essentially a function of capitalism as it evolved in Britain specifically or in Europe generally, what better way to document the process than to examine South African gold mining finance in some detail? Hobson made a start. Some of those following after him have questioned the nature and use of his evidence.[4] But neither followers, adapters, nor critics have made the effort to prove or disprove his arguments with better data. If economic imperialism is an important and controversial subject, if

1. A. G. Hopkins, "Imperial Business in Africa, Part I: Sources," *Journal of African History,* XVII (1976), 29.

2. For the essential works see the annotated bibliography in E. R. J. Owen and R. B. Sutcliffe (eds.), *Studies in the Theory of Imperialism* (London, 1972), pp. 331–38; the authors quoted in D. K. Fieldhouse (ed.), *The Theory of Capitalist Imperialism* (London, 1967); and the issues in W. J. Mommsen, "Europäischer Finanzimperialismus Vor 1914: Ein Beitrag Zu Einer Pluralistischen Theorie Des Imperialismus," *Historische Zeitschrift,* CCXXIV (1977), 2–81.

3. A. G. Hopkins, "Imperial Business in Africa, Part II: Interpretations," *Journal of African History* XVII (1976), 278.

4. See D. K. Fieldhouse, "Imperialism: An Historiographical Revision," *Economic History Review,* 2nd ser., XIV (1961), 187–209.

the most celebrated case[5] of the phenomenon before 1914 was the growth of South Africa's gold fields, and if the financial operations connected with that growth have been neglected or obscured, then this study should at least fill a void and contribute to more sophisticated discussion.

1. In the Aftermath of Hobson and Others

A review of historiographical trends in the study of the economics of European empires and an examination of the work done on the gold mines and their controllers will illuminate the points at issue and the lacunae in the published evidence. One of the most plausible models of the expansion of Europe in the late nineteenth century has been constructed by D. K. Fieldhouse.[6] Explanations of the velocity, the intensity, and the other components of European expansion can best be understood, he suggests, by dividing them into two general categories. Those in the first category assert that expansion resulted predominantly from Europe's needs and wishes. Within this Eurocentric literature economic and noneconomic subcategories may be distinguished. The economic arguments have stressed the compelling need of Europe's economies to find places to dump surplus capital or goods or services or the need to export in certain combinations all three of these commodities. Noneconomic explanations of Europe's outward thrusts have fastened upon rivalries among nation states, priorities and perceptions within governments, and the notions and commitments of social classes. But historians, Fieldhouse among them, have in recent years offered in rebuttal a second set of explanations which stress the pull effect of develop-

5. "Nowhere in the world," Hobson wrote, "has there ever existed so concentrated a form of capitalism as that represented by the financial power of the mining houses in South Africa, and nowhere else does that power so completely realise and enforce the need of controlling politics." *The Evolution of Modern Capitalism: A Study of Machine Production* (London, 2nd ed.; 1906), p. 267.

6. *Economics and Empire, 1830–1914* (London, 1973), pp. 3–87. See also *ibid.*, pp. xv–xvi for his rethinking of what he wrote in the article cited in n. 4 above.

ments overseas. According to this view, Europe's contact with other areas of the globe fostered local problems which triggered further metropolitan involvement. In other words, peripheral crises rather than internal stresses impelled Europe to act.

It is simplistic to stress one economic factor to the exclusion of others, or to dismiss noneconomic variables. Though Hobson stressed the central importance of surplus capital, his definition of imperialism allowed for the push effect of trade.[7] And, though economic determinism was fundamental to his understanding of the phenomenon, he offered strategic, military, philanthropic, and other noneconomic drives as causal factors in expansion. Similarly, while V. I. Lenin's explanation of imperialism is fundamentally monistic, he nevertheless observed that "the non-economic super-structure which grows on the basis of finance capital, its politics and its ideology, stimulates the striving for colonial conquest."[8] An explanation which excludes either Eurocentric pushes or peripheral pulls seems to be as inadequate as one that ignores economic factors or noneconomic variables. As Ronald Robinson, a leading exponent of the peripheral approach has observed, "imperialism was as much a function of its victims' collaboration or non-collaboration—of their indigenous politics, as it was of European expansion. The expansive forces generated in industrial Europe had to combine with elements within the agrarian societies of the outer world to make empire at all practicable."[9]

Fieldhouse's own theory is sophisticated but it does give priority to one variable. He concludes that economic factors were present in almost every situation in which European control was formally extended. Among these factors he believes trade patterns

7. "Imperialism," he asserted, "is the endeavour of the great controllers of industry to broaden the channel for the flow of their surplus wealth by seeking foreign markets and foreign investments to take off the goods and capital they cannot sell or use at home." J. A. Hobson, *Imperialism: A Study* (London, 3rd ed.; 1938), p. 85.

8. Quoted in E. Stokes, "Late Nineteenth-Century Colonial Expansion and the Attack on the Theory of Economic Imperialism: A Case of Mistaken Identity?" *Historical Journal,* XII (1969), 292.

9. R. Robinson, "Non-European Foundations of European Imperialism: Sketch for a Theory of Collaboration," in Owen and Sutcliffe, *Imperialism,* p. 118.

to be more pronounced than investment trends, but he maintains that neither trade nor investment factors were so vital to European economies that their governments were impelled by them to react with appropriate annexations. Instead, he asserts, the economic factor operated to create local or peripheral situations which were responded to by governments whose main concerns were to maintain influence and insure stability. The frequency of these interventions at the end of the nineteenth century is, Fieldhouse suggests, attributable to the disruptive effect of the vast disequilibrium in the power relationship between "representatives of the advanced economies of Europe and other less-developed societies."[10] To summarize (but hopefully not to oversimplify Fieldhouse's modified, peripheral approach), imperialism occurred more because its economic components disturbed the world order outside Europe than because the economy of Europe was in trouble. Or Europe expanded *not* so much because it was capitalist but because the less-developed world was *not* industrialized.

The peripheral approach to imperialism contains a large element of economic determinism—a point often missed, for example, in summaries of the work of Robinson and Gallagher[11]—but its determinism is not compatible with either the Hobsonian or neo-Marxist positions. These are much more Eurocentric and stress much more the importance of investment capital. They suggest that in the several decades before 1914 imperialism was the result of new, internal pressures in western European (and North American) society. These pressures were produced by changes in the capitalist and industrial countries which made them need foreign outlets for capital more than they needed markets for manufactured goods and trade routes for shipping. Accumulating capital as an impetus for expansion became more important than unsold goods or redundant technological capacity. Moreover, this expansion, fueled predominantly by investment capital, was more

10. Fieldhouse, *Empire,* p. 476; Cf. D. S. Landes's equilibrium analysis in "Some Thoughts on the Nature of Economic Imperialism," *Journal of Economic History,* XXI (1961), 510–12.

11. See Stokes, "Mistaken Identity," *Mistaken Journal,* XII (1969), 293.

disposed to require territorial acquisitions than informal dependencies, more inclined to be monopolistic than competitive, and more prone to generate armed conflict. Thus, by emphasizing the economic problems and opportunities generated outside the advanced capitalist countries, the peripheralists are basically at odds with Hobson and the Marxists.

But, if there are fundamental differences between Hobsonian and Marxian determinists on the one hand, and the peripheralists on the other, there are also important distinctions between Hobson and the Marxists, as well as among the Marxists themselves. The first distinction to note about Hobson and many of his followers is that they selected the British empire as their special target, while Lenin and his contemporary Marxist colleagues focused upon western Europe. Second, whereas the South African War shaped Hobson's entire understanding of Britain's domestic economy—flawed, as he saw it, by under consumption and an unhealthy preoccupation with overseas possessions—it was World War I that heralded for Lenin the end of advanced capitalism in western Europe. Third, to Hobson "surplus capital" emerged as a compelling impetus to overseas annexation beginning around 1870; to Lenin "monopoly finance capitalism" "did *not* coincide with the scramble for colonies between 1870 and 1900 but came after it."[12] Lenin was not always as precise in his chronology and perhaps he did not need to be. But differences in the structure and needs of the gold mining companies on the eve of the local war in 1899 on the one hand, and at the outbreak of the world conflagration in 1914 on the other, could illuminate strengths or weaknesses in his argument.

Lenin's notion of finance capital was apparently borrowed from Rudolf Hilferding. Hilferding stressed less the availability of capital and emphasized the importance of a particular kind of capital. Banks, on the basis of money acquired from savings of depositors and the reserve capital placed with them by industrial and commercial capitalists, were able to extend huge credit lines

12. *Ibid.*, p. 289.

to finance development. "I call this *bank capital*," wrote Hilferding, "*finance capital.*" This finance capital gave the banks tremendous leverage and fostered the monopolizing of industry.[13] If Lenin found much of Hilferding's exposition on finance capital congenial, the same cannot be said of his reaction to another fellow Marxist's notions on imperialism. Karl Kautsky's assessment "rested on the belief that imperialist rivalry among the leading powers was merely one possibility among others; there might be less dangerous and more profitable solutions—for example, 'the joint exploitation of the world by internationally united finance capital in place of the mutual rivalries of national finance capitals.'" Such a possibility was an anathema to Lenin who "was convinced that imperialism as a world system was fated to go down in a series of shattering wars and revolutions."[14]

2. The Historiography of the Mines

The foregoing reviews the essential points in the debate on economic imperialism before 1914; it remains for us to consider the literature on the classic case of imperialism, the gold mines. In the historiography of the mines and their controllers, at least four distinctive kinds of studies are discernible. One type may be called the sympathetic storyteller, the most familiar of this type being Paul H. Emden who published *Randlords* more than 40 years ago. Others include Theodore Gregory with his introductory chapters in a biography of Ernest Oppenheimer, and J. G. Lockhart and C. M. Woodhouse with their life of Cecil Rhodes.[15]

13. Quoted in Fieldhouse (ed.), *Capitalist Imperialism*, p. 76, "Just as capital in its highest form is transformed into finance capital, so the great capitalist—the finance capitalist—more and more consolidates his disposal of the entire capital of the nation by means of controlling bank capital." *Ibid.*

14. G. Lichtheim, *Imperialism* (New York, 1971), pp. 105–6.

15. T. Gregory, *Ernest Oppenheimer and the Economic Development of Southern Africa* (London, 1962); J. G. Lockhart and C. M. Woodhouse, *Cecil Rhodes: The Colossus of Southern Africa* (New York, 1963).

However, for our purposes the most important storyteller is A. P. Cartwright.[16] His journalistic expertise and his unrivalled access to the archives of the descendants of the companies which founded the gold mines have provided the most credible portraits of the controllers and the best accounts of their business dealings. On both counts they were a varied lot. Moreover, in the formative years of the industry their contrasting or conflicting personalities and financial strategies were important, or so the storytellers assert. But just how were they important? Here the storytellers are not helpful. Though occasionally critical of the wisdom or integrity of certain Randlords, they believe that overall the industry benefited South Africa's as well as Europe's economy. Their defense of capitalism, however, contains sparse quantitative evidence. They do not attempt a comprehensive analysis of the industry, and they are both uncritical and unenlightening on crucial aspects of the mines' performance and organization.

A number of neoclassical economists have been more illuminating on such matters as capital formation and profitability. The most important of these is S. Herbert Frankel who has made perceptive qualitative observations about the industry in its formative years. He has noted, for example, that "French and also German investors were important" as suppliers of the Rand's capital needs.[17] Yet he has not made an attempt to quantify that contribution or explore how it might have shaped the mines' development. This omission is understandable because Frankel has been primarily occupied in studying the industry's performance in the aggregate and in the interwar and contemporary periods. His analysis for the pre–World War I period consequently assumes that developments and practices common to the industry in its later phases were well entrenched in its formative years.

Frankel's calculations of profitability are also of limited use in

16. See his *The Corner House, The Early History of Johannesburg* (Cape Town, 1965); *Gold Paved the Way, The Story of the Gold Fields Group of Companies* (London, 1967); and *Golden Age, The Story of the Industrialization of South Africa and . . . The Corner House Group of Companies, 1910–1967* (Cape Town, 1968).

17. S. H. Frankel, *Capital Investment in Africa, Its Course and Effects* (London, 1938), p. 89.

the discussion of economic imperialism.[18] For example, dividend yields, because of enormous overinflation of share values in the industry's early years, are not very helpful in determining investor profits. Such profits, whatever they might have been, are also of marginal assistance in uncovering initial investment stimulants. Profitability calculations based on dividend yields are also of little help in determining whether economic imperialism paid too little or whether it took too much. For instance, companies whose dividends are modest but which employ "labor at rates lower than would obtain in a free bargaining situation" are by David Landes's definition exploitive.[19] Even companies which operate at a loss but whose activities provide large personal fortunes for their directors, deplete the savings of their shareholders, and disrupt the life of societies in regions where they operate—are these not also exploitive? If, however, aggregate profit calculations are inadequate indicators of company behavior, the same cannot be said of estimates of capital absorbed by the mines. Frankel has provided a sophisticated set of investment estimates which can be effectively employed in the post-Hobsonian debate.[20]

A third group of contributors to that debate is what may be termed the "geopolitical" critics of monistic economic interpretations. These include the "liberal school" of South African historians whose studies have emphasized the contribution of imperial policy to the growth of racism in southern Africa.[21] They are thoroughly familiar with the involvement of the mining magnates in South African politics, especially their participation in the Jameson Raid and the Johannesburg plot. They have, like the storytellers, stressed factors which differentiated among the

18. S. H. Frankel, *Investment and the Return to Equity Capital in the South African Gold Mining Industry, 1887–1965* (Oxford, 1967).

19. Landes, *Journal of Economic History,* XXI (1961), 499. He of course points out that the Marxian definition assumes capitalism by its very nature to be exploitive of labor. Cf. P. A. Baran and P. M. Sweezy, "Notes on the Theory of Imperialism," *Monthly Review,* XVII (March 1966), 16.

20. In addition to his calculations in works cited in n. 17 and n. 18 above, see his "Return to Capital Invested in the Witwatersrand Gold-Mining Industry, 1887–1932," *Economic Journal* (1935), 68–76.

21. Ethnic discrimination and its interconnectedness with economic exploitation in South African history is discussed in H. Adam, *Modernizing Racial Domination: South Africa's Political Dynamics* (Berkeley, 1971), pp. 18–36.

Randlords. However, these historians are not well informed on the capitalists' financial operations. Understandably, they take only a marginal interest in the links between the mines' controllers and European capital sources. Preoccupied with imperial policy, these historians view the noneconomic priorities of government officials, especially of Joseph Chamberlain and Alfred Lord Milner, as crucial catalysts in the confrontation between British imperialism and Afrikaner nationalism. In the count down to war the Rand capitalists became, in the view of a major member of this school, "instruments of British policy. They acted . . . as men under orders, relying on the superior political wisdom of the professional statesmen."[22] The main aim of British policy, this "liberal school" contends, was to reverse a trend of dwindling dominance in an important part of the empire.

This geopolitical argument might be dismissed on theoretical grounds. A Marxist would argue that these historians are so preoccupied with a political superstructure that they ignore its economic base. On the other hand, exponents of peripheral imperialism, do not overlook the economic base and also take a strong geopolitical stance. The leading adherents of the peripheral explanation as it applies to South Africa, Robinson and Gallagher, state:

> It would seem likely that the pressures which impelled the [British] ministry against the [Boer] republic were exerted not by Home, but by British south African opinion. There were economic interests which demanded action; but they were not those of the British economy. They were sections of the south African mining industry and the Cape and Rhodesian trading and railway interests. The British government was too closely tied to these factors not to protect and to promote them locally and commercially. But its purpose in doing so was primarily imperial and political. It had no other means of saving supremacy in south Africa.[23]

This explanation of the origins of the South African War, conceived by its authors as part of "a contribution to the general

22. J. S. Marais, *The Fall of Kruger's Republic* (Oxford, 1961), p. 324.
23. *Africa and the Victorians: The Climax of Imperialism in the Dark Continent* (London, 1961), p. 460; also see W. R. Louis, ed., *Imperialism: The Robinson and Gallagher Controversy* (New York, 1976).

theory of imperialism," is, like the analysis of the "liberal school," largely silent on the dynamics of mining finance and organization. It thus ignores an important part of the evidence.

The most recent revisionist works by those economic determinists who are probing the Randlords' activity do stress mining organization. Geoffrey Blainey has asserted that the Jameson Raid and the Johannesburg plot were the responsibility of a certain sector of the mining magnates—those heavily committed to deep-level mining operations which made them vulnerable to restrictive and corrupt practices of the Transvaal government. Magnates who concentrated upon the more profitable and less risky outcrop mines did not resort to subversive politics. Blainey also claims that Cecil Rhodes organized the plot to overthrow Kruger's government at great risk to his "political power in order to preserve economic power."[24] Blainey has acquired followers, the most prolific of whom is Donald Denoon, who has taken Blainey's argument for the pre-Raid period and shown how it can be used to explain post–Boer War politics. He suggests that a cleavage between the establishment, consisting of the deep-level mining magnates and a dissident group engaged in outcrop work and diamond development, continued to exist during the reconstruction period. The establishment, not the dissenters, cooperated with and dominated the state, with the result that Milner's plans for South Africa were defeated. Milnerism, Denoon concluded, failed not because it was too much influenced by capital but "because of the inability of Milner's Government to placate all necessary magnates."[25]

While Blainey and Denoon stress how crucial episodes in South African history before 1914 were the result of mining magnate interference in the political process, their economic determinism

24. G. Blainey, "Lost Causes of the Jameson Raid," *Economic History Review*, 2nd ser., XVIII (1965), 366.

25. D. J. N. Denoon, "'Capitalist Influence' and the Transvaal Government During the Crown Colony Period, 1900–1906," *Historical Journal*, XI (1968), 331. See also his "The Transvaal Labour Crisis, 1901–6," *Journal of African History*, VII (1967), 481–94; and his *A Grand Illusion: The Failure of Imperial Policy in the Transvaal Colony During the Period of Reconstruction, 1900–1905* (London, 1973).

seems at odds with, or at least is not obviously supportive of, Hobsonian and neo-Marxist argument. What were the Eurocentric pressures which contributed to the magnates' political initiatives? Were in fact different development strategies among the Randlords, rather than monopolistic trends in the gold mining industry, crucial determinants of the magnates' political involvement?

The cleavage among the mining magnates claimed by Blainey and maintained by Denoon is, on closer examination, largely inappropriate to an explanation of the Randlords' behavior. Blainey stressed mining techniques and technology in establishing his two categories of magnates. Although mine development practice needs to be emphasized, it should not obscure crucial financial arrangements and needs. Indeed, Blainey largely ignored the mines' capital structures.[26] The weakness in Denoon's work has been demonstrated by Arthur Mawby. He shows that Denoon's premises are faulty and his evidence suspect. The dichotomy between deep-levelers and outcroppers among the Rand capitalists is "irrelevant and incorrect."[27]

Whatever the differences among the Randlords, these should not obscure the fact that they were able to consult and cooperate. This point is emphasized in a revisionist probe of the political involvement of the Rand magnates during the years between the Raid and the outbreak of the South African War. Alan Jeeves contends that the need to show a united front was reinforced by growing fears of an alliance developing between the Transvaal government and nonmining elements among the large foreign community settled in the midst of the state's Afrikaner population.[28] These nonmining elements included *uitlander* commercial interests in Johannesburg: merchants, wholesale agents, and importers. Fear of this real or imagined alliance, he argues, drove the Randlords into support of that part of the *uitlander* commu-

26. See R. V. Kubicek, "Randlords in 1895: A Reassessment," *Journal of British Studies,* XI (1972), 84–103.

27. A. A. Mawby, "Capital, Government and Politics in the Transvaal, 1900–1907: A Revision and a Reversion," *Historical Journal,* XVII (1974), 415.

28. A. H. Jeeves, "The Rand Capitalists and the Coming of the South African War, 1896–1899," *Canadian Historical Association Papers* (1973), 61–83.

nity (organized into the South African League) which agitated for political reform and which identified with the imperial presence. Some mining leaders "favoured close cooperation with the League and with Milner from an early date." But their fear that the *uitlanders* as a whole might ally with the government against them "was a factor inducing several of the more timid of the capitalists to cooperate closely with the Imperial Government and with the South African League."[29] Caught between growing local hostilities and pressures from the imperial government, the Rand capitalists threw in their lot with Milner. Thus Jeeves, through noting the growth of local commercial interests, adds another economic dimension to the peripheral explanation offered by Robinson and Gallagher while he disputes the relevance of Blainey's argument. Not only was the imperial government on the defensive, so too were the Rand magnates. Jeeves has further argued that both before and after the Boer War the gold mining industry's wasteful, inefficient, and callous use of African workers created labor problems which required state support to alleviate if profits were to be sustained. Though that support was forthcoming, it came from a state upon which the Randlords were dependent rather than from a state which they dominated.[30]

While shortcomings in the theses of Blainey and Denoon have been demonstrated, no "new coherent perspectives" have been substituted for "this vital period in South African history."[31] An-

29. *Ibid.*, p. 79.

30. A. H. Jeeves, "The Control of Migratory Labour on the South African Gold Mines in the Era of Kruger and Milner," *Journal of Southern African Studies*, II (1975), 3–29.

The way in which the mines' controllers used labor, black and white, as opposed to the manner in which they employed capital is itself a subject which neoclassical and neo-Marxist studies have recently significantly illuminated. See especially: F. A. Johnstone, *Class, Race and Gold: A Study of Class Relations and Racial Discrimination in South Africa* (London, 1976); R. Davies, "Mining Capital, The State and Unskilled White Workers in South Africa, 1901–1913," *Journal of Southern African Studies*, III (October 1976), 41–69; P. Richardson, "The Recruiting of Chinese Indentured Labour for the South African Gold-Mines, 1903–1908," *Journal of African History*, XVIII (1977), 85–108; and C. Perrings, "The Production Process, Industrial Labour Strategies and Worker Responses in the Southern African Gold Mining Industry," *ibid.*, 129–35.

31. A. Atmore and S. Marks, "The Imperial Factor in South Africa in the Nineteenth Century: Towards a Reassessment," *Journal of Imperial and Commonwealth History*, III (1974), 139.

thony Atmore and Shula Marks also contend that the Robinson and Gallagher argument has weaknesses. They point out that *Africa and the Victorians* tries to approximate " 'the relative strength of the different drives [towards expansion]' " through one set of exclusive sources, the correspondence and documents left by imperial officials.[32] Though these sources are important, an historical approach which largely excludes other kinds of documentation is, to say the least, inadequate.[33] Neither the revisionist economic determinists, their critics nor the peripheral advocates have used or marshaled evidence that allows for an adequate assessment of those economic pressures developing in Europe which were being funneled into South Africa through the gold mining complex.

3. Some Evidence and Its Uses

The previous discussion of the debate on economic imperialism and of the studies of the South African gold mines demonstrates the need for more rigor in refining categories and for marshaling more evidence. First a definition of what is meant by the mines' controllers. Though sometimes referred to as mine owners, they used mostly other people's capital in promotion and development. They were, then, the men chiefly responsible for raising and allocating capital for and taking profits from such mining activities. One of the most important problems in categorization has to do with the roles and functions assigned them. Are they, for example, to be considered a homogeneous or a heterogeneous lot? Were they European or locally based? Hobson, stressing their power and unity of purpose, referred to them as a small "con-

32. *Ibid.*, p. 130.

33. I have shown elsewhere, for example, how a document in government files supplied by an important representative of the gold mining industry was deliberately misleading, though government officials had no way of knowing it. See R. V. Kubicek, "Finance Capital and South African Goldmining, 1886–1914," *Journal of Imperial and Commonwealth History,* III (May 1975), 386–95.

federacy" or "oligarchy."[34] Others deny that the controllers were cohesive by making, for example, a distinction between "Anglo-Saxons" and "cosmopolitans."[35] Blainey and Denoon differentiate between outcroppers and deep-levelers. Frankel and Gregory point out the fundamental distinction in the industry was the group system whereby several financial houses each controlled and managed a stable of mines.[36]

Whatever the distinctions that should be made among the mines' controllers, it is also essential to clarify their base of operations. Hobson, noting their Eurocentric disposition, called them "international financiers." Robinson and Gallagher imply the controllers were locally based as they were not "of the British economy." Terms such as "Randlords" and "Rand capitalists" also suggest the controllers were locals rather than expatriates. Even referring to the controllers as "financiers" or as "capitalists" may obscure an important part of their function. Several of them brought geological, technological, and managerial expertise to mining development. Should they not then be called entrepreneurs rather than simply financiers or capitalists?[37] On the other hand, were these entrepreneurs themselves dependent upon the backing and initiatives of others who might fit Hilferding's description of bank capitalists? In any event the role and function of the mines' controllers should become clearer if, to use Hopkins's phrase, the "business strategy of the firms" they founded is fully disclosed. The storytellers have revealed important aspects of the financial programs of some of the more visible companies. The neoclassical economists have provided overviews and aggre-

34. J. A. Hobson, *The War in South Africa, Its Causes and Effects* (London, 1900), p. 197, and his *The Evolution of Modern Capitalism* (London, 2nd ed.; 1906), p. 268.

35. J. van der Poel, *The Jameson Raid* (Oxford, 1951), pp. 8, 80.

36. Frankel, *Investment in Africa*, pp. 81–82; and Gregory, *Ernest Oppenheimer*, pp. 15–16.

37. The distinction is prompted by J. P. McKay, *Pioneers for Profit, Foreign Entrepreneurship and Russian Industrialization, 1885–1913* (Chicago, 1970), pp. 16–17. Also see D. G. Paterson, "European Financial Capital and British Columbia: An Essay on the Role of the Regional Entrepreneur," *B. C. Studies* (Spring 1974), 33–47.

gate estimates of performance. But the strategies of the firms of several important entrepreneurs—how they developed or speculated with claim holdings, how they obtained and employed capital, and how they took and used profits—have not been established.

The most glaring gap in the literature is the absence of a full-scale study of capital formation. Perhaps the difficulties inherent in the task—lack of readily usable data and problems of terminology—explain the hiatus. Despite the fact that the gold mining industry generated a great deal of published information in its formative years, it was very secretive or misleading about how it was financed. In the works of C. S. Goldmann, the annual mining manuals of R. R. Mabson, and the reports of the Transvaal Chamber of Mines, statements of "nominal," "authorized" and "issued" capital abound. The market value of share capital is also easily discovered. This information, however, does not reveal with any precision how much capital was put into mining shares and debentures or how much of this capital actually went into mining. We are here faced with "the familiar problem of not being able to produce a wholly reliable, modern, aggregative statistical series by totalling up whatever individual statistics may have been recorded without obligation, or responsibility, or aggregative intent, in an earlier age."[38] Despite the difficulties inherent in the task, Frankel has produced aggregative series which are very useful. But they must be used with caution, especially for the years before the South African War. Many flotations in the formative years were short-lived or provided little information about their capitalization. Capital represented by vendor shares was often enormously overvalued. Furthermore, Frankel's estimates are of little validity if used in isolation from series for other European investments abroad. However, used carefully and compared with other components of foreign and colonial investment, Frankel's series can be most revealing of the dynamics of gold mining finance.

38. J. H. Drabble and P. J. Drake, "More on the Financing of Malayan Rubber, 1905–23," *Economic History Review*, 2nd ser., XXVIII (1974), 108–20.

Any study of European overseas investment must take into account Rondo Cameron's admonitions. "The export of capital in the nineteenth century," he warns, "cannot be measured. . . . All that one can do is to estimate historical flows of capital on the basis of usually incomplete and highly imperfect evidence. . . . The most one can expect is a fair approximation, not absolute precision."[39] In this study a number of "fair approximations" have been derived from unpublished records left by the gold mining entrepreneurs.

Cameron also makes a set of distinctions by which to determine what "flows of capital" one should attempt to approximate, or at least describe,[40] and four of these capital flow patterns are important to this work. The first is capital poured into the industry from the personal sources of its founders. A second is the capital siphoned from the industry by its controllers for their personal fortunes or their other business activities. A third is the capital pumped into gold mining by European investors distinguished, where possible, by nationality, location, and socioeconomic status. This type of capital allocation may sometimes be called portfolio investment to indicate that it is "small, or fragmented, or passive," and that it is controlled by local management. Direct European investment, as distinct from portfolio investment, is large, concentrated, and presupposes effective foreign or metropolitan control. The "line between active foreign direction and passive portfolio participation is often unclear"[41] but, for purposes of analyzing gold mining finance the distinction is useful to make. A fourth flow pattern which needs to be mentioned is capital raised by the industry's financial operations but which did not leave Europe. In a strict sense capital spent upon mining equipment manufactured in Europe was not "exported" to or invested in South Africa. Also very substantial amounts of capital were accumulated and transferred by stock market operations in mining shares but were never put into the mining

39. R. E. Cameron, *France and the Economic Development of Europe, 1800–1914* (Princeton, N.J., 1961), p. 71.
40. *Ibid.*, pp. 71–82.
41. McKay, *Pioneers for Profit*, p. 13.

companies. Nevertheless, for purposes of gauging Eurocentric pressures in a case study of economic imperialism, capital flows confined to Europe but connected to overseas activity must be recognized and if possible approximated.

If the economic function, as well as the political role, of the mines' controllers are established, and the capital formation connected with the gold industry's growth is approximated, then a case study adequate to the task at hand should result. That task, attempted in the conclusion, will be to determine how compatible the South African case is with the theories of economic imperialism.

• 2 •

Patterns and Structures of International Finance

Neoclassical economists and economic historians define problems and conduct research with little reference to the concerns which animate the discussion of economic imperialism.[1] Yet their work of recent years on the dynamics and performance of the advanced economies of Europe before 1914 is not without relevance to this discussion. Data they have provided, though not entirely satisfactory, are much less crude than what were available to the critics of empire at the turn of the century. They have also struggled with such questions as whether or not capital exports debilitated domestic development, depressed wage rates, or yielded large profits. Answers to these questions are important to the understanding of the dynamics of European overseas activity. What follows is an attempt to use recent studies by neoclassical scholars to isolate the financial trends and structures inherent in the capitalist economies to which gold mining finance might be particularly sensitive or intimately related.

1. The Volume and Direction of Capital Flow

From its inception in 1886 to the end of 1913, the last full year of production before World War I, the Witwatersrand gold min-

1. For an exception to this trend see M. Simon, "The Pattern of New British Portfolio Foreign Investment, 1865–1914," in J. H. Adler (ed.), *Capital Movements and Economic Development* (London, 1967), pp. 44–45; reprinted in A. R. Hall (ed.), *The Export of Capital From Britain* (London, 1968). However, Simon was imprecise in categorizing capital flows by political status. It is not clear, for example, whether he considered the Transvaal before 1899 independent, dependent, or part of an informal empire. Thus, his analysis is not as specifically directed as it might have been to points at issue in the debate on economic imperialism.

ing industry absorbed between £ 116 and 134 million in equity and loan capital.[2] The volume of the flow of European financial capital abroad cannot be established with any confidence, but crude estimates have been made. The stock of British overseas investment by 1914 amounted to approximately £ 4 billion, French claims abroad to about £ 2 billion, and German foreign securities to £ 1 billion.[3] Much of this capital had been invested on the continent: "In 1913 some 60 per cent of outstanding French foreign long-term investments and half of the German, were still in Europe."[4] About £ 1 billion had financed American development.[5] Thus the amount of capital which was raised for Europe's overseas formal and informal empires before 1914 was considerably less than the £ 7 billion it invested. It was likely more in the order of £ 3 billion.[6] These estimates allow some order of magnitude to be imposed on the volume of capital invested in South Africa's gold mines. They suggest that about 4 percent of the capital that the major western European countries exported overseas to dependencies and spheres of influence before 1914 went to finance the mines. While gold mine investment may thus appear small, it was not insignificant when set on side illuminating indicators of other overseas capital flows during 1886–1913. For example, as Chart 2.1 illustrates, British security issues for Argentina (public and private) in the period were £ 239 million; private new issues for Canada amounted to £ 170 million; new issues for Australian mines totalled £ 43 million and new direct investment in Canadian mines £ 35 million. In the 28 years before World War I, South Africa's gold mines may have drawn from Europe's premier capital markets three times as

2. Calculated from Frankel, *Investment in Gold Mining,* Appendix D, Tables 1 and 6, pp. 116, 121.

3. P. L. Cottrell, *British Overseas Investment in the Nineteenth Century* (London, 1975), pp. 13–15; Cameron, *France and Europe,* pp. 64, 486–87, 533–34; and W. G. Hoffmann, *Das Wachstum der Deutschen Wirtschaft seit der Mitte des 19. Jahrhunderts* (Berlin, 1965), p. 262.

Estimates in francs or marks have been converted to pounds to facilitate comparisons.

4. A. I. Bloomfield, *Patterns of Fluctuation in International Investment Before 1914* (Princeton, 1968), p. 3.

5. Simon, *Capital Movements,* p. 44, n. 1.

6. Cf. Bloomfield, *Patterns of Investment,* pp. 2–3.

Chart 2.1. *Select Elements in European Overseas Investment, 1885–1913*

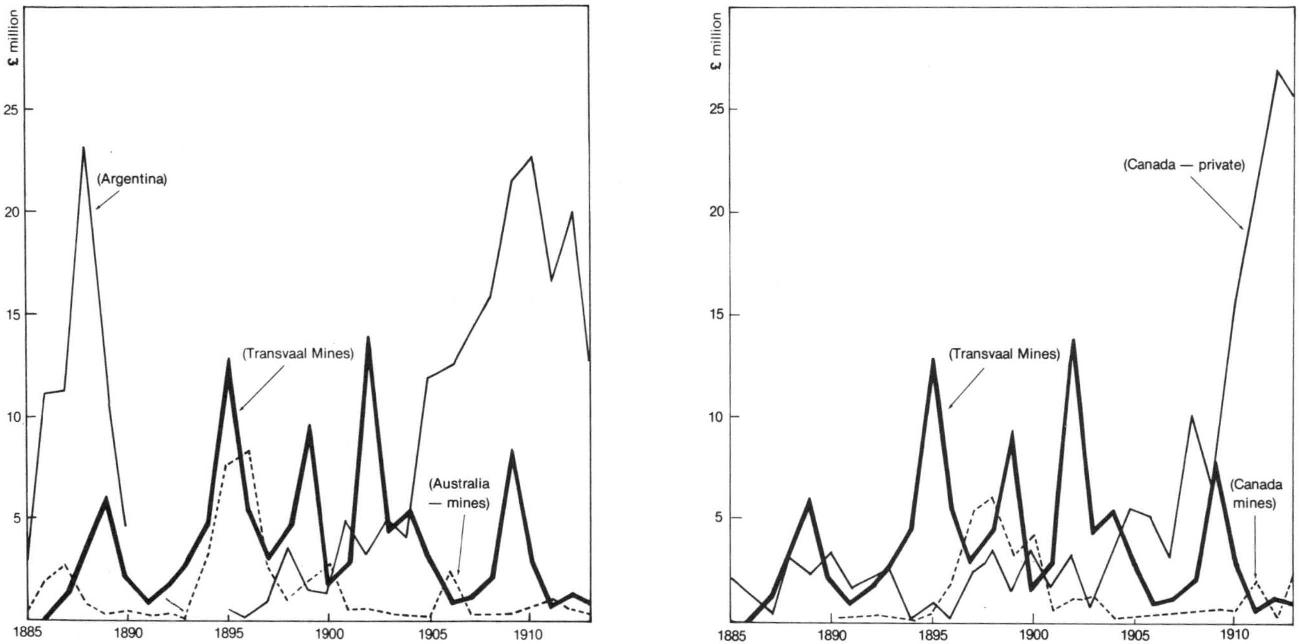

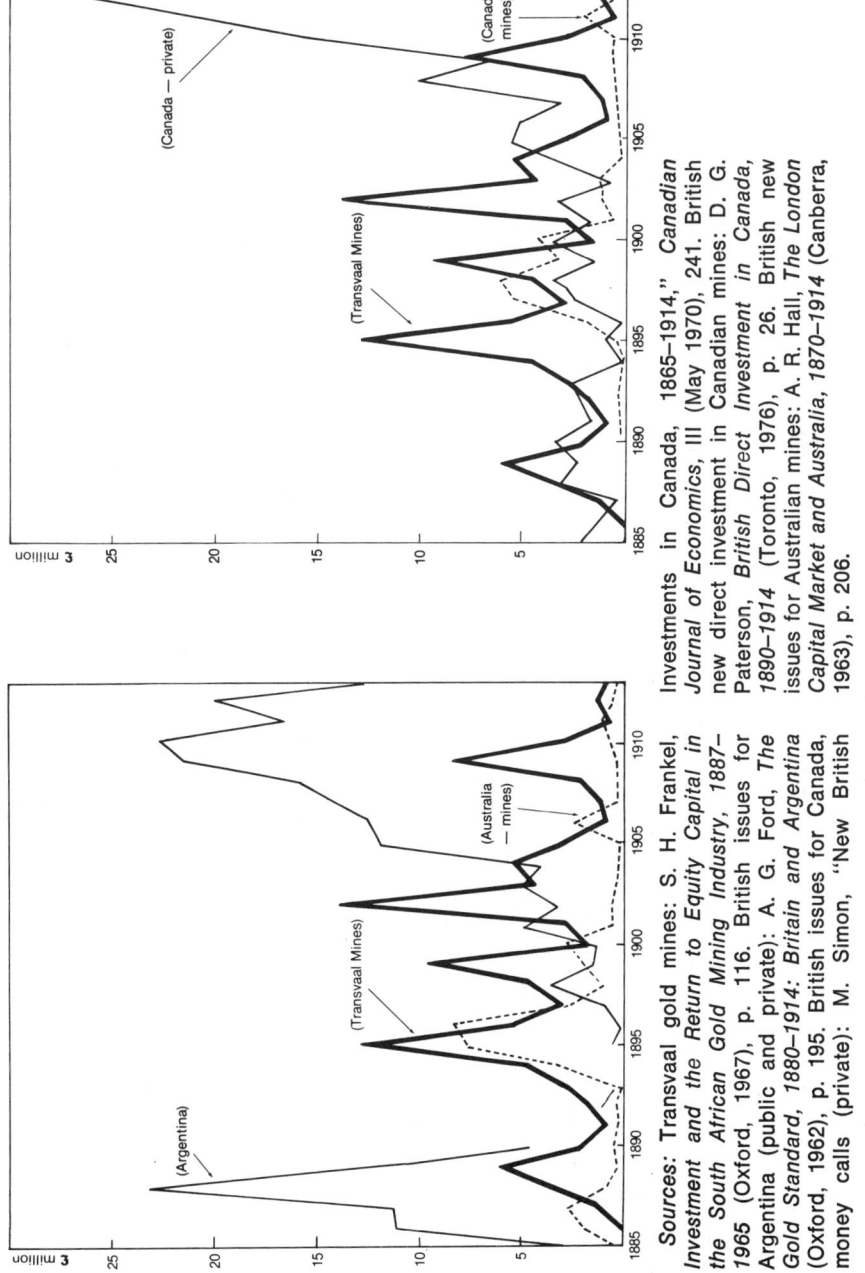

Sources: Transvaal gold mines: S. H. Frankel, *Investment and the Return to Equity Capital in the South African Gold Mining Industry, 1887–1965* (Oxford, 1967), p. 116. British issues for Argentina (public and private): A. G. Ford, *The Gold Standard, 1880–1914: Britain and Argentina* (Oxford, 1962), p. 195. British issues for Canada, money calls (private): M. Simon, "New British Investments in Canada, 1865–1914," *Canadian Journal of Economics,* III (May 1970), 241. British new direct investment in Canadian mines: D. G. Paterson, *British Direct Investment in Canada, 1890–1914* (Toronto, 1976), p. 26. British new issues for Australian mines: A. R. Hall, *The London Capital Market and Australia, 1870–1914* (Canberra, 1963), p. 206.

Chart 2.2. ***Transvaal Gold Mines: Capital Investment, 1887–1913***

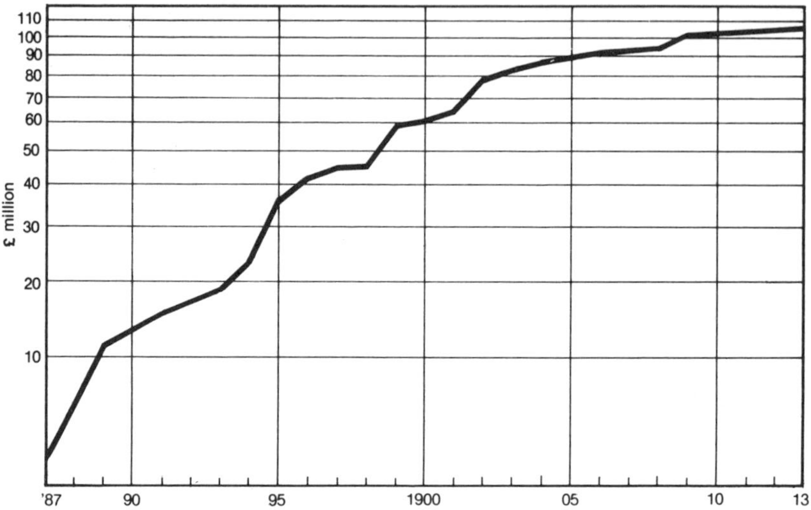

Source: S. H. Frankel, *Investment and the Return to Equity Capital in the South African Gold Mining Industry 1887–1965* (Oxford, 1967), p. 116.

much financial backing as all Australian or Canadian mining activity, almost as much as Canada's private sector and about half of what Argentina's public and private sectors raised.[7]

As Chart 2.1 indicates the Transvaal mines absorbed much of their share capital in five brief spurts: in 1888–89, 1895, 1899, 1902–3 and 1908–9. Chart 2.2 shows that the annual amount absorbed in the years before the Anglo-Boer War was higher than for the years after it. For example, between 1887 and 1898 the annual average was £ 3.9 million; between 1902 and 1913 it was £ 2.5 million. What, if any, was the coincidence between this gold mining investment pattern and fluctuations and trends in the general flow of European capital abroad? Pronounced fluctuations in capital flow may be illustrated through the behavior

7. The mines also absorbed about 60 percent as much European capital as all of Russia's private corporations and banks which received about £ 208 million during 1886–1913. Calculated from McKay, *Foreign Entrepreneurship*, pp. 26–27.
For European investment in Japan see D. S. Landes, "Japan and Europe: Contrasts in Industrialization," in W. W. Lockwood (ed.), *The State and Economic Enterprise in Japan* (Princeton, 1965), pp. 93–100.

of Europe's major stock exchanges. They helped to raise much of this capital. Not infrequently stock markets underwent periods of extraordinary expansion and contraction. Not surprisingly the periodicity and intensity of these fluctuations in the markets of London, Paris, and Berlin were closely interrelated and, with minor leads or lags, moved together. During the period 1887–1913 "major contractions and speculative crashes occurred simultaneously on all European exchanges" in 1889–90, 1895, 1907 and 1912.[8] In addition to the major breaks another of lesser magnitude occurred in 1904. Most of these panics, in which investors sold masses of securities in the firm belief that liquidity of assets was more important than expected capital losses, occurred toward the crest of an expansionary movement. The first, that of 1889–90, was so timed. It began in Paris in early 1889 with the failure of a major French bank involved in abortive attempts to corner the market in copper. It was intensified by the crash of the Panama Canal Company and, in the following year, by the drop in Argentine securities which forced the Baring crisis. The second stock market bust, that of 1895, also followed a boom and also began in Paris. It was initiated by overspeculation in mining shares, especially Rand scrip. Subsequently, in 1904 rumors of an outbreak of war between Russia and Japan prompted another panic which was more intense in Berlin and Paris than in London. Usually American stock market movements had minimal impact on the European exchanges. But a break in New York in 1907 induced panics in Paris and Berlin and a slump in London. Again these contractions had followed rising trends in market values. Forced sales of securities in 1912 also followed an expansionary period. This panic struck Berlin and Paris harder than London and was caused by the outbreak of the Balkan War.[9]

Gold mining financial practice, as shown in subsequent chap-

8. O. Morgenstern, *International Financial Transactions and Business Cycles* (Princeton, 1959), p. 526.

9. *Ibid.*, pp. 546–47, 574–80; A. R. Hall, *The London Capital Market and Australia, 1870–1914* (Canberra, 1963), pp. 157–85; and R. Goffin, "Les Valeurs Mobilières en France à la fin du XIXe et au début du XXe Siècle," in C. Morrisson and R. Goffin, *Questions financières aux XVIIIe et XIXe siècles* (Paris, 1967), pp. 126–31.

ters, largely induced the contraction of 1895. But mining share activity did not always coincide precisely with European stock exchange fluctuations, nor was the connection so direct even when it did. To be sure "Kaffir market" fluctuations often paralleled general market activity as Chart 2.3 suggests. Peaks followed by panics in 1889–90 and 1895, the crash of 1907, and the slump of 1912 were apparent in both markets. But gold mining investment in 1899 and 1902–3 suffered much sharper reverses and did not share in the investment surge before the crash of 1907. Obviously the Anglo-Boer War had a greater impact on the price and marketability of gold shares than other securities. Other differences between general market and "Kaffir market" fluctuations can be observed. The panic in gold shares in 1890 was more the consequence of a setback in gold mining production than the result of the general market contraction. The decline in gold shares which started in 1895 persisted into the following year though most market values recovered.[10] Thus, capital obtained from gold share issues was sometimes conditioned by developments to which general market activity was not as sensitive. These influences originated within the gold mining industry or were outgrowths of South African affairs. But more often than not the finance of gold mining development reflected market conditions which were the result of events remote from the industry.

While short-term capital inflows the gold mining industry received were frequently in phase with general stock exchange fluctuations, was there a similar coincidence in long-term trends? As previously noted the trend in gold mining finance over the 28-year period to 1913 featured two distinct phases. More capital and at a greater rate was put into the industry before the Anglo-Boer War than after it. Indeed, if we exclude the flurry of investment in 1902, occasioned by anticipation of the rapid recovery at the end of the war, the decline in investment during the second phase is very pronounced. From 1903 to 1913 only £ 30.3 million were invested as compared to £ 53 million between 1889 and 1899.[11]

10. See chaps. iii and iv, this volume.
11. Calculated from Frankel, *Investment in Gold Mining*, p. 116.

Chart 2.3. *Fluctuations in Investment Abroad, 1885–1913*

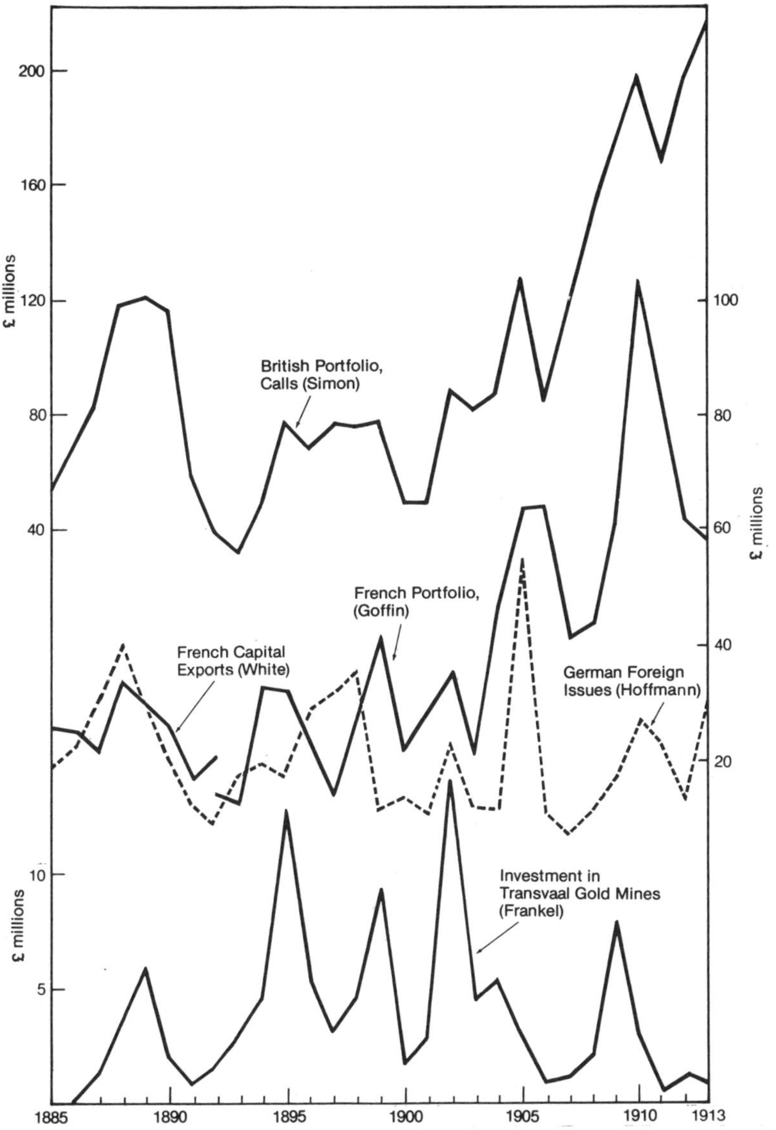

Sources: M. Simon, "The Pattern of New British Portfolio Foreign Investment, 1865–1914," in J. H. Adler and P. W. Kuznets (eds.) *Capital Movements and Economic Development* (New York, 1967), pp. 52–53. H. D. White, *The French International Accounts, 1880–1913* (Cambridge, Mass.: 1933), p. 122. R. Goffin, "Les Valeurs mobilères en France à la fin du XIXe et au début du XXe siècle," in C. Morrisson and R. Goffin, *Questions financières aux XVIIIe et XIXe siècles* (Paris, 1967), p. 131. W. G. Hoffman, *Das Wachstum der Deutschen Wirtschaft seit der Mitte des 19. Jahrhunderts* (Berlin, 1965), p. 262. S. H. Frankel, *Investment and the Return to Equity Capital in the South African Gold Mining Industry, 1887–1965* (Oxford, 1967), p. 116.

Three possible explanations for this decline may be offered. First, the industry in its postwar development phase did not require or actively seek as much capital. Second, it sought more capital but investors' portfolios would not absorb many more such issues. Third, investors may have preferred to send capital elsewhere in anticipation of higher returns. The industry's strategies will be established in subsequent analysis. Here we want to determine if the long-term trends in investment abroad coincided with the industry's long-term absorption pattern. Share market activity and investment trends generally during the period 1886–1913 featured two long waves, one cresting at its very beginning in 1889–90, the second at its end in 1912–13. The lowest ebb in the interval cannot be so precisely determined but roughly coincided with the turn of the century.[12] The "Kaffir market" and gold mining investment flows were more or less in sequence with the first crest and the lowest ebb. But they did not share in the second crest.

The remarkable surge in foreign and colonial investment in the decade before World War I that shows up in aggregate estimates and which is illustrated in Charts 2.1 and 2.3 is corroborated and amplified by a number of examples. British investment in American railways which reached at least £ 400 million by 1898 was to witness its biggest increases after 1904.[13] Russia's mines and metallurgical industries, though they had absorbed large amounts of European capital during 1893–1900, obtained new major infusions starting in 1909.[14] Interest in Malayan rubber shares started in 1904 and peaked in 1910.[15] Direct British investment in Canada, which had crested in 1897 almost solely as a consequence of a mining boom, peaked again in 1912 during a flurry of investment which went into a range of business activity in-

12. Cf. Chart 2.3; Cottrell, *British Investment*, pp. 35–40; Simon, *Capital Movements*, p. 48; and Goffin, *Questions financières*, p. 119.

13. D. R. Adler; M. E. Hidy (ed.), *British Investment in American Railways, 1834–1898* (Charlottesville, Va., 1970), p. 169. For estimates of German investment in American securities, £ 31–41 million in 1898, see *ibid.*, p. 191.

14. McKay, *Foreign Entrepreneurship*, pp. 26–27.

15. R. T. Stillson, "The Financing of Malayan Rubber, 1905–1923," *Economic History Review*, 2nd ser., XXIV (November 1971), 590.

cluding manufacturing.[16] The private and public sectors in Argentina raised £ 180 million in new issues between 1900 and 1914 of which 60 percent went for railway development.[17] The predominant element in the surge was private borrowing for social overhead (especially railways) and extractive industry (particularly mining) for areas of the globe whose infrastructures were already partly developed.[18] Thus, at a time when capital inputs in the gold mining industry of South Africa were falling off, Europe was exporting large amounts of capital to developing countries for purposes similar to South Africa's needs. Therefore, a lack of capital for investment abroad was not the reason why capital placements in the gold mines declined after the turn of the century.

2. Clients of the Capital Market

Several explanations for the availability of capital for export have been offered. These include the lethargy of domestic industry and its unwillingness, as in the case of French industry, to compete for financing in the capital market.[19] It is also argued that domestic investment was unattractive as in the case of Britain where Consols, real estate and, after 1900, railways offered declining yields.[20] Perhaps reinvestment of profits previously made abroad were significant. Whatever the reasons the increase in the volume of capital for export might have occurred as the income of Europe increased and was dispersed in the hands of more and more investors. Or was it concentrated in the portfolios of a more or less static number? It has been calculated that the real income of Britain's wage earners increased significantly

16. D. G. Paterson, *British Direct Investment in Canada, 1890–1914* (Toronto, 1976), pp. 25–26.
17. A. G. Ford, *The Gold Standard 1880–1914, Britain and Argentina* (Oxford, 1962), p. 155.
18. Cf. Simon, *Capital Movements*, p. 49.
19. Goffin, *Questions financières*, p. 137.
20. B. Supple, *The Royal Exchange Assurance, A History of British Insurance, 1720–1970* (Cambridge, 1970), pp. 341–48; and R. J. Irving, "British Railway Investment and Innovation, 1900–1914," *Business History*, XIII (1971), 39–63.

in the 1870s and 1880s but began to decline in the early 1890s. Thus, it is suggested that in Britain the per capita increase in income during our period (1886–1914) was greater for the investing classes or "went to the owners of capital."[21] In France and Germany "a significant increase in the share of income" apparently went to "salaried employees and wage-earners combined."[22] But inflation eroded some of the workers' gains in Germany, and the salaried employees obtained much of this increase in France.[23] Europe's bourgeoisie, possessed of "multitudinous shadings of income, origin, education and way of life," their ranks supplemented by absorptions from the working classes, and strongly committed to upward mobility,[24] did acquire more and more savings. During our period increasing numbers of the bourgeoisie became small-scale investors with the resources and ambitions that left them not satisfied to hoard or leave savings in banks, and not content with declining yields from property investment. Many, familiarized with what it had to offer by the financial press, were attracted to the stock exchange. The result was that the number of shareholders in public companies increased and the average amount of securities held decreased. Nonetheless, the great bulk of investment securities still remained in 1913 in the hands of a very small and very wealthy sector of the middle class made up of an elite group of merchants, industrialists, professionals, and rentiers. In Britain, for example, "in 1913 only about 2% of the value of stocks, shares, and other securities dealt in on the Stock Exchange belonged to those whose property was worth less than £ 1000, and only 10% to those whose property did not exceed £ 5000." Though there was some appreciable

21. S. Pollard and D. W. Crossley, *The Wealth of Britain, 1085–1966* (London, 1968), p. 235. Owners of capital obtained this increase "not because they earned more on their investments but because they had more of them, while the wage earners failed to benefit from increasing production." *Ibid.*, p. 236.

22. D. S. Landes, *The Unbound Prometheus: Technological Change and Industrial Development in Western Europe from 1750 to the Present* (Cambridge, 1969), p. 242, n. 1.

23. K. D. Barkin, *The Controversy Over German Industrialization*, 1890–1902 (Chicago, 1970), pp. 268–70; A. Daumard, *et al.*, *Les Fortunes françaises au XIXe siècle* (Paris, 1973), p. 589.

24. Landes, *Unbound Prometheus*, p. 9.

dispersion of accumulating wealth among Europe's middle classes and this was reflected in a larger and more diverse group of investors, there seems little doubt that very wealthy investors continued to own "the bulk of the capital" and to direct "the flow of investment."[25] We will have occasion to discover if this general trend in investor profiles was characteristic of the shareholders in South Africa's gold mines.

3. Market Organization and Practice

The volume of investment capital channeled through the capital markets of Europe increased, its geographical and sectoral distributions changed, and its sources altered. The markets themselves changed as the mechanism linking borrower and lender changed. What has been described as the "primary market"[26] featured numerous issuing institutions which dealt or even specialized in foreign and colonial securities. The most famous in our period were Europe's merchant banks. They sometimes joined together so as to be more able to compete and spread the risk in underwriting large issues. The bond issues of the Austro-Hungarian government were handled, for example, by a syndicate organized through the Rothschilds of Vienna, Paris, and London which also included such German merchant banks as S. Bleichröder and Sal. Oppenheim, Jr., and even corporate banks like the Disconto–Gesellschaft.[27] Merchant banks were usually known for their caution, but the well-known overcommitments of Baring Brothers and the Rothschild involvement in volatile South African mining finance indicate that some were prepared to take considerable risks.

The merchant banks notwithstanding, it was the new corporate investment banks of France and Germany and the invest-

25. A. K. Cairncross, *Home and Foreign Investment, 1870–1913: Studies in Capital Accumulation* (Cambridge, 1953), pp. 85–86, 223–25.

26. Cottrell, *British Investment*, p. 34; see also M. de Cecco, *Money and Empire: The International Gold Standard, 1890–1914* (Oxford, 1974), pp. 103–10.

27. J. Riesser, *The German Great Banks and Their Concentration* (Washington, 1911) p. 421.

ment trusts of Britain which in the late 19th century became the important intermediaries. France at mid-century pioneered the corporate investment bank. As these banks became more numerous and specialized, they also became more powerful. France's great corporate banks—the Crédit Lyonnais, the Comptoir d'Escompte, and the Société Générale—may have deemphasized their investment function by the turn of the century, but the Crédit Lyonnais particularly continued to be "highly successful in placing large blocks of the most varied types of securities." At the same time several "institutions designed specifically to exploit economic opportunities in foreign countries" emerged. Chief among them was the Banque de Paris et des Pays-Bas.[28] All these banks financed "the carrying of securities on the Bourse in Paris, partly to facilitate speculation in those securities in which they [were] interested." They even "lent a considerable amount of capital on the Berlin Bourse."[29] Germany's major banks were more committed to their country's industrial development than their French counterparts, but they too were "closely associated with the promotion of foreign investment."[30] The financial leverage these banks possessed is indicated by the fact that Germany's major six banks, the Deutsche, the Dresdner, the Disconto-Gesellschaft, the Darmstadt, the Schaafhausen and the Handels-Gesellschaft possessed capital and reserve in excess of £ 125 million in 1908.[31] They spread risk through joint ventures which included direct involvement in the formation and financing of industrial companies. They were even "reproached for their practice of 'pumping' funds entrusted to them too exclusively into industry and trade and into the Bourse."[32] In contrast to

28. Cameron, *France and Europe*, pp. 195–97.

29. R. J. Lemoine, "The Banking System of France," in H. P. Willis and B. H. Beckhart (eds.), *Foreign Banking Systems* (New York, 1929), p. 577.

30. W. O. Henderson, *The Rise of German Industrial Power* (Berkeley, 1975), p. 184.

31. *Ibid.*, p. 183. These banks in 1913 had loans in the money market raised on the deposit of stock exchange securities totalling some £ 35 million. Derived from P. B. Whale, *Joint Stock Banking in Germany* (London, 1930), pp. 340–53.

32. P. Quittner, "The Banking System of Germany," in Willis and Beckhart, *Foreign Banking*, p. 704.

banks on the continent, Britain's joint stock banks were not adventurous investment banks. But faced with declining yields on Consols, their preferred investment stock, these banks along with British insurance companies did venture further afield by taking up substantial amounts of foreign and colonial government securities.[33] Neither were prepared to try high-risk mining shares, but the banks did lend substantial amounts of short-term funds to stock market operators.[34]

The intermediary in Britain which assumed the role which joint-stock banks and insurance companies were reluctant to play was the investment trust. It is particularly significant for our purposes because such institutions became essential vehicles for the financing of South Africa's gold mines. These trusts evolved in the latter half of the nineteenth century by catering to the growing numbers of small investors, by offering to spread risks, and by promising yields higher than gilt-edged securities. By the late 1880s they not only carried various stocks but also promoted companies and underwrote share issues. Those which launched or took up interests in companies that required long development periods and large capital infusions before they produced profits could attract the impatient investor by promising him an immediate return on his capital from dividends obtained through investments in established firms. Many trusts were fraudulent or ill-managed. Many also had a "bias in favour of higher yielding oversea securities."[35] Thus, investment trusts, though they often claimed to be safe places for capital were, in fact, high-risk ventures.

What has been called the secondary market, that is, the stock exchange, which was primarily concerned with stocks and shares already issued, did little to ameliorate risk. On the contrary, this intermediary often served to accentuate it, both through inefficiency and abuse. Under relaxed entry requirements, member-

33. C. A. E. Goodhart, *The Business of Banking, 1891–1914* (London, 1972), pp. 127–41; and Supple, *British Insurance*, pp. 341–48.
34. Riesser, *German Banks*, p. 556.
35. Hall, *London and Australia*, p. 56.

ship in the London stock exchange increased from more than 2000 in the late 1870s to a peak of 5567 in 1905.[36] It leveled off to something under 5200 thereafter. At the same time the volume of securities handled was facilitated by the establishment of a clearing house for bargains. It was operative by 1885 but not always effective, as in 1895 when it failed to cope with the volume of speculative transactions. In London, and particularly in Paris where membership in the Bourse was strictly limited, outside or curb markets flourished. The continued existence of informal stock markets suggests that the official exchanges did not respond as effectively as they might have to investment pressures. Neither did they make a concerted attempt to prevent abuses. Government restrictions placed on company formation or on the type of shares that could be quoted and the kind of company which could be listed, rather than self-policing measures implemented by the exchanges, provided what little protection there was for the unwary investor. He could be fleeced on the official as well as the unofficial exchanges by the wares of bogus companies. "Before 1914 the [London Stock] Exchange made no attempt to restrict or control in any way the right to deal in any security, whether British or foreign. . . . It was in general more concerned with arrangements to ensure a reasonable free market in the securities than with the intrinsic merits of the company or with the adequacy or accuracy of the information provided."[37] But even the existence of a free market was not assured. Market operators cooperated with promoters and issuing houses to inflate the price of securities by using the premium dodge. Under this arrangement "it was usual for the issuing house to arrange with jobbers at what quotations dealing should commence, and to create an appearance of market activity. . . . One broker might be sent in to buy, and another to sell simultaneously, or the jobbers might be given the right to buy from, or to sell to, the underwriters at a certain price, so that they could rig the market

36. E. V. Morgan and W. A. Thomas, *The Stock Exchange: Its History and Functions* (London, 1962), p. 140.

37. F. W. Paish, "The London New Issue Market," *Economica*, XVIII (1951), 4.

without fear of being landed with stock. Dealing began before allotment, usually at a premium."[38] Distinctions were not maintained between brokers who bought and sold shares for the public and jobbers who made up prices and who were supposed to transact business only with brokers and not directly with the public. Brokers did, in fact, engage in making up prices, if not on the official exchange, then on the street. Jobbers did deal directly with the public. Such practices also restricted free market operations and allowed "low company promoters and camp followers of the financial army to market wares which [could not] bear inspection."[39] The Berlin Bourse was not allowed to quote the securities of companies which had not established assets and yielded profits. Foreign companies with shares of small denomination were seldom permitted a listing in Paris. But the continental investor had easy access not only to the curb market in Paris but the largely unregulated official exchange in London. The stock exchanges supplied a service for borrowers and lenders. But it is also clear that stock market operators were self serving. They collaborated with borrowers at some expense to lenders, rigged or took advantage of share price movements through operations on the unofficial markets, and used information to speculate in share transactions for their own accounts. Under minimal restraint, not given much to innovation, but strategically placed as intermediaries on investment conduits, stock market operators in London and Paris fostered a good deal of inefficient capital allocation.

Inefficiency and abuse were no more apparent than in the mining market sector of the London exchange. We will have occasion to explore the "Kaffir market" in depth in subsequent chapters; here it is instructive to note some of the practices in the Australian mining market. During the West Australian mining boom of 1895–96 London financiers took up marginal properties, assigned themselves huge amounts of vendor shares for minimal capital outlays, and puffed their properties in misleading prospectuses. By March 1895, 123 Australian exploration and prospecting

38. Cairncross, *Home and Foreign*, pp. 93–94.
39. H. Withers, *Stocks and Shares* (London, 2nd ed.; 1917), pp. 246–47.

companies with an aggregate nominal capital of more than £ 14 million were before the investing public. Some of these folded even before their shares were run up in the mining market. But others survived. Despite comment in the responsible financial press which should have put off investors, considerable capital was sunk in paper companies. Official members of the stock exchange, if they did not join in the deceptions which plagued the mining market and which made mining investment more risky than it would have otherwise been, did nothing to stop them. Indeed "jobbers, stockbrokers, both 'inside' and 'outside', and other members of the financial community formed the core" of "an important group of professional speculators centred in London." These could take up extremely large amounts of shares with little intention of holding them. They could, when over-extended with large holdings acquired with borrowed money, unload large amounts to exploit a rise or in anticipation of a fall. The insiders thus added an important volatile dimension to stock market transactions. Western Australian mines "reached their lowest point in the investors' estimation in 1901." They revived because "the worst financial element had been removed by the failures" and because continued press criticism "led to an improvement in the quality of the local managers and the London directors." But by 1903 the mines' output had peaked and they "were never again able to dominate the mining markets as they had done for a few years in the nineties."[40]

Some preliminary conclusions about gold mining finance and its relationship with Europe's primary and secondary capital markets can be derived from the foregoing discussion. Obviously the gold mines were predominantly financed through the speculative surges which afflicted Europe's closely interrelated stock markets. Behind these periodic surges were the gambling instincts and growing income of the bourgeois elite coupled with the ambitions and savings of growing numbers of unwary small investors. These aspiring capitalists may well have placed savings in what they thought were safe but what were in fact high-risk

40. Hall, *London and Australia,* pp. 46, 112–14, 178.

ventures. Market operators, company promoters, investment trust directors, and even powerful bankers were more than willing to provide the action for the gamblers and promises for the small investors. Indeed, many were speculators in their own right. They were in no small measure responsible for stock market fluctuations. The connection of these capital market manipulators with the more fundamental patterns of growth, decline, or adjustment in the capital markets of Europe is not as readily apparent. Fluctuations in investment are not of the same order as underlying trends in capital flows. Gold mining finance featured speculative surges connected with investment fluctuations, but this finance was of sufficient magnitude to warrant examination in relation to underlying trends. South African gold mining finance apparently marked time after 1900 when all indicators suggest that the greatest movement in European capital exports before 1914 was underway. We have still to explore fully this anomaly.

• 3 •

Technology and Gold Mining Development

Why mankind should greatly value gold, or why it would want to scour or burrow beneath the earth's surface for it, are questions beyond the scope of this study. But western civilization was deeply and unquestioningly committed on both counts. The frenzied gold rushes to South Africa, Western Australia and the Klondike testified to the second commitment. The gold standard bore out the first. Through this device the Bank of England maintained a substantial gold reserve, on demand paid out gold sovereigns for bank notes, and exchanged bar gold at the price of £ 3.17s.9d per standard ounce. It could pay less for foreign gold coin and pay more for gold bars as well as sell gold from its reserves. During our period the Bank "moved its prices for bars over a range of 4d. between the extreme points of the minimum buying price and the maximum selling price."[1] The national banks of other states, wholly or partly on the gold standard, set similarly narrow limits for gold points in their own currencies, thus ensuring their free convertibility. The gold standard facilitated international finance, trade, and commerce. Coupled with the demand for gold generated by industry and hoarders, national currency arrangements assured the world's gold producers a high and stable price for their product.[2] Before 1914 oversupply or de-

1. R. S. Sayers, *Bank of England Operations, 1890–1914* (London, 1936), p. 82. Standard gold assayed at 11⁄12ths or 916.6 fine. Fine or essentially pure gold was worth £ 4.5s an ounce.

2. For estimates of the amounts of gold used for currency, retained by governments, employed in industry and stored by hoarders, as well as accounts of how it was sold see L. de Launay, O. C. Williams (trans.), *The World's Gold* (London, 1908), pp. 160–86. For an account of the insurmountable difficulties involved in quantifying gold movements see O. Morgenstern, *The Validity of International Gold Movement Statistics* (Princeton, 1955). Also see Cecco, *Money and Empire*, Tables 13–16, pp. 244–47.

creasing demand were not concerns. Thus, the only factors which would limit or promote the influx of available capital into gold mining development in the Transvaal were the methods used to finance development, the nature of the resource, and the means available to work it. The essential means entrepreneurs required were an adequate labor force and an effective technology. An examination of the technology western civilization lavished on the mines brings a measure of insight to the financing strategies employed by the mining companies. Such an analysis also illuminates the local and metropolitan pressures which shaped mining development.

1. Discovery and Initial Development

South Africa's first gold rush occurred after prospectors of European descent found gold in the eastern Transvaal in 1882–83. They discovered alluvial gold in the Kaap Valley and gold-bearing quartz veins in the Sheba Valley. The Barberton boom of 1885 ensued. Thousands of miners flocked to the region. Promoters, who set up a local stock market, followed close behind. The rush soon petered out, though the vein gold in the Sheba Valley continued to be mined on a modest scale long afterwards. The Barberton finds, along with earlier discoveries of alluvial gold in the Murchison Range and in the Pilgrim's Rest–Lydenburg area, led to a great deal of prospecting activity in the Transvaal. Some of this was directed at quartz veins located to the southeast of Barberton. This search led to the discovery of the unique conglomerate outcrops of the Witwatersrand. These had been laid down in the deltas of rivers flowing into a vast, ancient lake. It silted up. The sedimentary beds were subjected to the major forces active on the earth's crust: they were warped, thrust, and slipped. Volcanic action pushed dykes of igneous material into the beds; lava in places covered them. Dolomite rock was also laid over them when they were submerged in water from the sea or another lake. Then the "whole bed of Witwatersrand rock was tilted at some stage; it became like a giant saucer with one edge buried deep and the other thrust near the surface. It was on the up-thrust northern lip of the saucer that the Witwatersrand gold deposits were discovered in an outcrop in 1886."[3]

Many miners who participated in the first phase of South Africa's second gold rush hoped the precious metal would yield to the techniques of alluvial or quartz mining. They were disappointed. The ore they extracted through open-pit works needed the methods of hard-rock mining. The gold it contained was in particles which the miners found to be firmly embedded in a matrix of minerals. This had to be finely crushed by heavy steam-driven stamps and introduced to mercury on copper plates, where the gold amalgamated with the quicksilver. The amalgam then required retorting before the recovered gold was poured into bars. Moreover, the gold particles were mostly minute and dispersed throughout the thin bands of conglomerate which were often found to be only inches thick. Tons of waste rock had to be moved and tons of ore had to be processed to obtain ounces or even pennyweights of gold. From its inception, mining development on the Rand was both labor and capital intensive. A large labor supply, elaborate machinery, and chemical works were required to profitably recover gold from the low-grade ore.

Given the unique properties of the Witwatersrand gold-bearing beds, the existence of expensive technology (like proven ore pulverizing machinery and the amalgamation process), and the high and dependable price of gold, it might be expected that developers would have assiduously sought to take advantages of monopoly and the economies of scale. But in the early phase of mining work a number of factors militated against such trends. In the remote interior with no rail link to southern Africa's ports, the Rand could not be readily supplied with the apparatus needed for large-scale operations. Archetypal, undercapitalized, small-scale miners clung to their claims. At the same time Transvaal mining law was not helpful to the bigger operator. A mining claim was 155 feet by 413 feet or equal to about 1½ acres. While

3. E. L. W., "Profile of A Gold Mine," *Optima,* XXIII (June 1973), 79. For explanations of how the gold came to be in the conglomerates see R. J. Adamson (ed.), *Gold Metallurgy in South Africa* (Cape Town, 1972), pp. 382–89.

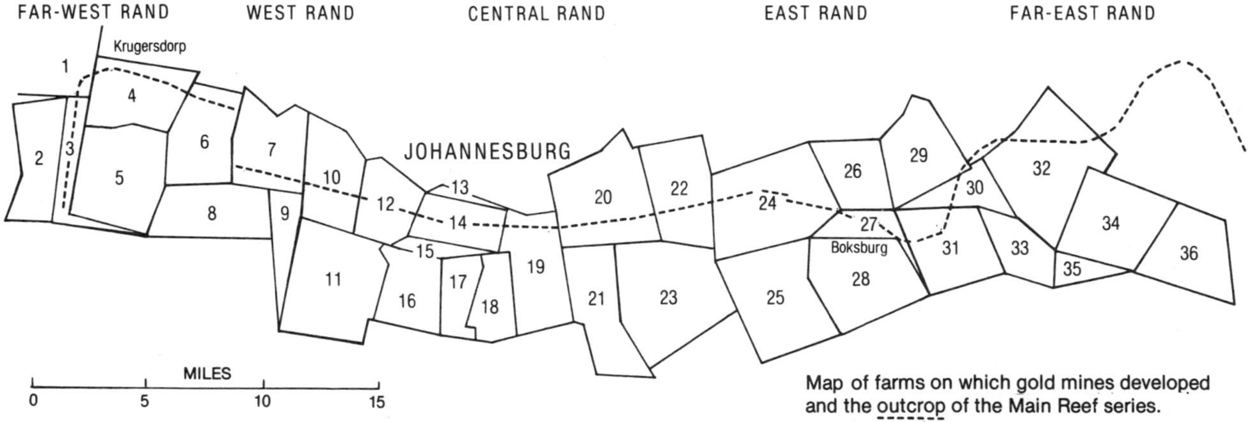

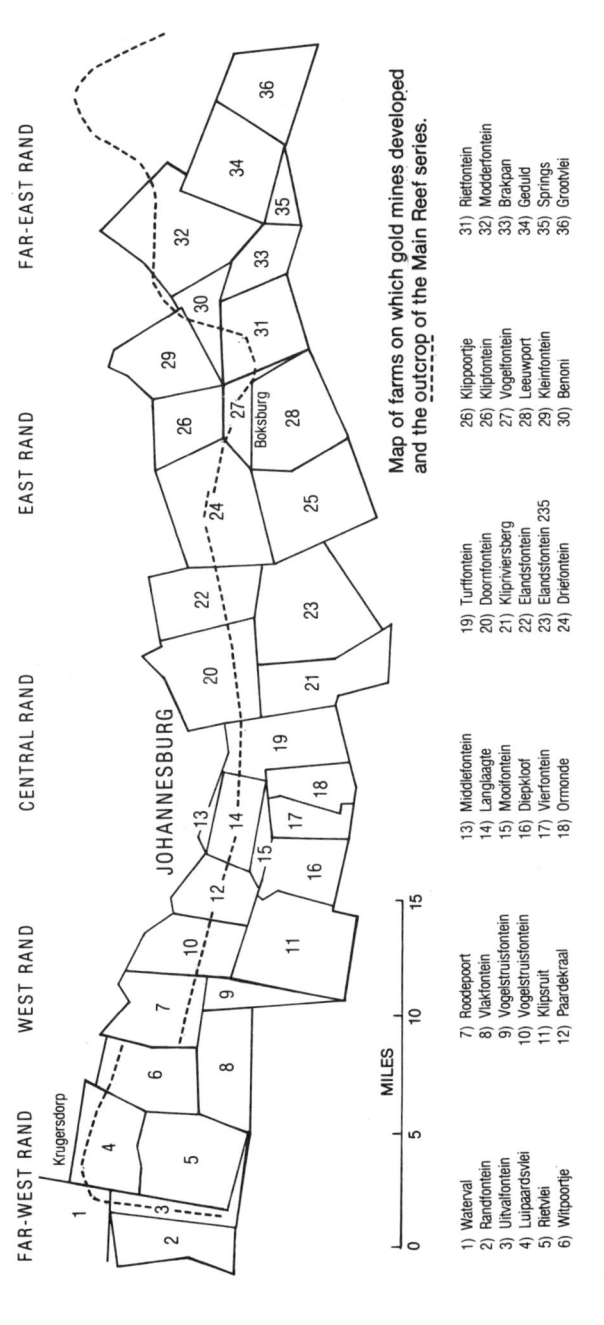

Map of farms on which gold mines developed and the outcrop of the Main Reef series.

1) Waterval
2) Randfontein
3) Uitvalfontein
4) Luipaardsvlei
5) Rietvlei
6) Witpoortje
7) Roodepoort
8) Vlakfontein
9) Vogelstruisfontein
10) Vogelstruisfontein
11) Klipsruit
12) Paardekraal
13) Middlefontein
14) Langlaagte
15) Mooifontein
16) Diepkloof
17) Vierfontein
18) Ormonde
19) Turffontein
20) Doornfontein
21) Klipriviersberg
22) Elandsfontein
23) Elandsfontein 235
24) Driefontein
26) Klippoortje
26) Klipfontein
27) Vogelfontein
28) Leeuwport
29) Kleinfontein
30) Benoni
31) Rietfontein
32) Modderfontein
33) Brakpan
34) Geduld
35) Springs
36) Grootvlei

its owner was entitled to work minerals found on or beneath it, he could not follow a promising find outside the limits of its surface boundary lines.[4] When it became apparent from surface excavations that the reefs dipped southward, additional hundreds of claims were pegged along the strike of the reefs and adjacent to existing mining operations. Transvaal mining law also allowed prospectors to peg private land proclaimed a public digging. Thus, when larger operators came to buy up large farms owned by subsistence Afrikaner agriculturists, they did not always obtain title to all the mineral rights associated with their purchase. The sheer size of the ground to be pegged also limited monopoly. In addition to the outcrops of the main reef series, which had been traced for several miles by 1887, several other real or imagined sets of conglomerate outcrops were pegged by hundreds of miners, many of whom turned promoter when development of their property proved beyond their resources. The peculiarities of Transvaal mining law, the unsettled state of knowledge as to where in fact the main chance lay, and the opportunities for miners to become company promoters prompted the formation of a multitude of mining companies. Some 90 ventures had been formed by the end of 1886; this number increased to 270 the following year; and by the end of 1889 "the shares of nearly five hundred companies were quoted, and more than three hundred were officially listed on the Johannesburg Exchange."[5] But only 44 companies were actually producing gold.[6] Though Rand development offered opportunities for capital concentrations in large-scale undertakings, its early phase featured a great deal of capital dispersion, a good deal of this fostered as much by speculation as by the elusiveness of payable gold.

A decline in the richness of ore mined brought an abrupt halt

4. Cf. American practice which allowed miners to pursue a lode found in their property beyond claim boundaries. R. W. Paul, *Californian Gold, The Beginning of Mining in the Far West* (Lincoln, Nebr., 1947), pp. 237–38. For financial practice in American mining see C. C. Spence, *British Investments and the American Mining Frontier, 1860–1901* (Ithaca, N.Y., 1958).

5. O. Letcher, *The Gold Mines of Southern Africa* (London, 1936), pp. 476–77.

6. Emden, *Randlords*, p. 348.

to the initial stage of development. Once it was discovered that the reefs of the main series dipped southward and to some depth, incline and vertical shafts replaced open-cut development work. Starting in March 1889 and at about a depth of 120 feet, these workings struck ore in which the gold resisted amalgamation. At the surface oxidation had "freed" the gold particles from other constituents of the mineralized matrix. At depth, where oxidation had not occurred, minute grains of gold "were either attached to or partially encased by pyrite crystals. Consequently during their passage over the amalgam plates insufficient contact was made with the mercury surface and the percentage extraction fell accordingly."[7] With no immediate solution at hand, yields of the producing mines declined sharply. This setback collapsed stock values, forced hundreds of companies to wind up, and left Johannesburg, a city of 17,000 founded in 1886 to serve the mines, in deep depression. The crash ruined hundreds of small miners and promoters who sold off what assets they could. The buyers were larger operators with financial resources sufficient to ride out the fall, purchase additional mining ground cheaply, and invest in a solution to the refractory ores.

The second phase of development, featuring a measure of consolidation and major new development, was made possible by readily available processes that could be used to treat the ore successfully. Australian and North American gold fields had been using a chlorination process on pulverized concentrates to dissolve the gold which was then reprecipitated. It was tried on the Rand with encouraging results. But a better solution was to hand. Developed in Glasgow laboratories and patented in 1887, the MacArthur–Forrest process for the extraction of gold by the use of cyanide was introduced to the Rand with remarkable results. After initial tests proved positive, cyanidation equipment was installed on a mine late in 1890. Tailings left from amalgamation work were put in a weak cyanide solution which dissolved the gold, thereby freeing it from its pyritic encasements. It was then precipitated by zinc metal shavings. Efficient amalgamation

7. Adamson, *Gold Metallurgy*, p. 90.

obtained 75–80 percent of the gold contained in oxidized, and less than 60 percent of that contained in unoxidized ore. Amalgamation in conjunction with chlorination got 75 percent of the gold from unoxidized reef. But recovery by amalgamation and cyanidation was almost 90 percent.[8] The MacArthur–Forrest process of course required extensive additional equipment. A separating system was needed to exclude sludge or slime which impeded cyanidation. A series of treatment tanks had to be constructed in which the residue of sands with which the gold was associated was introduced to dissolving and washing solutions. Some mines experimented with a German invention to precipitate the gold—the Siemens–Halske electrolytic method—instead of the zinc metal technique.[9] In 1894 the mines also installed equipment to treat the cast-off slimes through a process of decantation and cyanidation. Initial costs in installing new refining equipment were covered by revenue from gold, recovered by cyanidation, in the accumulated, untreated tailings of the mine dumps. The rapid and successful introduction of the MacArthur–Forrest process is indicated by production figures. Amalgamation accounted for 656,489 ounces of gold or 96 percent of total production in 1891; by 1894 its share, 1,291,708 ounces, represented only 70 percent.

2. Deep-Level Development

Without a high percentage of recovery from the low-grade ore, mining would have been unprofitable. Cyanidation provided the extra necessary yield, insured continued production, and stimulated new development. It thus inaugurated the second stage of Rand development, the plunge into deep-level mining. In 1890 a test borehole struck the main reef series at a depth of 571 to 635 feet; another, begun in 1892, 4100 feet south of the central Rand outcrops, reached gold-bearing conglomerate the follow-

8. *Ibid.*, pp. 88–89; and F. H. Hatch and J. A. Chalmers, *The Gold Mines of the Rand* (London, 1895), pp. 180–243.
9. Adamson, *Gold Metallurgy*, pp. 120–21.

ing year at a depth of 2343 feet. These tests confirmed the theories of knowledgeable mining engineers that not only did the ore beds dip southward for a considerable distance but that the angle of dip leveled out significantly.[10] Mining engineers from Britain, France, Germany and North America, who were either brought to the Rand by the developers or sent there by European governments and financial institutions, were already familiar with mining operations at levels below 4000 feet. If the Witwatersrand system was not permeated with excessive underground water, and if it was no hotter at this depth than other areas of the earth's crust where mining operations were underway, then the know-how was at hand to develop large deep-level mines on the Rand. By 1895 about a dozen undertakings located to the south of the outcrop mines were in the development stage. They were modest in their objectives as their shafts were being sunk to strike the reef at depths well under 1000 feet. Meantime, a second row of deep-levels designed to work the reefs at depths up to 3000 feet were in the planning stage.[11]

These deep-level initiatives, along with the elaborate equipping of the outcrop mines to make the most of cyanidation, would not have occurred when they did had not the Rand had access to a cheap energy supply and had it not come to be served by a rail link to the coast. Searches for the elusive outcrop on the east Rand turned up large coal deposits. These were used to fire the boilers of steam engines which drove the hoists on the mine shafts, activated the crushers and stamps in the mills, and ran the air compressors which operated rock drills. Coal-powered steam engines also ran generators. By 1895 electricity had come

10. In fact "the strata dip southwards at an angle of 70° at the top of the succession, the angle becoming progressively smaller lower down until it reaches 10° near the bottom." *Ibid.*, pp. 357–58.

11. Hatch and Chalmers, *Gold Mines*, pp. 87–110. These authors were British. B. Schmeisser, a German engineer sent to the Rand by his government, published, *Ueber Vorkommen und Gewinnung der nutzbarn Mineralien in der Sudafrikanischen Republik* (Berlin, 1894). The French engineer, L. de Launay wrote *Les Mines d'or du Transvaal* (Paris, 1896). The most well-known American experts on South Africa's gold mines were John Hays Hammond (see his preface in the work of Hatch and Chalmers), and Hamilton Smith (see his influential article in *The Times*, 28 March 1895).

"to play an important part in driving the various subsidiary machinery in and about a mining plant." For example, it was used increasingly to operate pumps essential to several phases of mining and refining. Below ground it illuminated loading stations and headgear, sorting-floors and tramways on the surface.[12] Freight rates from the coast to Johannesburg averaged £ 30 a ton in 1889. After the railroad reached the Rand in September 1892, these charges were cut by two-thirds. Moreover, the latest in bulky, heavy equipment could be ordered in Europe and transported to the mine sites at affordable prices.

Indeed, mine management was far more preoccupied with costs generated by below-ground operations than by expenses incurred through surface plant development. One of these outlays, representing about 12 to 20 percent of total operating expenses, was for explosives. The mines in 1894 consumed 48,000, and by 1898 225,000, 50-pound cases of dynamite and blasting gelatine. Alfred Nobel had perfected the former in 1867 and the latter in 1874. Blasting gelatine, used on the Rand in much greater amounts than dynamite, was 93 parts nitro-glycerine and seven parts of collodion cotton. It could efficiently break up the hardest rock and was, therefore, particularly suited to deep-level mining. In fact, Rand development could not have proceeded beyond the outcrops without high explosives.[13] They were supplied to the industry by the Nobel international dynamite trusts through a local monopoly granted by the Transvaal government at a cost considerably higher than the going rate elsewhere. The industry wanted the price reduced by about 30 shillings a case to effect a reduction in working costs of 4 percent.[14]

A second concern was the cost of labor. Management thought it paid both white and black workers too much. In 1894 about 5300 skilled whites were employed on the mines at an average

12. Hatch and Chalmers, *Gold Mines,* pp. 47, 161, 173.

13. *Ibid.*, p. 247; S. J. Truscott, *The Witwatersrand Goldfields: Banket and Mining Practice* (London, 2nd ed.; 1902), pp. 362, 457; and A. P. Cartwright, *The Dynamite Company, The Story of African Explosives and Chemical Industries Limited* (London, 1964), pp. 25, 33–35.

14. *Ibid.*, pp. 48–49; Hatch and Chalmers, *Gold Mines,* p. 270; Transvaal Chamber of Mines, *Annual Report for 1897* (Johannesburg, 1898), pp. 9–11.

wage of £ 23 per month. By the end of 1896 11,600 were averaging better than £ 26. These wages accounted for 20–25 percent of operating costs in 1894 and 30 percent in 1896. Far more blacks were employed for far much less. At the end of 1894 almost 41,000 Africans were on the mines, the great majority below ground where they were used to man hand drills, shovel waste rock and ore, and operate mine cars. By the end of 1896 almost 90,000 were employed. Black wage rates are elusive, but it would appear that earnings, exclusive of food allowances, averaged slightly above £ 3 per month in 1894 and represented about 32 percent of total working costs. By 1896 African wages represented less than 24 percent of such costs because they had been driven down to £ 2.10, but still not low enough to suit the Transvaal Chamber of Mines.[15]

Neither the costs of high explosives nor of labor had been reduced to the full satisfaction of mine management by the time the war broke out. However, by then deep-levels had come on line and were adding significantly to Rand production. Moreover, impressive dividend yields and firm share prices indicated that the mines' capital suppliers were being given satisfaction.[16]

3. The Problems of Postwar Development

When the industry resumed production and development at the close of the war, inflated prices for explosives were not one of its problems. Indeed, blasting gelatine, which cost the mines more than £ 5 a case in 1897, now cost considerably less than £ 3. Prices came down because the British administration in the Transvaal ended the local monopoly and because the Nobel trusts now had competition. The Kimberley diamond industry, backed by the major Rand producers, formed a high explosives company at the Cape. It was in production by 1903. By 1909 a

15. *Ibid.*, pp. 252–58; Truscott, *Witwatersrand Goldfields*, pp. 448–57; S. T. van der Horst, *Native Labour in South Africa* (London, 1942), p. 130; Chamber of Mines, *Annual Report for 1897*, pp. 106–113.

16. For more on this performance see chap. iv, p. 71, this volume.

third company, a subsidiary of Britain's largest manufacturer of ammunition, was operating out of Natal and successfully competing for a share of the Rand's voracious needs. By 1907 these exceeded 500,000 cases. On the eve of World War I, high explosives plants operating in the Transvaal, the Cape, and Natal represented the largest manufacturing industry in South Africa.[17]

While explosive costs were not a problem when mining resumed, a lack of labor was. Management faced an acute shortage of unskilled workers, one partly of its own making. The Chamber of Mines temporarily reduced wages to £ 1.10 and tried to monopsonize the recruitment and allocation of African labor. These measures, coupled with better and safer job opportunities for blacks in other sectors of South Africa's postwar economy and the disruptions war had caused in migratory labor patterns, left the mines chronically short.[18] The shortfall was partly made good by large-scale importation of Chinese indentured laborers who were first introduced to the mines in 1904. Applied technology on the world's sea lanes provided cheap shipping that could move people as well as goods. The Rand, for a time, was on the receiving end of oceanic labor migration made possible by the steamship.[19] Because they proved to be politically sensitive, the Chinese workers were all repatriated by 1911, but not before the mines had surpassed prewar production levels, increased their supply of African labor, and introduced several technological innovations.

These innovations were in part a response to labor shortages. But they were also prompted by growing evidence that the richness of the ore gradually declined with depth. Rather than selectively mine rich patches of reef and leave lower-grade ore untouched, a tactic widely practiced on the Rand before the war,

17. Cartwright, *Dynamite Company*, pp. 102–6, 115, 119.

18. D. Denoon, "The Transvaal Labour Crisis, 1901–06," *Journal of African History*, VII (1967), 481–94; and A. Jeeves, 'The Control of Migratory Labour on the South African Gold Mines in the Era of Kruger and Milner," *Journal of Southern African Studies*, II (October 1975), 20–21.

19. P. Richardson, "The Recruiting of Chinese Indentured Labour for the South African Gold-Mines, 1903–1908," *Journal of African History*, XVIII (1977), 85–86.

the mines now found they had to be much less selective. By milling more ore in less time, achieving a higher rate of recovery, and cutting working costs, management found it could mine the lower-yielding ores profitably.

Processes, techniques, and sources of power were readily available to facilitate the transition in mining strategy. These aids, however, were not always adapted as promptly as they might have been. To increase the amount of ore mined and at the same time cope with labor shortages, management had to forgo certain conventional notions. For example, air drills were thought to be too bulky and required too much time to set up. Consequently, much of the extensive drill work, especially at the ore face in the stopes, was done by hand. But a measure of the rethinking which occurred was a contest held by the Chamber of Mines in 1909. It sought to encourage the development of a light, efficient drill to be operated by one man and which would sharply reduce the number of "hammer boys" needed for hand-drill work. The number of rock drills used on the Rand increased from slightly less than 2000 in 1905 to more than 5500 in 1913.[20] Meanwhile electrical power increasingly displaced steam power. By 1909 electricity had begun to be introduced to replace steam for hoisting and achieved marked savings in working costs. The following year a company was formed to provide the mines with a central power plant.[21] More and heavier stamps were installed. These, coupled with tube mills introduced in 1904 and of which there were 296 along with 9946 stamps on the Rand's producers by 1913, gave the milling end of the industry more capacity and yielded a pulp from which amalgamation and cyanidation could extract more gold. Besides pursuing technological innovations which obtained increased production and greater efficiency, mine management also achieved important economies of scale through amalgamating the properties of existing mines

20. Transvaal Chamber of Mines, *Annual Report for 1909* (Johannesburg, 1910), pp. lxii, 1; and *Annual Report for 1913* (Johannesburg, 1914), pp. lvii, 239.

21. This was the Victoria Falls Power Company (afterwards the Victoria Falls and Transvaal Power Company) with a capital of £3 million. See A. P. Cartwright, *The Gold Miners* (Johannesburg, 1962), pp. 172–73.

Table 3.1. *Witwatersrand Mines: Statement of Tonnages Milled, Gold Values, and Working Costs, 1902–13*

Year	*Tons milled*	*Value* £	*Value per ton milled* s.d.	*Working cost per ton* s.d.
1902	3,416,813	7,179,074	42.0	25.9
1903	6,105,016	12,146,307	39.8	24.9
1904	8,058,295	15,520,329	38.6	24.4
1905	11,160,422	19,991,658	35.10	23.6
1906	13,571,554	23,615,400	34.6	22.2
1907	15,523,229	26,421,837	33.11	20.10
1908	18,196,589	28,810,393	31.5	18.0
1909	20,543,759	29,900,359	28.11	17.1
1910	21,432,541	30,703,912	28.6	17.7
1911	23,888,258	33,543,479	27.11	18.0
1912	25,486,361	37,182,795	29.0	18.8
1913	25,628,432	35,812,605	27.9	17.11

Note :Figures for 1913 effected significantly by strikes.

Source: Transvaal Chamber of Mines, *Twenty-Fourth Annual Report for the Yəar 1913* (Johannesburg, 1914), p. 234.

and starting new ones with much larger claim areas. Instead of mines with a few hundred, mines with a thousand or more claims became the norm. The end result of these various adaptations and strategies is illustrated by Table 3.1 which shows that production rose and working costs fell in the decade before 1914, despite a steady decline in the richness of the ore mined.

Though production was going up and working costs down, mine management continued to argue it paid too much for labor. But labor costs per man had not noticeably increased from the prewar figures. In 1913 the average wage of 24,000 whites employed was a little above £ 26 and for 210,400 blacks about £ 2.5. We will have occasion in subsequent analysis to determine why management continued to press for wage reductions given the apparently impressive performance with existing rates. Here we need note that management, in order to achieve savings or effect efficiencies, rejected employment of unskilled white labor,[22]

22. R. Davies, "Mining Capital, the State and Unskilled White Workers in South Africa, 1901–1913," *Journal of Southern African Studies*, III (1976), 58.

contemplated employing blacks in some of the more skilled jobs, and made minor efforts to preserve the health of miners. Hot cocoa was provided in large quantities to black workers on the notion it could reduce a high incidence of pneumonia. An attempt was also made to ameliorate miners' phthisis or pneumoconiosis to which white miners, whose length of service in the mines was longer than that of African migratory workers, were particularly prone. Dust reduction schemes included adding water jets to rock drills, better ventilation, and improved blasting procedures. Studies into the disease were also commissioned.[23] Meanwhile white labor became better organized and more active in seeking improved working conditions and protecting themselves against Chinese or African competition. They struck in 1907, in 1913 when riots and bloodshed occurred, and again in 1914.[24] Moreover, in the aftermath of the repatriation of Chinese workers, management failed to control satisfactorily the acquisition of black labor. For example, "recruiting anarchy" prevailed in south-central Africa, an important source of labor.[25]

Technology had its limitations. It provided management no ready panacea with which to control labor as effectively as it desired. Nonetheless, applied technology was fundamental to the Rand's development. Early industrial Europe, even the preindustrial world, mined alluvial or vein gold. But the Rand's gold could only be won with power and products of the "second industrial revolution."[26] Nobel's blasting gelatine invented in 1874; the MacArthur–Forrest cyanide process patented in 1887; hard steel alloys, essential for dies and shoes in the mortar boxes of the mills' stamps, produced in quantity only after about 1880; centralized power stations, which the Rand adopted in the new century, also first devised in the 1880s; without these devices the Rand could

23. Various issues of the *South African Mining Journal* and several numbers of the Transvaal Chamber of Mines, *Annual Reports*, especially that for 1913.

24. F. Wilson, *Labour in the South African Gold Mines, 1911–1969* (Cambridge, 1972), pp. 8–9.

25. Richardson, *Journal of African History*, XVIII (1977), 107.

26. Landes, *Unbound Prometheus*, p. 235 and chap. v, *passim.*; G. Barraclough, *An Introduction to Contemporary History* (Harmondsworth, Middlesex, 2nd ed.; 1967), pp. 46–64; W. H. McNeill, *The Rise of the West* (Chicago, 1963), pp. 764–70.

not have developed as the world's major gold field. Without the reactions and energies unleashed by chemical processes, without metallurgical developments and electrical power, the Rand could not have become the economic juggernaut of South Africa. In a real sense it was Europe's new technologies rather than its capital exports which seemed to dictate the timing of the Rand's development and, therefore, its role in the late-nineteenth-century economic imperialism.

· 4 ·

The Rise and Decline of the Corner House Group

During the period 1902–13, 37 percent of the Rand's gold yield or 11 percent of the world's output, was produced by companies controlled by the Central Mining and Investment Corporation, by its affiliate, Rand Mines Limited, or by the creator of these two investment trusts, the private financial house of Wernher, Beit and Company.[1] These three firms (see Table 4.1), along with Eckstein and Company, the Johannesburg representatives of the London-based private house, made up the most important of the several financial groupings which developed the Witwatersrand. By 1913 the business of Wernher, Beit, despite large gold share holdings was largely confined to the South African diamond trade which had launched the firm. Its founding partners had left vast personal fortunes. Alfred Beit died in 1906 and left an estate of £ 8 million. Julius Wernher, when he died in 1912, left £ 11.5 million.[2] A stable of immensely profitable gold mines provided investors in Rand Mines, including partners of the private firms who were its major shareholders, a yearly average dividend of 168 percent, or £ 9,388,000, between 1902 and 1913.[3] Before the South African War, Rand Mines, founded in 1893, provided similar profit rates for its clients and controllers. Central Mining, formed in 1905, was confined neither to Trans-

1. See Table 4.1 and Transvaal Chamber of Mines, *Report for 1913*, p. 237.

2. Beit's estate paid out £ 644,000 in death duties, Wernher's £ 2 million, *South African Mining Journal*, 17 December 1910, p. 663; and F. Eckstein to L. Phillips, 11 July 1913, Archives of Barlow Rand Limited, Johannesburg (subsequently referred to as BRA).

3. R. R. Mabson, *The Statist's Mines of the Transvaal*, 1909–10, pp. 468–72; and W. R. Skinner, *Mining Manual*, 1915. Also see Table A.1 (in Appendix A) which indicates the market value of Rand Mines's share holdings in 16 mines was about £ 10 million.

Table 4.1. *Production and Dividends of Witwatersrand Gold Mines by Group, 1902–13*

Name of mining group	*Producing mines (1913)*	*Nonproducing mines (1913)*	*Issued capital all mines (£)*	*Issued capital (%)*	*Gold produced (£)*	*Gold produced (%)*	*Dividends (£)*	*Dividends (%)*
Corner House (Wernher, Beit; Rand Mines; Central Mining)	14	1	14,083,527	23.28	111,877,916	37.19	37,874,858	48.62
Consolidated Gold Fields of South Africa	6	0	7,739,306	12.79	32,468,902	10.79	8,977,306	11.52
Farrar and Associates (East Rand Proprietary Mines; Anglo-French Exploration)	2	5	5,026,584	8.30	29,942,747	9.95	6,924,209	8.89
Johannesburg Consolidated Investments (Barnato family)	8	2	5,002,763	8.27	22,283,929	7.41	5,519,930	7.09
J. B. Robinson	3	0	8,032,700	13.28	30,250,581	10.06	3,397,830	4.36
S. Neumann & Co.	6	2	4,849,802	8.02	18,421,325	6.12	3,486,144	4.47
General Mining & Finance Corporation	7	0	4,980,226	8.23	18,723,769	6.23	2,850,178	3.66
A. D. Goerz & Co.	4	4	3,469,033	5.73	12,950,406	4.30	2,325,228	2.99
Consolidated Mines Selection	1	1	1,550,000	2.56	2,214,448	.74	543,750	.70
Abe Bailey & Associates	1	2	1,548,400	2.56	2,189,525	.73	59,760	.08
Henderson's Transvaal Estates	0	2	846,507	1.40	—	.00	—	.00
Lewis & Marks	0	2	654,500	1.08	—	.00	—	.00
Unaffiliated Mines	6	6	2,721,896	4.50	16,456,695	5.47	4,268,459	5.48
Miscellaneous Production & Dividends	—	—	—	—	3,047,905	1.01	1,668,454	2.14
Total	58	27	60,505,244	100.00	300,828,148	100.00	77,896,106	100.00

Sources: Transvaal Chamber of Mines, *Annual Reports*; and R. R. Mabson, *Mines of the Transvaal*.

vaal gold nor Cape diamonds. By 1913 the corporation's investments also included farms and real estate in the Transvaal, gold mines in West Africa and Alaska, cotton plantations in the Sudan, metallurgical companies in western Europe, British and German government bonds, and railways and oil leases in central America. However, its multisector, multinational investment mix produced meagre profits. Indeed, it had to write off the value of its securities in 1908 and again in 1913 by a total of £ 2 million.[4]

These preliminary remarks about the financial history of the Corner House group prompt a number of questions. What were the capital sources and development strategies which enabled the group to become the dominant gold mine developer and its founders to achieve great personal wealth? As the dominant developer, was the Corner House able to exercise effective control over the other mining groups? Did its dominance increase, fluctuate, or decline over the period 1886–1914? What factors account for its investment diversification program? Did, for example, Central Mining's varied investment strategy indicate an expansion based on continued Rand commitments or a redirection of its Rand-derived assets? Finally, did government action frustrate Corner House initiatives or fulfil its expectations? Answers to these questions should illuminate the role and function of the Corner House group as a vehicle for European economic expansion.

1. The Kimberley Connection

Before gold was discovered in quantity in the Transvaal, a major diamond field had come into production at Kimberley. Here the Corner House group had its beginnings. Here it de-

4. See Tables A.1–A.7 in Appendix A. The oil interests of the Corner House were in the Carribbean and, since they were not acquired until 1913, do not show up in the tables. They were put into Trinidad Leaseholds which was formed with a capital of £ 550,000.

The market value of Central Mining's holdings was about £ 5 million of which £ 2 million was in Transvaal gold mines. The market value of securities held by the private firms was about £ 5.5 million of which £ 3 million was in Rand Mines and Central Mining shares and £ 650,000 in diamond interests.

veloped its business style and established financial links between South Africa and Europe. The private firm, Wernher, Beit and Company, was founded in 1890, but was in effect the reorganization of Jules Porges and Company.[5] This company, formed by Porges, a Bohemian-born diamond merchant operating out of Paris, had been active on the Kimberley fields from about 1873. One of its rising young representatives was Julius Wernher, the son of a German general, who forsook a career in the military (he served in the Franco-Prussian war) for banking and commerce. By 1880 Alfred Beit had joined the firm. He had learned the diamond trade in Amsterdam, and used his expertise with great effect in Kimberley where many sellers and buyers had only a hazy notion of what stones would fetch in Europe. Beit's German-Jewish parents had converted to Lutheranism and were among Hamburg's successful upper middle-class families engaged in industry and commerce which, in this case, included gold refining, silk and wool importing, dye making, and banking. The partnership established a branch in London as well as in Kimberley and Paris, and dealt in diamond shares and claims as well as precious stones.

Porges had formed a Paris-based mining company in 1880 called the Compagnie Française des Mines de Diamants du Cap, and this company controlled strategic claims in the Kimberley pipe, figuring prominently in the schemes, tried or contemplated during the 1880s, to monopolize production on the diggings. When the French Company remained the only impediment to Barney Barnato's control of the Kimberley pipe, and when Cecil Rhodes achieved control of the De Beers pipe, the only other major source of diamonds in the region, Porges and Company came to occupy a crucial position. It backed Rhodes. Not only did it support him against Barnato through its own holdings, but Porges and Company also found Rhodes the capital he needed to pull off his coup. Beit got a syndicate of French and German

5. Unless otherwise noted, biographical and financial information in what follows is from Emden, *Randlords;* Cartwright, *Corner House;* B. Roberts, *The Diamond Magnates* (London, 1972); and H. A. Chilvers, *The Story of De Beers* (London, 1939).

financiers to provide substantial backing. Through Porges's firm. Rhodes also got Rothschild support for a loan which enabled him to purchase the French company. He paid £ 1.4 million for it. Since the French company had been originally capitalized at £ 560,000,[6] Porges and partners, who likely held a significant part of its share capital, along with their Paris backers turned a tidy profit. Moreover, Wernher and Beit were made life governors and were entitled to a share of the profits in De Beers Consolidated, the company Rhodes formed to effect his monopoly of diamond production.[7]

Like many Kimberley entrepreneurs, the partners speculated in gold shares in the Barberton mining boom of 1885. Unlike most, they could easily afford the gamble and made money from it. They employed James B. Taylor, a former Kimberley diamond broker as their Barberton representative. Acting on his timely advice, they unloaded their stocks before the boom broke.

When the Rand began to open up, Porges and Company used the profits from their Barberton deals, some £ 30,000, along with about £ 20,000 from Beit's personal capital, to get in on the ground floor. They minimized possible loss, should the venture prove a bust, by spreading risk. They formed a syndicate with Sigismund Neumann, a Bavarian-born financier and diamond buyer working out of London and Kimberley, and Rodolphe Kann, a Paris financier and cousin to Porges, who had been a helpful contact in eliciting Rothschild support for Rhodes's schemes. As Porges explained from Pretoria to Wernher early in 1887:

> The only investments I have made for the syndicate so far consist . . . of £ 15,000 for claims of which £ 5000 is tied up, and £ 20,000 for machinery—at most, therefore, £ 35,000. . . . In the last year about £ 65,000 was earned on [Barberton] gold [shares] of which at the highest estimate [£]35,000 was lost. . . .
>
> In the Witwatersrand we have invested, as our share of the syndicate's £ 20,000 for machinery, at the most £ 10,000, and in the

6. *Economist,* 12 June 1880, p. 683.

7. Gregory, *Oppenheimer,* pp. 54–56. Wernher was instrumental in forming the Diamond Syndicate which helped control prices by arranging sales quotas.

Beckett Lewis syndicate [for holding stands in the Johannesburg township and farms in the Transvaal], at the most £ 8000. If everything turns out badly the gold profits, which we have never taken into account, may be lost completely. Certainly this is not likely to happen. I believe, rather, that we are looking ahead to a great future; yet even though one is certain of success, it is always just as well to think of a good retreat.[8]

Porges's letter was not only revealing of a cautious, risk-spreading approach,[9] but it was also indicative of how little capital it took, compared to the resources it possessed, for a company to begin development in a remote region like the Transvaal.

Along with the firm's caution went a good deal of flexibility, particularly when it came to recruiting personnel. It was partial to men with Kimberley experience but ability, not background, seemed the key criterion. At the same time local managers were allowed considerable scope for initiative. Thus, to take charge of the partnership's interests on the Rand, Porges and Beit brought in Hermann Eckstein of Stuttgart. The son of a Lutheran pastor, he was managing a diamond mine near Kimberley when he was recruited along with the South African James Taylor who had proved his worth both at Kimberley and at Barberton. They formed Eckstein and Company, were to act as the local representatives of Porges and Company, and be entitled to one-fifth the profits made on the Rand. Taylor appears to have been one of the very few on the Rand in 1887 capable of determining the gold content of the reefs. This skill, and Eckstein's shrewd deals, provided Porges and Company with extensive interests at the cheapest prices in the richest properties along the whole length

8. J. Porges to J. Wernher, translated from the German, 19 February 1887, BRA. With regard to claims, £ 10,000 had been paid out in shares to Japie de Villiers, the owner of half a mining property the remainder of which the partners had already obtained a half interest in through another syndicate (i.e., the Robinson Syndicate) to which Beit had contributed on his own account some £ 20,000–£ 25,000. These holdings were used to float the enormously profitable Robinson Gold Mining Co. in 1887. Also see chap. vi, this volume.

9. Porges also spent £ 1000 in another syndicate to participate in the ownership of a farm adjoining a silver mine near Pretoria. The real estate and farm ventures were done in conjunction with Samuel Marks (see chap. vii, this volume), and Alois Nellmapius (see n. 39 below).

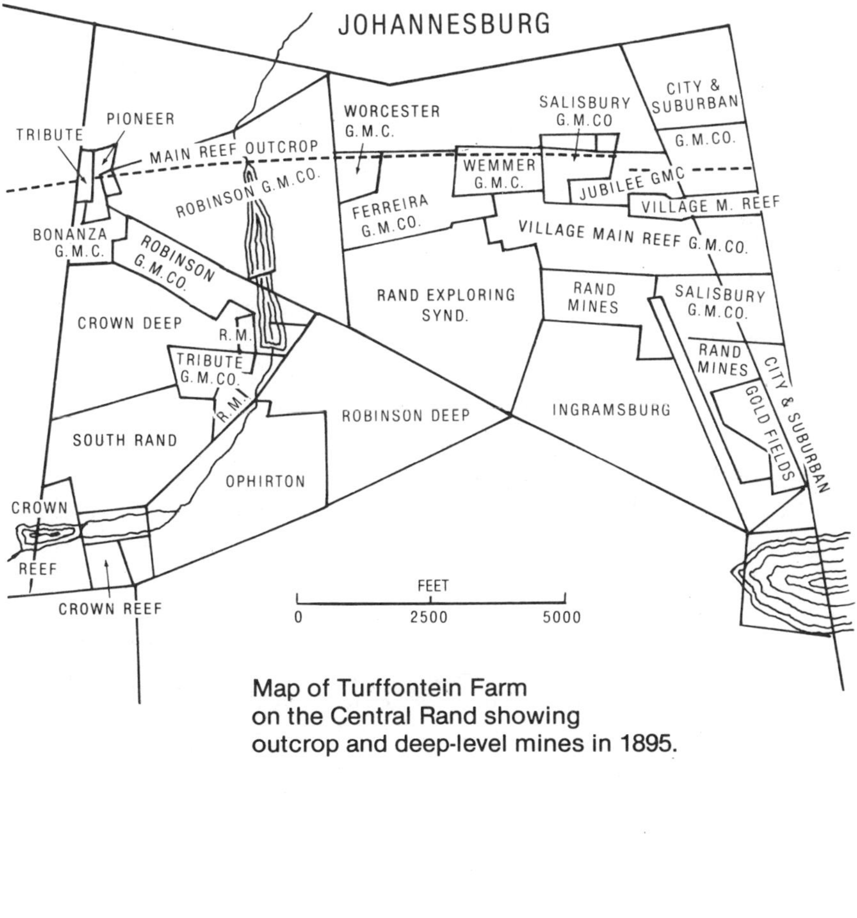

Map of Turffontein Farm
on the Central Rand showing
outcrop and deep-level mines in 1895.

of the central Rand. By mid-1888, Eckstein's had formed three mines (Bantjes, Langlaagte, and Robinson), bought out two (Ferreira and Henry Nourse), and held large interests in three others (Jubilee, Salisbury, and Wolhuter). Eckstein's also launched the Modderfontein on what became the far-east Rand.[10] It also held numerous claims and options through several syndicates in which it was a significant participant.

Through the commitments Eckstein's made, Jules Porges and Company tied up £ 360,000[11] in Transvaal gold shares, a sum which represented 7 to 10 percent of all the capital (some £ 5 million) thus far invested on the Rand.[12] The remainder of the firm's investments, approximately £ 840,000, was in diamonds. Porges, observing a downturn in the market value of diamond securities and rampant speculation in gold shares, advocated withdrawing "a sizeable amount of the business and invest[ing] this elsewhere, in unquestionably good securities."[13] No doubt the firm adopted its senior partner's recommendation.[14] But Beit saw that the speculative craze, so much a feature of any new mining center, obscured the Rand's potential to provide an investment haven. Not only could the price of the product be known in advance but, despite dispersion in the reefs, it was available in huge and relatively uniform amounts. Thus, with product and price assured, successful development depended upon only two other variables: the cost and availability of labor and of

10. C. S. Goldmann, *The Financial, Statistical, and General History of the Gold and Other Companies of Witwatersrand, South Africa* (London, 1892), *passim.* These nine enterprises had an aggregate issued capital of £ 3,881,000.

11. J. Porges to J. Wernher, translated from the German, 20 May 1888, BRA. This amount included £ 250,000 paid to Joseph B. Robinson for his interest in the Robinson mine.

12. Cf. J. B. Taylor to R. Kann, July 1888, quoted in Cartwright, *Corner House*, p. 74: "Today we have a town [Johannesburg], built in the most substantial way, consisting of no fewer than 3,000 houses and a population of at least 17,000 inhabitants. In two years upwards of five million pounds sterling have been invested in stocks, shares, buildings and mining concerns." Cf. also the gold mining investment estimates of Frankel: total capital at par value to the end of 1888 of £ 5,589,421 in *Investment in Africa*, p. 95; and £ 5,083,-634 in *Investment in Gold Mining*, p. 116.

13. J. Porges to J. Wernher, 20 May 1888, BRA.

14. See p. 69 in this volume.

equipment. These could be obtained and utilized through effective management. Taylor's words to Kann are instructive:

> From the reports of the Jumpers, Langlaagte, Ferreira [and] Robinson . . . you will find what work has been done and the amount of ore sighted and ready for breaking only. I repeat it here to further illustrate my arguments . . . 238,100 tons of ore, or a money value of about £ 951,000!
>
> This, it must be remembered, is only down to the present levels [i.e. 60–100 feet]. . . .
>
> Up to the present work has been carried on in a primitive way, and the expense has been very heavy. In the course of another year everything will be regulated. The supplies will become cheaper, labour more abundant and fuel will be reduced to 30 shillings per ton for coals.[15]

Eckstein's, with Beit's blessing, would further commit the partnership to the Rand's development. For this was no Barberton. But could "everything be regulated"?

2. The Search for Clients and Capital

Porges, admitting he did not possess the "commercial temperament" that drove Beit, and having "enough capital to live well," withdrew from the company at the end of 1889. However, from retirement in Paris, he helped arrange syndicates to take up shares in Rand ventures. Kimberley capital had started Rand mining activity and dominated it during the 1886–88. Thereafter, as the capital intensive industry's needs got beyond the Cape's resources, Wernher and Beit turned to Europe. Kann, as well as Porges, facilitated the process; but so too did "the Beits of Hamburg and their banking friends in Germany."[16] Beit, Taylor later recalled, gave "participations to the Rothschilds of Germany, Austria, and France. Through [Rodolphe Kann] of Paris he secured the support of many banking houses: in fact, all those

15. J. B. Taylor to R. Kann, July 1888, quoted in Cartwright, *Corner House*, pp. 75–76.
16. *Ibid.*, p. 79.

houses which had made money out of diamond shares became eager to participate in gold shares."[17]

Besides cultivating a coterie of wealthy financiers, Wernher and Beit participated extensively in stock market operations. During the 1888–89 boom they operated with a large, cheap inventory of Rand shares, much of it from companies in which they were not directly interested. They were enormously successful operating on exchanges in Johannesburg, London, and Paris. While the whole Rand for all of 1888 produced gold worth £ 727,800, Eckstein's declared a net profit for the five months to 31 December of £ 860,500. It could "easily have been fixed at over £ 1,000,000 but," Eckstein reported, "I preferred following my usual role by valuing everything at what I may term safe values. . . ."[18] When the boom broke early in 1889, the firms held approximately 400,000 £ 5 shares in the Robinson mine, the Rand's most prolific producer, and 100,000 £ 1 shares in about 20 other Rand undertakings. Eckstein's had been among the first to learn of the pyritic ores which resisted amalgamation. So the partners had been able to act on the stock exchange before the news became widespread and set off a panic. Wernher thought that they were caught with more scrip than desirable but judged the firm's gold share position to be "very strong." He also regretted not exploiting the peak more effectively. "It was," he observed, "a great mistake not to sell at a value 10 to 12 times above what was paid cash a short time before."[19] Still, even when other stocks became unsaleable, the partners lodged 50,000 Robinson shares in Paris at an average slightly above par.[20] Wernher, Beit and its Johannesburg representatives exploited the boom effectively and weathered the crash with little difficulty.

17. J. B. Taylor, *A Pioneer Looks Back* (London, 1939), pp. 109–10. As early as February 1889, advertisements pushing South African gold mines, including several controlled by Porges & Co., were circulating in Berlin. Printed circular in German by Felix Abraham, Berlin, 19 March 1889, in BRA.

18. Cartwright, *Corner House*, p. 85; and Hatch and Chalmers, *Gold Mines*, p. 284. By operating in Johannesburg, London, and Paris markets simultaneously, the parent firm was able to profit from arbitrage transactions as well as the inflationary trends in share values.

19. Porges & Co. to Eckstein & Co., 12 and 18 April 1889, BRA.

20. Same to same, 15 October, and 8 and 15 November 1889, *ibid.*

By 1890 the firms were more than successful financial institutions skilled at market operations and supported by a select group of European capitalists. Early knowledge of the refractory ore was no accident. Eckstein's assiduously accumulated mining intelligence. At the same time Wernher, Beit took a keen interest in mining plant and metallurgical processes. Thus, the mines Eckstein's controlled were among the first to try out the cyanide process which successfully treated the refractory ores.[21] The London firm also invested in, and Wernher served on the board of, Fraser and Chalmers, one of the Rand's main suppliers of mining machinery.[22] It also invested in Charles Butters and Company, a firm which developed several refining processes which were adopted on the Rand.

With extensive expertise and capital resources behind it, Eckstein's was able to take the lead in deep-level development. It had added another diamond mine manager from Kimberley to its staff, the London-born Lionel Phillips. The findings of J. S. Curtis and Hennen Jennings, two American consulting engineers the firm employed, convinced Phillips that deep-level mining was feasible and profitable. Buying for his own account and later, with Beit's backing, for Eckstein's, he began in 1889 to acquire claims south of the outcrop mines. By the time a test borehole struck reef at depth early in 1890, Phillip's firm "had acquired not only such deep-level mining companies as then existed but also a solid block of ground south of the producing mines from Langlaagte to Modderfontein."[23]

It was one thing to acquire the deep-level mining ground cheaply and to know the technology was at hand to exploit it. It was quite another to raise the capital necessary for development. Several outcrops had been brought into profitable production on £ 20,000.[24] But deep-level mines, with larger claim areas

21. Hatch and Chalmers, *Gold Mines,* pp. 213–14. Eckstein's was also behind legal action which invalidated the patent rights on the process. By 1895 the mines were freed of heavy royalty payments incurred in its use.

22. Fraser and Chalmers erected the first large battery on the Rand in 1887, *ibid.,* p. 2; and *Statist,* 2 December 1905, pp. 1002–4.

23. Cartwright, *Corner House,* p. 109.

24. Derived from Goldmann, *Witwatersrand Companies, passim.*

requiring more expensive shaft development and equipment, would need 15 to 20 times that amount. Moreover, capital would have to be committed for a much longer period before profits could be generated. Such sums for such long-term commitments could not easily be raised on the stock exchanges. The crash of 1889 had left the Rand in bad repute in London and ruined many Johannesburg promoters. Not only the mining market but most security markets on the stock exchanges were inactive in the early 1890s. These unfavorable market conditions left Wernher, Beit two possible options: to fund development largely through the firm's own substantial resources, or to seek capital from its financial contacts in Europe. The firm compromised. Beit, who had to convince the cautious Wernher of the merits of deep-level mining, devised the development program adopted. The partners would put up half the initial capital needed, to a maximum of £ 200,000, which would be used by a public company with the responsibility to finance and develop several mines on properties Eckstein's had acquired. Partners in the two private firms would dominate its board and be entitled to 25 percent of the profits. Capital sources already known to the firms would be invited to take up the rest of the share capital.

The London partners founded Rand Mines in February 1893, registered it in the Transvaal, and provided it with a nominal capital of £ 400,000 in £ 1 shares. Eckstein's put 1300 claims and a majority shareholding interest in five mining companies already floated into the new trust. Since Eckstein's received only 200,000 shares for this vendor interest, it was not, as was usually the case in mining company formation, overvalued. On the other hand, the partners had insured themselves a generous share of any forthcoming profits.

In addition to the vendor allotment, Rand Mines issued 100,000 shares. Kann in Paris got 3000. Ernest Cassel, an important German-born London merchant banker, received 6000. Four men, representative of the Diamond Syndicate which Wernher had helped found to control sale prices, obtained 8400. They were H. Hinrichsen, R. Hinrichsen, Harry Mosenthal, and Sir Horace Farquhar. The Rothschilds took up 27,000. Four influential consulting engineers, three of whom had been or were employed by the Rothschilds, were allotted 15,000. These were E. G. de Crano, Hamilton Smith, H. C. Perkins and Hennen Jennings.[25] Surprisingly enough a number of Rand developers and promoters were also offered allotments. Eckstein's timely move into deep-levels gave it a tremendous advantage over its competition. Rather than exploit that advantage by excluding or absorbing rivals or hangers on, the firm gave them a piece of the action. If, reasoned Eckstein, we exclude "others from good bargains now and then a good thing will slip by me. . . . In the long run it will pay better to let other people earn something as well. It will bring grist to the mill in the shape of timely information. . . ."[26] In this instance Gold Fields of South Africa, the second largest developer on the Rand, obtained 30,000 shares. Two of its directors were also named to the board of Rand Mines. Three local promoters, Abe Bailey, Carl Hanau, and Sigismund Neumann, took up 10,700. A number of small allotments were also made, mostly out of the partnership's own allocations, as a public relations gesture. Such recipients included the Transvaal's chief justice, J. G. Kotze; the state secretary, J. G. Leyds; and the editor of the Johannesburg *Star,* Frederick J. Dormer. In all about 50 individuals, including all the partners in Wernher, Beit and Eckstein's participated in the first allotment. Neumann, Bailey and another Johannesburg promoter, H. B. Marshall, and others, were issued an additional 32,700 shares for claims in 1893. Though the partners retained a large holding in Rand Mines and the number of its shareholders remained small, there was some subsequent dispersal. By 1896, for example, there were 213 additional investors on its books.[27] They were largely French and held very small amounts. By then the market value of Rand Mines's shares had reached as high as £ 45.

25. Derived from Rand Mines's original allotment book, BRA. Nathaniel M. Lord Rothschild, Alfred de Rothschild, and Leopold de Rothschild each took up 8000 shares.

26. Quoted in Cartwright, *Corner House,* p. 119.

27. They were listed as being present or represented by proxy in the *Report of the Third Annual Meeting of Rand Mines,* 19 March 1896. Jules Porges was among them.

The initial allotments made at par were insufficient to meet the needs of the subsidiaries Rand Mines developed. Within a year of the trust's formation, Perkins, its general manager, told shareholders that over the next two- and one-half years, that is, from early 1894 to mid-1896, five deep-level mines would need £ 900,000. On the basis of its share and claim holdings in these companies, Rand Mines would need to supply 62 percent (£ 560,000) of this sum.[28] Later, as new mines were formed and established undertakings expanded or proved more costly to develop than anticipated, these requirements were revised upwards. The development of Geldenhuis Deep was a case in point. The first of the shallow deep-levels to begin production, it was controlled by Rand Mines, outfitted with Fraser and Chalmers machinery, and provided with 218 claims on which two shafts intersected the main reef series at 589 and 900 feet. The mine absorbed £ 350,000 before its mill started up in September 1895, several months later than first expected. Full-fledged deep-levels were of quite a different order of magnitude. Their shafts would be sunk to a depth of 3000 feet, their claim areas would be much larger, and they would take several years to develop. Mine experts calculated in 1895 that such mines would absorb more than £ 850,000 each, before their mills began crushing ore.[29] Perkins, at the beginning of 1896, projected that Rand Mines would need to more than double its financial commitment. It would, that is, have to spend more than £ 1.2 million.[30]

The second boom in gold shares, which occurred during 1894–95, supplied some of this development capital. But it also featured enormous speculations based upon very flimsy assets. Many London brokers and jobbers not previously involved with the mining market took up vast quantities of shares for themselves and their clients. Banks specializing in gold shares were founded in Paris. Several German great banks backed Rand developers.

28. *Report of the First Annual Meeting of Rand Mines,* 2 February 1894.
29. Hatch and Chalmers, *Gold Mines,* pp. 105–7; and C. S. Goldmann, *South African Mines; Their Position, Results, & Developments . . . and Kindred Concerns* (London, 3 vols.; 1895–96), I, 113–18.
30. Rand Mines, *Third Annual Report,* 19 March 1896.

While the influx of new participants offered Rand promoters great scope for profitable dealing, it also limited their opportunities to control the market. It was, observed Wernher, "so big and so cosmopolitan that it becomes more hopeless than ever to prophesy."[31]

Following its customary caution, Wernher, Beit used the boom to strengthen its financial position. But the firm also missed opportunities to raise capital for development. Through well-organized syndicates and pools, it prevented indiscriminate large sales from depressing the price of shares in which it was interested. It reduced participations in undertakings it did not control, selling off, for example, even shares in Goldfields.[32] It also unloaded worthless shares, what Wernher called "rubbish." Nor was it, he admitted, "quite guiltless" when it came to pushing up values artificially, a practice "not worthy of a great firm." He could note with more satisfaction that neither the reserves of the partnership nor those of Rand Mines were ever "engaged or encumbered." But he regretted that the firm missed "to a great extent" the opportunity of raising additional large amounts of capital by underestimating demand for meritorious deep-level shares.[33]

When the inevitable crash came, it was exacerbated by the political repercussions triggered by the Jameson Raid and the discovery that deep-level mines would require more capital than originally expected to bring into production. The position was "much more difficult" than it had been in 1889. "Then," Wernher noted, "it was a question of £ 10,000s; today it is one of millions."[34] Many investors, and even a number of brokers who were left with stock for which their clients would not or could not pay, lost heavily. The break not only deflated and made unsaleable previously overpriced speculative scrip, it had a similar effect upon shares with great dividend potential. Promising deep-

31. J. Wernher to Eckstein & Co., 15 June 1895, BRA.
32. A. Beit to L. Phillips, 15 December 1894, *ibid.*
33. J. Wernher to G. Rouliot, 15 November and 15 December 1895, and 21 May 1897, *ibid.*; and Kubicek, *Journal of British Studies,* XI, 97.
34. J. Wernher to G. Rouliot, 30 October 1896, BRA.

level mines, needing capital to complete development before milling began, were caught short.

To offset the effect of the market break, the Corner House pursued two initiatives. First, along with other interested parties such as Goldfields, Neumann, and Sir Edgar Vincent, whose Ottoman Bank had speculated heavily, the House took up "good or fair stocks" when "no buyers [were] to be found in the market."[35] Second, to ensure Rand Mines would "not suffer for want of capital,"[36] it arranged for the company to issue £ 1 million 5 percent bonds. Of this amount £ 670,000 was placed at £ 98 in January 1897. In Paris Porges, his associates, and a bank specializing in South African gold shares took £ 120,000. German banks absorbed £ 200,000, and the Rothschild interests £ 35,000. Other subscribers closely linked to Wernher, Beit took the remainder. These included Neumann (£ 100,000); Taylor, now retired from Eckstein's (£ 25,000); the Exploration Company, a mining trust established by Hamilton Smith (£ 50,000); and Perkins, Rand Mines's general manager (£ 20,000). The remainder (£ 100,000) was absorbed by another mining trust, Consolidated Deep-Levels, a joint venture of Smith and Wernher, Beit.[37]

3. Limiting Investments on the Rand

Wernher, Beit's own resources were likely so large that it need not have called upon outside sources or close associates for the additional capital the deep-level mines required. Securities the firm had deposited with the Union Bank of London in 1895 are instructive.[38] On face value these securities were worth £ 1,170,000. Almost half this amount, or £ 547,000, was in Con-

35. Wernher, Beit & Co. to Eckstein & Co., 18 October 1895, *ibid.*

36. J. Wernher to G. Rouliot, 3 December 1896, *ibid.*

37. Same to same, 15 January 1897, *ibid.* For more about Consolidated Deep see Goldmann, *South African Mines,* I, 51–53.

38. Lists of securities of Wernher, Beit & Co. with the Union Bank of London, 31 November 1895 and 9 January 1896, BRA. Wernher was appointed a director of the bank in 1895.

sols and earning 2¾ percent. Bonds issued by the governments of Argentina, Chile, Cape Colony, the Transvaal, Egypt, Russia, and India had a value of £ 233,000. American securities, mostly railway bonds, totaled £ 230,000 and promised an average yield of 4.8 percent. Diamond company debentures included in the portfolio were worth only £ 25,500 and must have represented only a small part of the firm's investments in production and sales. Other small commitments included Netherlands and South African Railways debentures (£ 50,000), Beira Railway bonds (£ 23,000) and Fraser and Chalmers securities (£ 5300). The only gold stock in the portfolio was 5½ percent Geldenhuis Deep debentures worth £ 55,500, part of a £ 152,000 issue the mine had placed to complete its working capital needs before it began production. It would appear that from an early date, Wernher, Beit showed a reluctance to confine or concentrate its resources in South African mining. Rather it was increasingly becoming a London-based private investment house with diversified interests overseas. At the same time its commitment to Consols revealed its penchant for caution, its wish to avoid risk.

Part of the Corner House's diversification strategy included South Africa. While it profited from Rand outcrop undertakings and Kimberley diamond production and awaited dividends from its deep-level investment, it also invested in land. Wernher, Beit and Eckstein's were major participants in the Transvaal Consolidated Land and Exploration Company formed in 1892 and which owned more than 2.3 million acres.[39] Eckstein also involved the Corner House in diverse holdings in Johannesburg. In 1892 he formed the Braamfontein Company. It planted trees on farm land north of the main reef series, and sold residential lots. Through Beit's cousin, Edouard Lippert, a promoter to whom Kruger's government granted concessions, the partners established the first cement factory in the Transvaal and acquired

39. The land holdings had been acquired by Alois Nellmapius in the 1880s with the support of Porges & Co. Originally from Bohemia, Nellmapius was an adventurer, farmer, and mining promoter who got along well with President Kruger from whom he obtained concessions. C. T. Gordon, *The Growth of Opposition to Kruger, 1890–1895* (Cape Town, 1970), pp. xvii, 144, 195.

a controlling interest in a public utilities company. Both these enterprises operated in Pretoria near which the Corner House also had an interest in a silver mine. Eckstein's helped Kruger's government establish a state bank and took up £ 100,000 of its capital of £ 4 million. In 1895 Wernher, Beit also held £ 50,000 in debentures of the Netherlands and South African Railway which had just linked Lourenço Marques with the Transvaal. These investments in real estate, industry, banking, and transportation did not, however, represent large sums. Land was very cheap; and the other Transvaal holdings, alongside other items in the firm's investment portfolios, very modest. Apart from the gold mining industry, the Transvaal's capacity to absorb capital at this stage in its development was very limited. Therefore, it is understandable that Wernher, Beit's nonmining holdings would not be large. This was especially true because Beit had a falling out with Lippert that might have prevented the Corner House from participating in the lucrative dynamite concession, which charged the mines very high prices.[40] However, limited or missed opportunities do not entirely account for the Corner House's small investments in the non-Rand sectors of the Transvaal's economy.

From the vantage point of London, the Transvaal, where "politics unfortunately seem to sway everything,"[41] was too much of a risk. Early in 1896 in the aftermath of the Jameson Raid, Wernher, the Corner House's chief financial architect, told Georges Rouliot, a partner in Eckstein's, "we want to get out rather than in." "Of course," he continued, "it requires time and much discretion and no doubt we will do yet a good many transactions before we accomplish our object. We don't want to go out of business but do it with a reduced capital—later on in the form of a company with reduced cares, risks and liabilities." Wernher expected that "with improved output and returns" from the mines, and a "more active" stock market, the firm "should succeed in reducing nearly as much as we like in two years." At the same time there were "plenty of chances for a big firm to

40. Cartwright, *Corner House*, pp. 123–25.
41. J. Wernher to G. Rouliot, 16 May 1896, BRA.

make money here as a great deal of business is constantly offering." French interests might well be induced to take over Wernher, Beit's position on the Rand. "So," he reasoned, "under all circumstances a reduction in the Transvaal will be useful."[42]

As Wernher anticipated, the mines' performance and market trends did allow the Corner House to reduce its position in the Transvaal. Rand Mines declared a maiden dividend of 100 percent in 1898 "obtained almost entirely through cash dividends received from [its] subsidiaries." Its shares, which bottomed at £ 15.10s in 1897, never declined below £ 25.10s in 1898 and reached £ 45 in 1899, a fraction below their highest quotation in 1895. These values reflected Rand Mines's strong performance during 1898 and its expected future yields which, its chairman predicted, would increase "with regularity, year after year, for a long time to come, before we reach [the] highwater mark." His optimism was based upon Rand Mines's deep-levels. Since 1895 when Geldenhuis had started up, six more deep-level mines had begun milling, four of them in the past year.[43] The mining market, revived by the deep-levels coming on line and cheaper borrowing rates, took up gold shares at increasing premiums. Wernher, Beit used the opportunity to raise working capital for the mines. Rand Mines sold off about 40,000 shares of its own or of its subsidiaries for more than £ 300,000. It also used cash from the sale of 5380 reserve shares to take up additional claims, including a number owned by Wernher, Beit. More significantly, the London firm extinguished its founder's interest in Rand Mines for eminently marketable shares. Through this single transaction the partnership turned a book profit in 1899 of about £ 5 million.[44] Moreover, it would permit Wernher, Beit and Eckstein's to diminish their management responsibilities for Rand Mines.

42. Same to same, 8 May 1896, *ibid.* For more on the French interests Wernher had in mind see chap. viii in this volume.

43. Two more commenced later in 1899. See *Report of the Sixth Annual Meeting of Rand Mines,* 23 March 1899; and *Mines of the Transvaal,* various years.

44. For the right to 25 percent of the profits after a 100 percent dividend was paid, they received about 11,000 shares which then had a market value of £ 45.

Given the Corner House's financial strategy, namely to build up a large portfolio of gilt-edged government securities, to reduce gradually its capital in the Rand, and to exploit promising new business elsewhere which its international connections allowed, the attitude of its most important partner to political events in South Africa is not surprising. Wernher, from London, implored the partners in Eckstein's to work for peace and stability in South Africa. Just before the Jameson Raid he told Phillips, who conspired in the Johannesburg plot, he did not see why it was not possible and desirable for the Kruger regime "to strengthen itself and ally itself to that most conservative element: capital." After the Raid he had explained to Rouliot that "we are all interested to maintain the [South African] Republic because that keeps the land free to all nations."[45] Just months before the South African War began, he told Rouliot that such an event would "be a great misfortune" and stressed again that a "guarantee of independence" for the Transvaal was a necessity.[46] But other partners in Eckstein's, especially South African–born Percy FitzPatrick, identified the Corner House with local anti-Republican political groups and cooperated closely with the imperial factor.[47] Though the financial policies of the Corner House dictated against British intervention and war, they did not dictate events.

4. Retrenchment and Withdrawal

British intervention and war appeared to be singularly ill-timed and inappropriate developments in the light of the Corner House's investment program. They also generated several difficulties and disappointments. The war had, of course, shut down the mines; but it also sharply curtailed share business. This forced Wernher, Beit to suspend its efforts to reduce its position on the Rand. The war had cooled French investment interest and its prolongation forced the Paris financial institution, which Wern-

45. Kubicek, *Journal of British Studies,* XI, 98.
46. J. Wernher to G. Rouliot, 13 May 1899, BRA.
47. Cf. Jeeves, *Canadian Historical Association Papers,* 1973, pp. 79–80.

her hoped would assume his firm's responsibilities, to liquidate.[48] Moreover, with the value of its assets depreciated and not readily saleable on the stock exchanges, the Corner House bought more shares than it wanted in an effort to at least maintain prices. A market recovery during 1902–3 in anticipation of profitable resumption was short lived, the slump which followed long and pronounced. At the end of 1905 Wernher found the mining market "bare of buyers." The book value of the partnership's mining shares, once valued at £ 3.7 million, had been knocked down by £ 700,000.[49]

Not only throughout the reconstruction period but also after Union, mining finance remained difficult. Only a modest recovery in 1908–9 relieved an otherwise gloomy situation. After having "almost the monopoly of speculative interest, both in London and Paris" for many years, the South African mining market ran into stiff competition. As Louis Reyersbach, a partner in Wernher, Beit, put it in 1912:

> To-day you have huge speculation going on in oil; English and Russian industrials; Home Rails, to a smaller extent in Rubber. Canada has come along and is absorbing immense amounts of money; Japan takes all the world will give it; South America is by no means to be considered as out of the running; and even from the United States of America a large number of propositions are constantly put forward, as with all their wealth, the Americans find difficulty in financing themselves. In addition to this you have gilt edged securities yielding fully ¾% to 1% more than they did ten or twelve years ago. You have Sweden, Bavaria and other States borrowing at 4%; and the City of Paris issuing a loan at 3% below par, which carries a lottery chance which is always attractive.[50]

Whether it was the pull effect of other developing economies, as Reyersbach seemed to suggest, or the push effect of Europe's advanced economies, which primarily accounted for the investment surge in the decade before 1914, it largely bypassed the Rand. Was it at a disadvantage? Reyersbach thought so. The mines' actual performance, assurances of their potential, and the local po-

48. See chap. viii, this volume.
49. J. Wernher to L. Phillips, 1 December 1905, BRA.
50. L. Reyersbach to R. Schumacher, 31 May 1912, *ibid.*

litical environment—none of these inspired confidence: ". . . the total of the dividends distributed by the Rand [were] declining, and, what is just as bad, we have to realise that the Government is far from friendly, in fact, that a large section of it is absolutely inimical to the industry."[51] Performance was disturbed by several dividend-yielding outcrops exhausting their claims, by the second-row deep-levels proving more costly to bring on line, and by the reefs showing signs of declining yields at greater depth. Unskilled labor shortages and disputes between white labor and management also contributed adversely to production and the mines' reputation. Yet aggregate figures obscured the impressive dividend performance of Rand Mines's stable, and, after all, such figures did show the field's production was increasing.

Wernher, Beit's financial strategies were not only impeded by competition from elsewhere for capital, by local government, or by performance records and labor problems. The firm, along with other South African mining groups, had gained international notoriety and was the subject of frequent press and political attacks in Britain and on the continent. The indifference and hostility shown the industry by the new Liberal government in Britain was particularly galling to Wernher who knew several of its leaders well. His companies on the Rand used Chinese labor. The partners had been, in Wernher's words "thorough Milnerite[s]." So the Corner House, and the Rand generally, were attractive targets in the election campaign of 1905. Indeed, to quote Wernher again, the Liberals had "sacrificed" South African mining interests "for party purposes." After the Liberal landslide, he thought the Corner House had "to deal with an over powerful party, a great section of which does not care two pence for the Colonies and less for the Cape."[52] The government's decisions to stop the use of Chinese labor and to introduce Responsible Government in the Transvaal at an early date were also, at least initially, felt as body blows by the industry. In France, where many investors had lost money through worthless or overvalued gold shares, and

51. *Ibid.*
52. J. Wernher to S. Evans, 9 July 1904 and 20 January 1905; *ibid;* Same to L. Phillips, 21 December 1905 and 27 January 1906, *ibid.*

where a strong reaction to the British intervention in the Transvaal set in, a good deal of vituperation was also heaped on the Randlords. Adverse commentary was also apparently fueled by the lifestyles of some of the mining magnates. Friedrich Eckstein, a senior partner in Wernher, Beit, agreed with Lord Rothschild that the "unspeakable vulgarity" of the Barnato family was a chief cause of the mining financiers' unpopularity.[53]

The ability of the Corner House to deal with various disappointments and difficulties was restricted by internal problems of leadership. Beit, whose health had never been the same after the traumas he underwent during the post-Raid inquiries, became increasingly unable to conduct business. After May 1905 he was entirely lost to the firm. He died in July 1906. Wernher found it difficult to take up the slack. His energies declined with advancing years and, without Beit's venturesome initiatives, his penchant for caution increased. Following a lingering, painful illness, he died in 1912. No obvious successor to either Wernher or Beit emerged.[54] Max Michaelis, who had been a partner with the firm in London since 1890, had "not felt well for a long time" and retired from the business at the end of 1901.[55] Another original partner, Charles Rube, was unsuitable if for no other reason than the fact he had ruined himself speculating in American securities.[56] Georges Rouliot, who had become the senior partner in Eckstein's after the war, retired shortly thereafter to Paris.[57] Friedrich Eckstein, who had been brought into the Johannesburg partnership by his brother, had the experience. He acted as chairman of Rand Mines, then joined the London partners in 1899 and became a director of Central Mining in 1905. But, on his own admission, he wanted to enjoy his fortune in his later years rather than devote himself fully to business.[58] Lionel Phillips had both the ex-

53. F. Eckstein to L. Phillips, 2 November 1906, *ibid.*

54. Wernher had once hoped his eldest son would succeed him in the business, but the courts declared him bankrupt when Wernher refused to pay his gambling debts.

55. J. Wernher to G. Rouliot, 13 December 1901, BRA.

56. F. Eckstein to L. Phillips, 14 March 1913, *ibid.*

57. He remained connected with Wernher, Beit through a directorship in Central Mining.

58. Cartwright, *Golden Age*, p. 21.

perience and the ability. But he probably lacked the desire. Indeed, had he and his wife not consumed so much of their capital at a time when his share holdings had depreciated sharply, he might well have left the firm. But Wernher, who agreed to carry some of Phillips's debts, got him to take up the gaping hole in the firm's management in South Africa left by Rouliot's retirement.[59] Louis Reyersbach was certainly aggressive and ambitious. But his lack of tact and his conflicts with Phillips could not have recommended him to the senior partners for a dominant role.

Despite problems in top-level management, the Corner House was able to take a number of initiatives in attempts to shore up the personal fortunes of the partners, to stabilize the market in gold shares, to improve the mines' profit picture, and to placate government. One of these steps was begun while the war was still in progress. The Corner House arranged for a dispersal of Rand Mines's capital through a stock split. Its nominal £ 1 shares, which were quoted in the market at £ 40 or even more, were converted in October 1901 into 5s shares. French stockholders had urged it,[60] and it did enable the partners to realize on some of their holdings, although these remained large. By 1905 more than 2900 registered shareholders were recorded in Rand Mines's ledgers. They held one million of its issued shares; 1730 held 50 or less. The remaining issued shares (almost 800,000) were in the form of bearer warrants and were also likely held in relatively small amounts and by numerous French investors.[61]

A number of operators who had acquired significant numbers of gold shares and debentures in Corner House enterprises urged Wernher to form a syndicate to buy gold shares "with a view of steadying the market and regaining the confidence of the Trans-

59. *Ibid.*, pp. 50–52; T. Gutsche, *No Ordinary Woman, The Life and Times of Florence Phillips* (Cape Town, 1966), pp. 165–91. M. Fraser and A. Jeeves (eds.), *All That Glittered: Selected Correspondence of Lionel Phillips, 1890–1924* (Cape Town, 1977), pp. 141, 215.

60. Rand Mines, *Sixth Annual Report*, 23 March 1899.

61. Rand Mines, *Eleventh Annual Report*, 21 March 1906 and chap. viii, this volume. In 1896 there had been fewer than 300 shareholders in Rand Mines. Beit's estate held 181,307 Rand Mines shares and Wernher's a large number as well. Notes on Beit's Transvaal estate by L. Reyersbach, 20 September 1907, BRA; and L. Reyersbach to R. Schumacher, 27 March 1914, *ibid.*

vaal Mines."[62] A further indication of investor pressure may have been the fact that the syndicate he formed was registered in London. Wernher, Beit's previous public flotations, including Rand Mines, had been registered in the Transvaal. The African Ventures Syndicate may have also been registered in London because the recently conquered Transvaal would soon adopt English company law. The advantages of registering under the relaxed arrangements of Kruger's government had been lost. In any event, the Syndicate's capital was £ 200,000 in 2000 shares of £ 1000 each. Though only £ 400 per share was ever taken up, the nominal value indicated the Syndicate was not designed to attract the general investing public. Active and retired partners in the Corner House took up 395 shares. Some 96 other individuals, a number of whom represented banks and other financial institutions, acquired the rest. They included or represented the Rothschilds (40), French financiers active in the gold share market in Paris (92), four French banks and other French investors (487), six German banks and other German financiers (717), and other South African mine magnates, none of whom were from the other major houses (155). Sir Ernest Cassel (25), a Swiss bank (28), and London diamond merchants accounted for practically all the remaining shares.[63] It is significant to note that among the possible recruits for such a venture, conspicuous by their absence were not only the other important mine magnates, but many brokers and jobbers who had been active on the London mining market. Wernher, Beit had, at one time, dealings with more than 70 of these city operators.[64] Thus, the Syndicate had firm links with European financiers but extremely limited connections with either London's financial community or other big South African mining interests.

Whatever the African Ventures Syndicate's capital sources, and even had they been more fully utilized, they were insufficient to

62. Wernher, Beit & Co. to J. & E. Wertheimber, 16 October 1903, *ibid.*

63. African Ventures Syndicate, Return Allotment, 12 November 1903 and 14 February 1905, Public Record Office, Board of Trade 31/10472/79005.

64. J. Wernher to G. Rouliot, 4 January 1902, BRA: "We used to have a/cs with 20 or 30 brokers—last settlement we dealt with 74—the number is ever increasing, each one bringing new blood."

restore confidence. Perhaps the formation of a much larger and more visible undertaking might. The Central Mining and Investment Corporation was launched by Wernher, Beit in 1905 with a capital of £ 6 million. It was the biggest trust of its kind the Rand or even London and Paris had seen. Its £ 20 shares were allocated to about 1540 individual and corporate shareholders.[65] Through this enlarged capital source, in which the African Ventures Syndicate took a half interest, Wernher hoped to halt the downward thrust of mining share values. But he was at best marginally successful. There were, for example, far too many gold shares at inflated prices still in the market, many of these held by operators or even other houses who awaited the first opportunity to unload, even well below cost. "Losses," reported Wernher in 1906, "are terrible. I know a jobber who sold for £ 21,000 what cost him £ 82,000; even big and hitherto quite undoubted firms are in a sore plight. . . ."[66] Though capital was flowing to mines in Siberia and Australia, South Africa was "left in the cold." With no relief in sight Wernher, Beit ordered Eckstein's to "put a stop to all capital expenditure."[67] Central Mining itself, at a time when the market had recovered somewhat, was forced in 1908 to depreciate the value of its securities by £ 1.5 million and to reduce its capital to £ 3.6 million by valuing shares at £ 12 rather than £ 20. Other indications of its failure to bolster the South African gold share market was its resort to a debenture issue of £ 1.2 million at 4½ percent, its retention of 20 percent of its investments in safe government securities, and its modest plunge into extractive enterprises in other areas of the globe.

In order to make their own gold stocks more saleable at a time when market values were declining and demand falling off, and also to curtail the private firm's business, the partners decided in 1907 to sell out to Central Mining. Through this transaction finally carried out in 1911, the partners exchanged assets valued at £ 1,154,000 for Central Mining shares issued at par (i.e. £ 12).

65. For an analysis of Central Mining's shareholders see chap. viii, this volume.

66. J. Wernher to L. Phillips, 24 February 1906, BRA.

67. F. Eckstein to same, 23 November 1906, *ibid.*

Though most of the assets were transferred at depressed market prices, these were above the cost price in Wernher, Beit's books. Wernher expected the exchange to "realize a handsome profit above book values."[68] His survivors in the partnership were, however, to be disappointed. Central Mining shares declined in market value and dividends, which averaged only 5 percent during 1906–13, fell from £ 1 per share in 1908–9 to nil in 1913. Then a further £ 550,000 was written off the value of the securities.

Central Mining was used not only to stabilize the market and to make the partnership's gold share interest more liquid, but also to improve the management of assets in the Transvaal. That is, it was used for the extension of the group system. This system, pioneered on the gold fields by Rand Mines, was designed to provide a pool of expertise, a purchasing depot, and secretarial and accounting services, as well as financing arrangements, for the individual mines the parent company controlled.[69] This centralized set of services no doubt contributed to Rand Mines outstanding success. Central Mining applied the group system in part to the badly run East Rand Proprietary Mines.[70] The management of dispersed mining interests outside the Rand, and varied real estate holdings throughout the state, which Wernher, Beit had also sold to Central Mining, were transferred to a new Corner House land office in Johannesburg. But other interests Central Mining acquired were varied and dispersed, or already managed by Rand Mines.[71] Thus, before 1914, Central Mining had not evolved a group system encompassing all the many companies whose securities it held.

Nonetheless, Central Mining, along with Rand Mines, introduced a number of efficiencies and economies into gold mining. Spendthrift American engineers were replaced with more cost-conscious British experts. The Corner House was the first of the mining houses to introduce tube mills. It also took a lead in rock

68. Quoted in Cartwright, *Corner House,* p. 267.
69. For a statement of the group system as it was later perfected on the Rand see Frankel, *Investment in Africa,* pp. 81–82.
70. For more on ERPM see chap. vi, this volume.
71. See Appendix A, Tables A.1–A.6.

drill development and in using electricity instead of steam power for hoisting. Top-level local management from the Corner House was also active in the Chamber of Mines, which sought to monopsonize the recruitment and allocation of black labor.[72] In its mines, which were better managed than the average Rand undertaking, ventilation, safety, and health programs likely showed some positive results.

The Corner House, like other mining groups, also sought to achieve higher yields and lower working costs through amalgamating existing mining properties. Indeed, in 1909 Eckstein's created Crown Mines, the largest unit formed on the central Rand. Its surface and mining rights, mainly on second-row, deep-level ground, covered about six square miles. The equipment and shafts of six mines, four of them producers, were included. Development proceeded from these shafts. Crown Mines 10 shilling shares traded at over £ 9 on expectations of a 40–50 year life span; dividends between 1909 and 1913 averaged 103 percent. In 1913 it produced gold valued at £ 3.3 million, more than any other mine on the Rand, and at a working cost per ton milled of 16s.5d. compared to the field's average cost of 17s.11d.[73]

In the 1890s the performance of a single mine, like the wealthy Robinson, could significantly help push up the market value of a host of dubious enterprises. In the years before 1913 Crown Mines could not duplicate the feat. It could not even restore confidence in a number of promising properties whose development work had to be curtailed or halted for lack of capital. Neither investor nor speculator could be enticed. "The fact is," concluded Friedrich Eckstein, "South African mines are a dead letter and nobody wants to touch them." It was pleasant, though wishful, to think that the South African government might nationalize them.[74]

72. See the speech of Lionel Phillips to the Chamber when he was its president. Transvaal Chamber of Mines, *Report for 1908*, pp. lxv–lxvi.

73. *Mines of the Transvaal*, 1909–10, pp. 159–61; Crown Mines, Value of Contributing Interests and Allocation of Shares, 30 June 1909, BRA; Shares Accruing in Crown Mines to Rand Mines, 1 January 1909, *ibid.;* and Transvaal Chamber of Mines, *Report for 1913*, pp. 204–12, 234.

74. F. Eckstein to L. Phillips, 3 October 1913, BRA.

Map of mines on the Central and East Rand showing the amalgamations of 1908-10

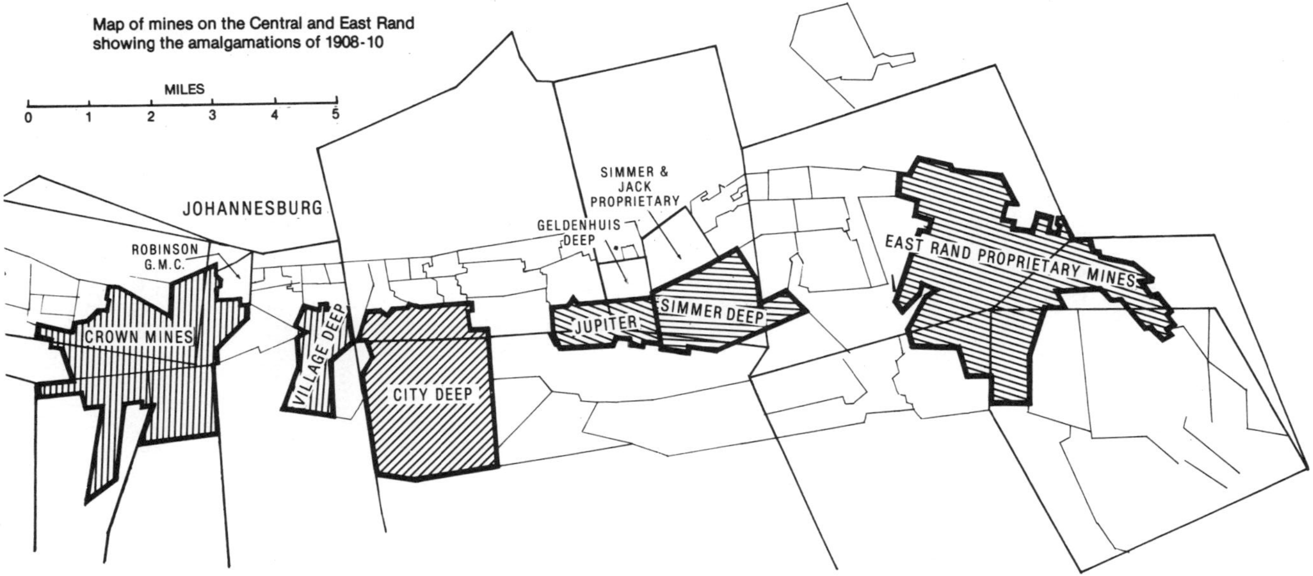

Eckstein's assessment was prompted by the knowledge that two other initiatives the Corner House pursued had not been very successful. One tactic it employed to restore investor confidence was to ensure a favorable press. Ever since Eckstein's had acquired an interest in the Argus Publishing Company in 1889, it and the London firm took an interest in the appointment of the editor of that company's newspaper in Johannesburg, the *Star*. But the men selected did not always turn out to be willing mouthpieces of the industry.[75] The London partners were sufficiently unimpressed with the value of the connection that in 1911 they agreed on no account would further investments be made in press ventures. They would, instead, be delighted to reduce the interest in the Argus Company.[76] In London, the Corner House had a particularly sympathetic interpreter in the *Statist*, and it came in for less criticism than other mining houses in the pages of the *Economist*. But it seems to have made little effort to purchase goodwill there. Paris was another matter. Here substantial subsidies, given to journals commenting on mining stocks, helped to arrest the rate of decline in gold shares.[77] But even the French press was later very critical of the transfer of Wernher, Beit's assets to Rand Mines and Central Mining. It charged, with some justification, that the private firm was trying to clear out of the Transvaal altogether by converting its holdings into marketable scrip.[78] Even in Paris total allegiance could not be bought.

Another initiative the Corner House pursued was to improve relations with and benefits from the state. With a government in power in Britain unsympathetic to the industry and committed to withdrawing much of its presence from South Africa, the London office saw it was essential to forsake Milnerism. Moreover, it

75. For examples of the Corner House's dissatisfaction with editors of the Johannesburg *Star*, see J. Wernher to S. Evans, 15 April 1904, *ibid.*; F. Eckstein to S. Evans, 22 July 1904, *ibid.*; and same to L. Phillips, 22 November 1907, *ibid.* Cf. A. N. Porter, "Sir Alfred Milner and the Press, 1897–1899," *Historical Journal*, XVI (1973), 329–39.

76. L. Reyersbach to L. Phillips, 20 October 1911, BRA. Wernher thought that the editorials in the *Star* had very little influence on parliament. J. Wernher to same, 20 January 1911, *ibid.*

77. See chap. viii, this volume.

78. F. Eckstein to L. Phillips, 17, 24, and 31 March 1911, BRA.

must seek an accommodation with the Boer government in the Transvaal which came to power there under the aegis of Responsible Government in 1907. Wernher, however, disliked politics and complained of how direct involvement in it had only got the Johannesburg partners a bad name. He was relieved when his most politically minded colleague, FitzPatrick, left Eckstein's, particularly because he thought the Boer leaders, Louis Botha and Jan Smuts, acted "with moderation and with some regard for the wishes of all."[79] Eckstein and Phillips also agreed that the best approach would be to seek frequent interviews with Botha in which "a conciliatory but frank attitude" was adopted. Such tactics, Eckstein expected, would achieve "a better recognition of the mining industry and its wants."[80] But he was to be disappointed.

Belated but effective government intervention in 1913, and the prompt action it took in 1914 against the strikes and protests of white miners were much appreciated by the firm. But the Transvaal government and (after 1910) the Botha-led Union government, appeared from the financiers' point of view to expect too much from the industry. Government was limiting profits too much, preventing the mines from pursuing new development and from offering higher dividends so as to compete for capital with lucrative investment opportunities elsewhere. "Under the existing working conditions," complained the Chamber of Mines in 1913, "the field is not attractive to capitalists." "Direct and indirect taxation," the Chamber continued, "through the customs, railways and profits tax, heavy outlay owing to the immense number of mining regulations that have been promulgated, and expenditure under the Miners' Phthisis Acts, are all factors tending to discourage new mining enterprise."[81] Little wonder Eckstein remarked upon the desirability of nationalization. The Rand entrepreneurs thought the Union government was thoroughly insensitive to the needs of capital.

79. J. Wernher to same, 2 March and 26 December 1906, 1 January 1907, and 22 May 1908, *ibid.*

80. F. Eckstein to same, 15 November 1907, *ibid.*

81. Transvaal Chamber of Mines, *Report for 1913*, pp. 419–20.

Appearances can be deceiving. The adage seems particularly applicable to the Corner House complex. It held a dominant position in mining development on the Rand. It enjoyed important European financial connections. Its senior partners amassed enormous wealth. Despite its advantageous position and its great wealth, the Corner House behaved very cautiously and as if it were very vulnerable. It was on the defensive before the South African War, an event, incidentally, that was thoroughly out of phase with the group's financial strategies. After the war, and despite the creation of the huge Central Mining trust, the Corner House was in retreat. Indeed, Central Mining was formed to save a crumbling position rather than as a vehicle for expansion or monopoly in South Africa. The Corner House group failed to capture the share it wanted of readily available European capital. That is, as we have noted in Chapter 2, there was no lack of investment capital for abroad. And, as we have noted above, the Corner House did not lack the means to tap the supply. But by the admission of its senior partners, the group was largely unsuccessful.

Wernher, Beit missed mining opportunities in South Africa because of its longstanding desire to cutback its position there and seek new ventures elsewhere. It also did not make the most of the interests it retained on the Rand or new ones acquired elsewhere because of a decline in management abilities at the top. But with much of its assets tied up in the mines and not saleable, the Corner House was forced to make changes. It effectively utilized technological innovation, mine amalgamations, and lower-level management reforms, all of which helped to offset labor difficulties and declining yields. The performance of Rand Mines's stable showed the gold fields could still produce huge profits. Why then, as Eckstein pointed out, did nobody want to touch South African mines? Why did all his firm's initiatives produce meager results in restoring investor confidence?

The answer lies partly in the profit picture, or at least how it was interpreted. Dividend yields, though not insubstantial, failed to match investor expectations built upon the halcyon performance of the mines and the mining market in the mid and late

1890s. Share prices, though they did not collapse, remained sufficiently depressed to discourage market speculators. Yet the spotty profit performance and depressed market conditions do not in themselves offer a total explanation. Given the buoyant and expansive capital export patterns, European capitalists seemed sufficiently attracted to investment abroad not to be easily put off by indifferent or lowered expectations. Given the flimsy assets which underpinned so many mining share booms, the Rand's potential was surely not to be ignored. But, on the basis of the Corner House's assessment of the situation, the political environment significantly disturbed investor confidence, an environment, incidentally, which the House tried but failed to improve. Government in South Africa and in Britain appeared indifferent if not hostile to the industry. The Randlords' notoriety also appeared to contribute to investor behavior. Thus, the unfavorable political climate and the Randlord's unpopularity, as well as an indifferent profit picture, turned off both investors and speculators. At least that seemed to be the experience of the Corner House, the Rand's most important financial group.

·5·

Consolidated Gold Fields: Rhodes and the City Connection

Herbert Davies, one of the builders of Consolidated Gold Fields of South Africa, thought the corporation had a good chance "to overshadow the Rand Mines,"[1] the firm through which the Corner House so successfully developed its deep-level interests. Goldfields's founders were early visitors to the Rand. They obtained substantial amounts of capital to develop the properties they acquired, but despite these advantages Goldfields did not surpass Rand Mines. Though it returned spectacular profits on occasion and enriched the fortunes of its founders and directors, it did not live up to its early promise.[2] As Table 4.1 indicates, during 1902–13 the mines Goldfields controlled on the Rand accounted for only 13 percent of issued capital, 11 percent of gold produced, and 12 percent of the dividends allotted. By 1914 it had withdrawn more capital from the Rand than the Corner House. It may seem paradoxical that an organization once intimately connected with the so-called colossus of southern Africa should become a relatively modest enterprise which directed its capital elsewhere. However, whatever Cecil Rhodes's talents, and many of them were overrated,[3] he was not an able gold mine developer.

1. H. E. M. Davies to E. F. Rhodes, 29 November 1894, Consolidated Gold Fields of South Africa, Johannesburg Archive. (Hereafter CGFSA—JA).

2. Goldfields was, of course, to become a much larger and more successful corporation in the interwar period. For its later history as well as many useful insights into its formative years see Cartwright, *Gold Paved.*

3. Cf. J. Flint, *Cecil Rhodes* (Boston, 1974), p. xviii. This study avoids the excesses of either adulation or spite which are characteristic of most biographies of Rhodes.

1. Backing from the City

Goldfields's cofounders, Cecil Rhodes and Charles Rudd, were among the first men of means from Kimberley who visited the Rand in 1886–87. They purchased cautiously. The nature and potential of the reefs were unproven and could be another flash in the pan like the Barberton finds. Neither partner grasped the possibilities of the reefs nor did they act effectively on the advice of knowledgeable men who did. Other claim buyers were uncooperative. Joseph Robinson, a bitter foe from Kimberley, would have nothing to do with Rhodes. He and Jules Porges had "driven up all prices." Even Porges would "join us in nothing," Rhodes complained to Rudd.[4] Their means were limited. The diamond fields, offering possibilities for a virtual monopoly, devoured energy and capital. Rhodes, therefore, used the Kimberley connection to further his diamond schemes rather than to back gold ventures on the Rand.

While his partner added to their holdings, Rudd went to London to found a company to raise new capital. Rhodes urged him to "1. Get as much money as you can. 2. Order a large quantity of machinery. 3. Draw a Trust with very wide powers. 4. Obtain us a good remuneration or else the Company is not worth working for."[5] Rudd obliged. He registered Gold Fields of South Africa in London in February 1887. Its authorized capital was £ 250,000 which, by its articles of association, could be used to acquire, develop or explore for any kind of mineral anywhere. Not knowing what properties Rhodes had acquired, Rudd was unable to assign himself and his partner a large vendor interest. He did,

4. C. J. Rhodes to C. D. Rudd, 5 February 1887 and n.d., CGFSA—JA. Numerous missed opportunities and the unproductive properties Rhodes and Rudd acquired might be put down to bad luck. Corner House success, on the other hand, was clearly the result of the cautious application of skill and insight, rather than good luck. See chap. iv, this volume.

In addition, Rhodes had a falling out with Hermann Eckstein during the early development of the mines which certainly left him out of touch with the best man to know on the Rand. The dispute is mentioned in J. Wernher to C. J. Rhodes, 26 September 1890, Rhodes Papers, Rhodes House, Oxford, MSS. Afr. S. 228: XXIII–XXIV and H. Eckstein to H. Currey, 14 April 1891, *ibid.*

5. C. J. Rhodes to C. D. Rudd, 7 February 1887, quoted in Cartwright, *Gold Paved*, p. 28.

however, insure that as originators and managing directors they were entitled to a third of the profits, before common share dividends were taken, through the issue of 200 founders shares of £ 100 each.

Before the Anglo-Boer War, most South African mining promoters set up their companies in the Transvaal rather than in London. Kimberley in the beginning, and later the Continent, provided them backing. Many were not British. They could avoid the inconvenience and constraints imposed by English company law. For example, they did not have to hold annual meetings in London or provide the register of companies with lists of their shareholders. But Rudd, from a family of genteel English landowners and a graduate of Cambridge, was British born. He also had contacts in the City, the nation's financial center.

Within a week of Goldfields's formation, 70,000 of its shares were taken firm, another 25,000 reserved for South African associates, and 30,000 offered to the public. By April 94,000 shares had been taken up in Britain;[6] by the end of October all of Goldfields's 250,000 £ 1 shares had been distributed for cash at par. Rudd had managed a very successful flotation despite the fact that to that date virtually no gold had been extracted from the properties he and Rhodes acquired. Moreover, the bust of Barberton was still fresh in the minds of London's mining market plungers.

Why was Rudd successful? Who were his backers? These questions have not been satisfactorily answered. Rhodes's financial reputation and the Rand's profit potential had not yet become well known in the City. His fame did not develop until after he arrived in London late in July 1887 when he came in any event, not to promote Goldfields, but to obtain backing from the Rothschilds to finance his diamond take-over.[7] That monopoly was not consummated until March of the following year. Initially, at least, it was Rudd's work and not Rhodes's fame which gained support

6. Summary of the Capital and Shares, Gold Fields of South Africa, 2 April 1887, BT 31/3813/23923.

7. "In 1888 he was still almost unknown outside the circles of the diamond merchants." J. S. Galbraith, *Crown and Charter: The Early Years of the British South Africa Company* (Berkeley, 1974), p. 56.

for Goldfields. Rudd made his brother, Thomas, who was a director of the London Joint Stock Bank, chairman of Goldfields. This link drew in a number of investors with a banking background. Most noticeable among them was a firm of merchant bankers, Arbuthnot, Latham and Company. One of its partners, William Reirson Arbuthnot, was also a director of the Joint Stock Bank. The private firm took up 2100 of the first allotment of 94,000 shares. It was interested in Indian railways and general and marine insurance companies. So it is not surprising to find East Indian merchants, who took up 1050 shares, and several insurance brokers among Goldfields's first investors. The Arbuthnots and their associates were likely represented on the original board by Sir Richard Pollock, a former Indian civil service officer and a director, as well, of the Southern Mahratta Railway. About 14,700 shares were taken up by Scottish interests. Chartered accountants, judges, and lawyers, as well as bankers from Glasgow and Edinburgh were prominent in this interest. What the *Economist* called the Hatton Garden group, London's diamond merchants, did subscribe for a small number of shares. They included Anton Dunkelsbuhler with 300. Formerly active in Kimberley, he would, within the decade, found his own gold mining house.

A more significant group of City backers was several stockbrokers and jobbers who specialized in the mining share market. They took up more than 8700 shares at a time when, the *Economist* noted, an upsurge in mining stock activity had been underway for more than a year.[8] Rudd apparently made a calculated effort to use these brokers to help launch the company. He appointed John James Hamilton, a member of the stock exchange, to Goldfields's board. Market operators like Robert and Thomas Hilders, Frederick Coles and Henry Whitehead, the latter two listed in a prospectus as the company's stockholders, cooperated closely with Goldfields's directors in selling stock. Other market operators who would acquire Goldfields's shares would buy and sell with no reference to management's blandishments and be-

8. *Economist,* 21 May 1887, pp. 650–51.

come, when it suited their purposes, vociferous critics of company policy.

But at its formation not even Goldfields's important backers were in a position to control Rhodes and Rudd. Their powers as managing directors gave them complete control of the company's affairs in South Africa. In fact, Rudd also controlled the London board. Not only was his brother its chairman, but two friends he had made on the diamond diggings also sat on it. These were William Farmer, who continued to have business interests in South Africa, and Leigh Hoskyns,[9] a barrister, who had been a magistrate in Griqualand West. In the beginning the managing directors could use their backers' capital anyway they saw fit.

2. Development Strategies

The success which attended Goldfields's formation was not followed during 1887–90 by successful gold mining, but this failure did not prevent the company from doubling its capital and declaring dividends. Such anomalies abound in mining company promotion and some of the reasons for Goldfields's performance were common enough. By mid-1888 the company had invested £ 98,700 in gold mining leases, properties, and shares. Most of this amount was put into three companies on claims Rhodes acquired on the west Rand. He had chosen unwisely. Ground pegged on the farm Luipaard's Vlei contained very low grade ore. Claims on the neighboring farm, Witpoortjie, were over a break in the main reef series. Production results were disappointing. But Goldfields had appropriated large vendor share interests for very little, paying, for example, £ 67,000 for 202,034 £ 1

9. Hoskyns and his father (a clergyman) and his brother-in-law, Thomas John Bowles (also a barrister) and relatives took up 2125 of the first issue of 94,000 shares.

Contemporary directories which assist in tracking down business and family connections include H. H. Bassett, *Men of Note . . .* (London, 1900–1901), which has a complete list of members of the official stock exchange, editions of T. Skinner, *The London Banks and Kindred Companies,* and of course various numbers of *Who's Who.*

shares in the Luipaard's Vlei Estate mine.[10] It sold these and other share interests on a rising market, one buoyed up by impressive yields on the central Rand. In a six-week period during 1889, Goldfields sold £ 300,000 worth of Rand stock.

Instead of using unspent capital and profits from stock deals to relocate on more lucrative parts of the Rand, the managing directors invested them in diamond shares. By December 1887 they had spent £ 57,000 on De Beers and Kimberley Central shares, by June 1888 the amount was £ 142,000. By November 1891 Goldfields's investment portfolios contained only a little more than 100,000 Rand shares at a cost of £ 33,000. Its holdings in De Beers and other diamond interests cost £ 287,000. To that date it had spent a total of £ 439,000.[11] Criticized by shareholders for the withdrawal from the Rand, Rudd argued that the move had been profitable and the diamond assets were sound.

He would find it difficult to justify a second strategy on similar grounds which also committed Goldfields's resources to ventures outside the Rand. Rudd used the company for Rhodes's schemes in the north. It created 120,000 new £ 1 shares in 1889 " 'to develop the Matabele concession lately obtained,' " and spent £ 239,000 on it.[12] By November 1891 it had spent a further £ 7525 on shares in the British South Africa Company. These capital allocations contrasted sharply with what John Galbraith has called the "pyramiding of paper capital" which featured prominently in the formation of the Chartered Company.[13] Insiders provided lots of watered stock but little of their own capital. Vendors of various concessions puffing flimsy evidence to suggest the existence of a second Rand, duped the investing public.

But some of Goldfields's backers knew enough not to want others to "pyramid paper" on their capital. Rhodes did not have it

10. Gold Fields of South Africa, Director's Report, 30 June 1888, Consolidated Gold Fields of South Africa, London Archive (hereafter CGFSA—LA); Luipaard's Vlei Estate Accounts to June 1899, CGFSA—JA.

11. List of Stocks Held and Expenditures compiled by F. Lowrey, 20 October 1890 and 30 September 1891, *ibid.*

12. Cartwright, *Gold Paved,* p. 51.

13. Galbraith, *Crown and Charter,* p. 86

all his way in diverting Goldfields funds to the north. To obtain support for the new share issue, Rudd had to meet certain demands. He had to sell off some De Beers holdings, give investors a chance at the new issue on a pro rata basis at par, declare a maiden interim dividend of five shillings, and promise to get the company as large an interest in the Matabele concession for as little as possible. Rhodes was furious. He protested the dividend, and wrote bitterly to his partner:

> I think the G.F.S.A. have behaved disgracefully. I am thinking of resigning but shall await your decision. I always said you made a mistake giving them up the concession and I must add I think I ought to have been consulted. I had merely to accept your decision. We might have had the best people in England. I have no intention of working for these fellows for the balance of my life. A more ungrateful crew I have never come across. I do not think I shall attend the yearly meeting. . . . The one point you forgot was though you obtained the concession I may have to spend my life developing it and you have handed me over to a crowd I will not work for.[14]

Rhodes's outburst revealed how important Rudd was in the formation and running of Goldfields. But he, perhaps to mollify Rhodes, pegged Goldfields's well-watered interest in the Matebele concession at 28 percent. Originally Rudd had promised the shareholders 50 percent. They also had to be content in 1890 with 55,000 Chartered Company shares with a market price of £ 2.10 in lieu of a cash dividend. Rhodes, not one to tolerate opposition, never did attend a general meeting of Goldfields.[15]

Yet for the most part his wishes continued to be met. Despite a number of pointed inquiries by shareholders at extraordinary general meetings in May 1891, they accepted part of a proposal to increase Goldfields's capital in order to buy a controlling interest in Frank Johnson and Company, a firm that had pegged gold claims in Mashonaland. The directors proposed to raise £ 260,000 through issuing 130,000 shares at a £ 1 premium. About £ 100,000 was to acquire the Mashonaland interest, per-

14. C. J. Rhodes to C. D. Rudd, 4 March 1889, CGFSA—JA.
15. Cartwright, *Gold Paved*, pp. 49–51.

haps £ 55,000 might be needed for railway work, and the balance was to be applied as Rhodes and Rudd thought best. "Are we entirely in the hands of the managing directors?" complained Edward Godefroi, a stockbroker holding 100 shares. He was not prepared to accept the proposal without "a great many more explanations" about what Rhodes and Rudd intended.[16] His sentiments were likely representative because shareholders took up less than half of the new issue at a premium. The remainder had to be issued at par.

By 1891 the makeup of Goldfields's shareholders had changed (see Table 5.1).[17] They had increased from about 400 in April 1887 to 3200. The Arbuthnots were still much in evidence as was the Scottish interest.[18] The City stockbrokers were still an important fixture and the Hatton Garden group was more pronounced. Investors were still very much London-based—about half the company's shares were held by people residing or working within a ten-mile radius of Charing Cross. But there were new financial groupings among them. A shipping interest, led by Sir Donald Currie, whose firm managed the Union–Castle line, had emerged. Currie, who was to be for many years a large shareholder in Goldfields, had interests, at one time or another, in diamond mining at Kimberley, and a gold mine on the Rand (Vogelstruis Estate) of which he was for a time chairman. He became director of De Beers but declined a seat on the board of the British South Africa Company, though he had held a significant share of the watered stock it absorbed.[19] The Rothschilds, who had raised money for

16. *Ibid.*, p. 58; Gold Fields of South Africa, Reports of Extraordinary General Meetings, 7 and 29 May 1891, CGFSA—LA; and Summary of Capital and Shares of Gold Fields of South Africa, 14 December 1891, BT 31/3813/23923.

17. Based on *ibid.*

18. For an account of how Scottish interests could play a wholly disproportionate role in the increase of British capital exports in the 19th and early 20th centuries, see B. Lenman and K. Donaldson, "Partners' Incomes, Investment and Diversification in the Scottish Linen Area, 1850–1921," *Business History*, XIII (1971), 1–18.

19. In 1891 the Currie family held more than 7500 and William Cunard 5000 Goldfields shares. For more on Currie's mining interests in southern Africa see Goldmann, *South African Mines*, I, 439–40; G. F. Williams, *The Diamond Mines of South Africa* (New York, 2 vols.; 1906), I, 281; and Galbraith, *Crown and Charter*, pp. 114, 283.

Table 5.1. ***Geographic Distribution of Shareholders: Gold Fields of South Africa, 1891***

Geographical area	Number of share-holders	Amount held £	%
Great Britain			
City of London			
Co. officials	12	20,516*	4.97
stockbrokers and jobbers	194	33,937	8.22
other	439	80,858	19.60
London (excluding the City)	866	96,579	23.41
England (excluding London and the City)			
Birmingham	98	7,698	1.86
other	951	87,965	21.32
Scotland			
bankers and stockbrokers	5	12,145	2.94
other	89	10,213	2.47
Ireland	64	5,731	1.39
Wales	13	653	0.16
subtotal	2,731	356,295	86.34
Continent of Europe			
France	183	17,341	4.20
Germany	138	14,428	3.50
other	49	7,211	1.75
subtotal	370	38,980	9.45
Other			
South Africa	95	13,601	3.30
Unclassified	20	3,751	0.91
subtotal	115	17,352	4.21
TOTAL	3,216	412,627	100.00

* includes founders shares

Note: Authorized Capital: £ 500,000 in 480,000 £ 1 ordinary and 200 £ 100 founders shares. Issued Capital: £ 412,627 in 412,427 £ 1 ordinary and 200 £ founders shares.
Source: PRO BT 31/3813/23923.

the Kimberley amalgamations, were also large shareholders.[20] Outside of London the South African interest, mostly mining promoters in Kimberley and Johannesburg, was maintained. But manufacturers from the Midlands now also participated. Such

20. They took up 5000 shares.

Birmingham worthies as the Chamberlains and Nettlefolds were among their ranks.[21] The ever-broadening share distribution pattern was not confined to Britain and South Africa. Some 370 continental investors held 40,000 or 9.5 percent of Goldfields's issued shares.

3. Easing Rhodes Out

Goldfields's withdrawal from the Rand had less to do with the poor-yielding properties the managing directors acquired, and more with Rhodes's objectives in Kimberley and the north. But the retreat had been timely. It prevented the company from suffering the setbacks associated with pyritic ores which the mines encountered in 1889. If this apparently astute move had been lost on the shareholders, Rudd made a point of reminding them when he announced, in August 1892, that the company had started buying back into the outcrops and taking a large interest in deep-level development.

Two significant developments prompted the return. First, while opportunities elsewhere diminished, the Rand's prospects improved. A new diamond pipe, discovered near Kimberley in 1891, threatened the industry with a glut and depressed De Beers shares. A second Rand did not materialize in Rhodesia and development there was, in any event, slowed by the preoccupation of the London directors of the Chartered Company with speculation. On the Rand, meanwhile, a rail link with the Cape was about to be completed, the cyanidation process to deal with pyritic ores was successfully introduced, and the possibilities of the deep-levels touted. Second, following on the complaints shareholders leveled at the financial strategies of the managing direc-

21. Arthur Chamberlain held 992 Goldfields shares in November 1891. He seems to have relinquished his share interest in Goldfields about the time his brother became colonial secretary. He was later involved with one of the companies which supplied explosives to the mines. See Cartwright, *Dynamite Company*, pp. 106–8. Joseph Chamberlain also invested in Transvaal gold mines. In 1897 he held 500 shares in East Rand Proprietary Mines. Proxy form signed by Chamberlain, 9 December 1897, BRA.

tors, the London board, with some new men among its members, took a more effective role in policy making. Rudd, whose business priorities were more and more coming in conflict with his partner's geopolitical ventures in southern Africa, encouraged this trend. Goldfields would not continue to subsidize indiscriminately Rhodes's central African vision.

Significantly enough, the initiative to return to the Rand and get in on the deep-levels lay with neither Rhodes nor Rudd. Among the first to recognize deep-level possibilities was Percy Tarbutt, a London-based civil engineer and mining promoter, who had been among Goldfields's original shareholders and whom the company had come to employ as a consultant.[22] Initially he was unsuccessful convincing Rhodes and Rudd, who again seemed unaware of the Rand's potential. Tarbutt and his partners, Cecil Quentin and Arthur Boucher, and other associates on their own account acquired the rights to a large number of deep-level claims. He also developed the Village Main Reef mine, the first to be formed on mining ground south of claims right on the conglomerate outcroppings. Herbert Davies, a chartered accountant and Goldfields's first secretary, joined its board in 1889 and maintained a vital interest on the Rand as well. He formed two companies in 1888, the South African Gold Trust Agency to deal in mining properties and company flotations, and the African Gold Share Investment Company to hold gold shares for dividends. These firms remained active on the Rand during Goldfields's absence.[23] When it became clear that Wernher, Beit had plunged into deep-levels and was prepared to undertake joint ventures with Goldfields, Rhodes's scepticism and Rudd's caution were overcome.

Davies put together the scheme by which Goldfields came back to the Rand. He formed a new company, Consolidated Gold Fields of South Africa, an amalgamation of the old Goldfields,

22. Tarbutt took up 400 of the 94,000 shares first allotted in London, BT 31/3813/23923.

23. The role of Tarbutt and Davies is developed from Goldmann's works, see especially *South African Mines*, II, 153–54; Cartwright, *Gold Paved*, pp. 42–43, 63–64, 73, and *passim;* and Consolidated Gold Fields of South Africa, *The Gold Fields, 1887–1937* (London, 1937).

Tarbutt's development company on the Rand called the African Estates Agency, and the two firms Davies himself had founded. These two companies, as well as Tarbutt's Agency, did very well. They received 246,500 shares, or almost half the number old Goldfields's shareholders obtained for the assets it merged in the new company, and a right to subscribe at par for 61,125 more. The South African Gold Trust, of which Davies continued as board chairman, also retained a separate existence and the right to operate outside Goldfields's activity. A further indication of the influential position Davies and Tarbutt had attained was their insistence that the managing directors give up their founders' interest. This entitled Rhodes and Rudd to 3/15ths of the profits. The founder share provision had been much criticized by shareholders for it took precedence over dividends in allocating profits. In exchange for 20 percent of the profits before dividends, Rhodes and Rudd got the opportunity, through an allotment of 80,000 shares, to receive 8 percent of dividends awarded ordinary shareholders. The partners also retained the right to 2/15ths in lieu of salary, and they were entitled to take up an additional 25,000 shares at par for cash. Under these arrangements, worked out during the latter part of 1892, the breakdown of authorized capital became:

—to Goldfields's shareholders (1 new share for 1 old)	500,000
—to South African Gold Trust Agency	110,000
—to African Gold Share Investment Company and African Estates Agency	136,500
—to Rhodes and Rudd for their founders' rights	80,000
—subscribed at par:	
South African Gold Trust	27,500
African Gold Share Investment, and African Estates Agency	34,125
Rhodes and Rudd	25,000
—shares held in reserve and issued in 1893	336,875
	£ 1,250,000[24]

24. Goldmann, *South African Mines*, II, 140–45.

The reserve shares were used to acquire substantial holdings in seven outcrop companies. Most went to Johannesburg operators such as Sigismund Neumann, Frederick English, and Edwin Dunning, to London stockbrokers including Leopold Hirsch and Joseph Pollak, or to other developers prominent among whom was the Corner House. The companies of Tarbutt and Davies also acquired a number of these reserve shares.[25] Goldfields's deep-level assets were put into a wholly owned subsidiary, Gold Fields Deep, formed in 1893. Since deep-level potential had not yet been realized, it might be assumed that the subsidiary was formed to shelter the parent firm from the worst effects of failure. But the subsidiary was also a convenient device through which to inflate Goldfields's vendor interest in deep-levels.[26] Speculation, as well as development, continued to dominate the financial strategies of Goldfields's London directors.

On the development side, Goldfields took on mining properties with northern boundaries a mile or more from the outcrops. This decision was made at a meeting between Rhodes, Rudd, and Davies in London in November 1894.[27] An agreement, reached between Beit and Goldfields a few days later, provided that second-row, deep-level properties would be acquired on joint account. Goldfields and the Corner House each agreed to take a 45 percent interest while Neumann got 10 percent. Other operators like Neumann were dealt with differently.[28] A contemporary map of the central Rand district showing the area of the contemplated second-row ventures, reveals that a good deal of the ground was taken up by these small operators or other mining houses.[29] These interests were awarded shares in subsequent flotations for their vendor interest, but on an ad hoc basis.

25. Agreements on distribution of Consolidated Gold Fields of South Africa's vendor capital of February, March and April 1893, BT, Register of Companies, File No. 36936.

26. Gold Fields Deep was merged into the parent company in 1898 by which time some deep-level mines were into profitable production and Goldfields had become less oriented to speculation.

27. H. E. M. Davis to managing directors [C. J. Rhodes and C. D. Rudd], 23 November 1894, CGFSA—JA.

28. Cf. A. Beit to L. Phillips, 1 February 1895, BRA.

29. See map in cover pocket of Hatch and Chalmers, *Gold Mines.*

Working capital, on the other hand, was acquired in three ways: by new share issues for cash, by debenture sales, and by stock market operations. Goldfields's share capital was converted and increased by a division of the existing 1,250,000 ordinary shares into 625,000 six percent preference shares, a like number of ordinary shares, and the creation of an additional 625,000 preference shares, half of which were offered to shareholders at par. All had a nominal value of £ 1; the preference shares, of course, ranked before the ordinary for dividends. These capital arrangements, along with a 5½ percent £ 600,000 debenture issue at 95, were completed by the end of 1894. By not flooding the market with new, ordinary shares, the company gave investors who had bought at a premium some protection. By issuing the preference shares and debentures, the directors seem to have tried to attract more investment, as opposed to speculative, capital into mining development.

Whatever Goldfields's development plans and financial strategies, they coincided with, indeed they took advantage of, the ebullient gold share boom of 1894–95. Goldfields's directors sold off much of the company's outcrop holdings at a large premium and used the proceeds to award huge dividends or finance the newly formed deep-level mines. Between 1893 and 1895 the company unloaded some 350,000 shares.[30] In November 1895 its directors announced a spectacular profit of £ 2,540,918, one which was "larger," said Thomas Rudd, "than any ever realized by any limited liability company in the City of London."[31] It allowed a dividend of 125 percent on the ordinary shares (i.e. a distribution of £ 625,000) and £ 1,145,742 to be carried forward. Its investment portfolio by late 1895 included 25,000 shares in De Beers Consolidated, 134,000 in Rhodesian companies (47,150 of these were Chartered Company shares), and 50,000 in undeveloped fringe outcrop mines on the Rand. On the other hand, Goldfields

30. Derived from annual lists of principal holdings of Goldfields in Reports of Directors and Statements of Accounts for 27 October 1893, and 30 June 1894, CGFSA—LA; and List of Investments, 30 April 1895, CGFSA—JA.

31. Consolidated Gold Fields of South Africa, Proceedings of Third Annual General Meeting, 6 November 1895, CGFSA—LA.

and its subsidiaries held about 1,200,000 shares in the Rand's deep-levels. Diamonds and the north had been largely left behind.

By 1895 Goldfields's shareholders had increased to about 10,000.[32] The commercial and financial groups prominent in 1891 were still much in evidence among these subscribers, but the number of small investors had noticeably increased. For example, among the 3940 registered shareholders who held 520,000 of the company's 625,000 ordinary shares (the rest were out in bearer warrants), 3856 held 185,000 or 36 percent in quantities of less than 1000.[33] Many of these did not enjoy the bounty suggested by Goldfields's record profits. The position of the small investor holding shares to obtain a profit from dividends is illuminated by an exchange which occurred a few years later between Davies and a South African Gold Trust subscriber.

> A lady approached me the other day [he told the company's general meeting] and said 'I have given your Trust Company £ 8.10s for my shares, and I am only getting 5s per share in return'.
>
> I replied [he continued], 'Dear Madam, if you had given the Company £ 8.10s you would have had a very different dividend; but the Company only received £ 1 per share of your money; the premium of £ 7.10s has gone into other people's pockets, and I venture to think that 25 percent is, after all, a very substantial return on the money which has actually been given the directors to invest'. We cannot make profits on money which does not come into the coffers of the Company.[34]

Though the average dividend paid by the Trust company for the previous five years had in fact been 53 percent, the woman in question, had she invested in 1894, would still have been out of pocket £ 5.17 for every share she bought. As the *Economist* observed in remarking upon the apparently attractive dividend

32. The Company claimed it had 10,000 to 11,000 shareholders, *ibid.* But estimates based on share allotment records deposited with the register of companies put the number at between 9000 and 10,000. The discrepancy may be with the Company counting shareholders by allotment. Some shareholders, especially market operators, held many more than one allotment.

33. Summary of Capital and Shares of Consolidated Gold Fields of South Africa, 20 November 1895, BT, Register of Companies, File No. 36936.

34. *Statist,* 18 February 1899, p. 263.

Goldfields's ordinary shareholders received in 1895: "Of course 125 percent is a very large distribution; but, after all, upon a £ 1 share at £ 20, it means just 6½ percent, while even at the present price of £ 17, the yield works out at less than 7½ percent."[35] Given the large increase in the number of Goldfields's shareholders, and given further that in the year ending November 1895 the company had recorded 30,000 share transactions,[36] it can be confidently assumed that large market operators made a lot of money before the small investor acquired his high-priced shares.

Some of these operators were directors or close associates of Goldfields. Davies, in putting off his Trust company's subscriber, omitted to point out that the premium she paid might well have gone into his own pocket. He dealt in shares both for his companies and his own account on a large scale. Some indication of how directors moved in the market is given by Rudd. He and Davies "with other friends arranged the purchase of not less than 80,000 shares" to keep up ordinary share values when the capital increase and stock conversion went through late in 1894.[37] Moreover, Rhodes and Rudd sold off most of the shares they obtained in Goldfields when their founders' interest had been extinguished, and, no doubt, at prices well above par.[38] Had the *Economist* known for certain that Rhodes and Rudd speculated for their own account, which it likely suspected, the journal would have been more critical than it was when it attempted to calculate their in-

35. *Economist,* 2 November 1895, p. 1429.

36. Consolidated Gold Fields, Proceedings, 6 November 1895, CGFSA—LA.

37. C. D. Rudd to E. F. Rhodes, 16 November 1894, CGFSA—JA.

38. By 1896 the Company, in extinguishing Rhodes's and Rudd's rights to profits, had awarded them 180,000 shares; they had also been given the option to subscribe for 25,000 at par. They would, of course, have had opportunity to acquire additional shares at modest prices. However, in 1898 their combined holdings of Goldfields's shares, including shares held by members of their respective families, was less than 110,000. Significantly enough, during the previous 12 months the two partners had completed 11 transactions involving more than 37,000 shares, while they held virtually no preference shares. Their holdings were subsequently even further reduced. These figures are derived from the lists deposited with the Register of Companies which could have concealed some of the partners' holdings. However, the lists are sufficiently detailed and complete to suggest that this was not the case.

comes. It figured that though Rhodes and Rudd had agreed to take out of profits only pro rata with dividends paid to shareholders and leave the remainder of what they were entitled to under emoluments as managing directors to their credit with the company, they would still receive £ 112,000. Perhaps the investors who did not speculate and those who did and were caught short when the market panicked, would have derived some consolation from Rudd's private admission to a brother of his partner: "In getting out of the outcrops we have, of course, sold long before we should have done if we could have foreseen what was coming. But this cannot be helped, and the increase of capital is, both for ourselves and all concerned, a most favourable one."[39]

Despite the unenviable position of Goldfields's small investors, the company's financial position appeared sound enough. The break in the share market and disruptions triggered by the Jameson Raid did not prevent Goldfields from declaring another dividend of 125 percent in 1896 and maintaining a large capital reserve. But, hereafter, actual mining results, rather than stock market operations, would have to provide profits.

Goldfields's local management had been faulty. Neither Rudd, who spent his time in Cape Town or London, nor Rhodes, who moved between Cape Town and Kimberley with occasional trips to London, would spend much time on the Rand. Against Rudd's better judgment, Rhodes made his brother Ernest the managing directors' representative in Johannesburg. Rudd thought Ernest "a very pushing fellow but without the ballast and shrewdness of his brother."[40] He also objected strenuously when, without his prior knowledge, Cecil Rhodes put another brother Francis (or Frank) on the Rand as a resident director in 1895.[41] Colonel Frank Rhodes was sent in to help with the Johannesburg plot rather than to assist in the management of Goldfields's business affairs. But neither Rudd nor the London directors knew this, which indicated, among other things, how little they kept up with

39. C. D. Rudd to E. F. Rhodes, 16 November 1894, CGFSA—JA.
40. Same to A. Boucher, 9 February 1893, *ibid.*
41. Same to E. F. Rhodes, 6 October 1895, *ibid.*

local development.[42] Rudd was not pleased either with the flamboyant and expensive ways of John Hays Hammond who Cecil Rhodes picked to be Goldfields's chief consulting engineer.

The American mining expert joined Goldfields in 1894 and was instrumental in providing solutions to some of the problems of deep-level mining. He, for example, doubled and then more than tripled the rate at which mine shafts were sunk. He also committed Goldfields to its major undertakings, the Simmer and Jack on the central Rand and the Sub Nigel to the southeast in the Heidelberg district. His influence was in part, of course, the result of his expertise. He dominated Ernest Rhodes and exploited the support of Cecil Rhodes, support perhaps obtained because of the large scale upon which he proposed to operate the mines, his willingness to conspire in the Johannesburg plot, and his disregard for Goldfields's London directors. Wernher, who could base his judgment upon the unrivaled mining intelligence his firm commanded, thought Hammond to be a windbag.[43] His successors said his development program was extravagantly conceived and carelessly implemented. As a member of the local management team which replaced Hammond and Ernest Rhodes complained, "I must once again say that I am firmly convinced that Hammond is the chief man to blame for all this vast, & in some cases useless expenditures at the Simmer [and Jack Proprietary Mine] and secondly the 'Captain' [i.e. Ernest Rhodes] for not looking carefully into the whole business."[44] Not only was Hammond involved in "gross mismanagement and reckless expenditure" on the Sim-

42. There is in the CGFSA—JA a copy of a lengthy statement by Rudd exonerating the London directors of foreknowledge of Rhodes's conspiracy and pointing out that Rudd himself only got wind of it in early December 1895 on a visit to the Cape. Even then he did not realize how Goldfields's resources were being used to foster rebellion on the Rand. The Company, he argued "has been more sinned against than sinning"; and the sinner was Rhodes who "seldom takes any active part" in its management. The statement has no date but cites several pieces of correspondence which corroborate his defence and of which there are copies in the archive.

43. J. Wernher to G. Rouliot, 18 December 1896, BRA. Wernher's comment should be kept in mind when reading J. H. Hammond, *The Autobiography of John Hays Hammond* (New York, 1935).

44. Major H. L. Sapte, local managing director of Goldfields, to H. E. M. Davies, 4 October 1896, CGFSA—LA.

mer and Jack,[45] but he misled London on his calculations of what it would cost to bring the deep-levels into production. There had been, wrote Ernest Rhodes's successor, an "enormous under estimate of cost."[46]

Hammond's activities which were detrimental to Goldfields's financial position did not stop at a bungled coup d'état and inefficient management. As part of his emoluments (he was the Rand's highest paid engineer), Rhodes had provided that he be allowed stock options at par in Goldfields's flotations. Stock options were a common form of remuneration for mining engineers, but Hammond wanted to make the most of his by telling the company how it should operate in the stock market. Ernest Rhodes, his willing accomplice, received rebukes from Rudd and Davies for local interference in what they considered to be London's job. As Davies put it, "engineering and finance should not be combined. It would be ridiculous for us from London to instruct Hammond in regard to shaft sinking, and I contend it is equally ridiculous for a Consulting Engineer upon the Rand to take *a market view* and judge what stocks should not be sold, and the sooner the two functions are separated, the better it will be for the Company." Davies further claimed that by not providing London with prompt and precise information about mine developments, and advising premature stock sales on four properties in which Goldfields had interests (New Rietfontein Estate, Knights Deep, Roodepoort Deep, and Simmer and Jack), it had lost out on £ 120,000 of profit. That meant, he told Ernest Rhodes, that given their personal holdings, "a loss to you and me of £ 3000 each."[47] Davies and Rudd had managed to get Cecil Rhodes to agree that it would, hereafter, be company policy that share transactions be made only in London and not on the Johannesburg stock market. The local exchange allowed many local mine officials to exploit price differences and launch stock

45. H. L. Sapte to J. C. Prinsep, secretary of Goldfields, 8 November 1896, *ibid.*

46. E. S. Birkenruth, local managing director of Goldfields, to J. C. Prinsep, 1 November 1896, *ibid.*

47. H. E. M. Davies to E. F. Rhodes, 29 November 1894, CGFSA—JA.

manipulations to the disadvantage of City operators. It was also agreed that Goldfields would no longer give options to managers and staff on the chance shares would rise, and that it would only job in the market to ease inflationary pressures.[48]

These restraints were established late in 1894, but they were likely inoperative until Rhodes's downfall in 1896, following the Raid and the plot, gave the London directors the chance to exert effective control. In the aftermath of the Raid, Rhodes and Rudd resigned as managing directors and their rights to 2/15ths of the profits were revoked.[49] Rhodes offered to break completely with the company. But the board, after consulting major shareholders, retained both Rudd, who had not been party to, and Rhodes, who it belatedly discovered had organized the conspiracy.[50] The company's capital was also increased so Rhodes and Rudd could be allotted 100,000 shares for their past services and for any claims they might have on the company. Davies, who worked out these arrangements, succeeded Thomas Rudd as chairman of the board. A distinguished soldier and administrator formerly with the raj in India, Lord Harris, was also brought on to the board as a director and vice-chairman.[51] He would succeed to the chairmanship when Davies died in 1899. Rudd retired from Goldfields in 1902, the same year that Rhodes died.

Recent historiography has shown how Rhodes had no scruples about misleading and using British government officials as well as

48. Same to same, 22 November 1894, *ibid.*

49. C. D. Rudd to E. S. Birkenruth, 5 January 1896, *ibid.*

50. Lord Rothschild was among the major shareholders consulted. Consolidated Gold Fields of South Africa, Board Meeting, 21 March 1896, Minute Books, CGFSA—LA; and Goldfields (London) to Goldfields (Johannesburg), telegram, 20 March 1896, CGFSA—JA.

It is at least interesting, if not significant, to compare how government, on the one hand, and business, on the other, handled Rhodes once it was publicly known he was guilty of subversive politics and, therefore, capable of causing much embarrassment. Each seems to have rid itself of his influence while discrediting him as little as possible.

51. Lord Harris may have been recommended through the Arbuthnots with their Indian connections. However, he had been known to Cecil Rhodes since the 1880s and was a cousin of F. Rutherfoord Harris, a crony of Rhodes, who was secretary of the British South Africa Company and part of the group of London speculators involved in Rhodesian ventures.

African rulers to further his schemes.[52] He could also mislead and use a British company, disregarding its City directors and its shareholders. In the process he, of course, disregarded his own investments. Through his ineffectual brothers he not only committed Goldfields to political conspiracy, but he also contributed to its faulty management. It was his demands on the company, not "the demands of his investments," which involved it in an attack on the Transvaal government.[53]

4. New Directions

By 1893 the London directors had curtailed Rhodes's use of Goldfields to push his northern venture. With his downfall in 1896, they were in a position to eschew politics, improve local management, and get on with development, but more capital was needed and these directors had to put their own house in order if it was to be obtained and effectively used. Davies and Rudd had made a habit of playing the market for the company as well as their own accounts. This tactic had worked when it coincided with market booms, but it was inappropriate during a market depression. The judgment of Goldfields's official history is instructive: "Too much reliance had been placed on raising money by issues of shares at a premium after the reefs had been struck, a process which became impossible on the collapse of the boom. It was equally impossible for the company, under these conditions, to realise any of its holdings for the purpose."[54]

The Company's business habits also made it unattractive to the stronger and better financed Corner House. Wernher thought Goldfields did "things too much in the happy go lucky style . . . & in bad times few will care to join them with money to help."[55]

52. See especially Galbraith, *Crown and Charter*, pp. 310–39; and Flint, *Rhodes*, pp. 227–47.

53. Cf. I. R. Phimister, "Rhodes, Rhodesia and the Rand," *Journal of Southern African Studies*, I (1974), 87.

54. Consolidated Gold Fields, *The Gold Fields*, p. 69.

55. J. Wernher to G. Rouliot, 26 December 1895, BRA.

The link between the two mining houses which had been forged by the friendship between Beit and Rhodes was broken when the latter was stripped of his controlling interests in Goldfields. Indeed, when Goldfields reneged on providing its share of loan capital for mines in which the two houses held joint interests, they had a falling out. "There is," Wernher told Rouliot, "no thought of our *financing* the G. F. They will have to pay heavily for any help they get." "We shall not forget their conduct you may be sure."[56]

With market operators and possible large backers like the Corner House uninterested in providing financing, Goldfields tried to entice its small investors. In 1897 Goldfields offered shareholders a ground-floor participation in a new issue of 750,000 ordinary shares at par. During 1897 its common shares fluctuated in the market between 3¾ and 5⅞. The following year, perhaps in part to promote confidence in deep-levels, Gold Fields Deep was absorbed by the parent company through the issue of an additional 550,000 shares, increasing Goldfields's capital to £ 3,250,000. But still "available funds had fallen far short of the full requirements of the deep level programme and . . . much of the work had to be slowed down or stopped entirely."[57]

To offset capital shortfalls because of disappointing market demand for shares, Goldfields resorted to debenture issues. During 1897–98 five deep-level undertakings it controlled issued a total of £ 1,660,000 in debentures bearing interest of 5½ or 6 percent. More than two-thirds of these issues carried the option that they could be converted into shares at fixed price. As the *Statist* observed, there was "no great risk in taking a first mortgage charge" on a Rand mining enterprise. The "investor has the reasonable safe character of his fixed charge—5½ or 6 percent—and, in addition, the chance of his being able to take shares during the term of the option at option price, and sell them, if he is so disposed, at a considerable enhancement in value within a limited time."[58] It is, therefore, not surprising to discover that

56. Same to same, 18 December 1896 and 3 May 1897, *ibid.*
57. CGFSA, *The Gold Fields*, p. 73.
58. *Statist,* 11 March 1899, p. 367.

the preponderance of the debentures in the best properties were taken up by Rand promoters or Goldfields's London backers.

The Robinson Deep issue is a case in point. This mine, along with the Simmer and Jack, was soon to become Goldfields's main source of profits. Its shafts had reached rich ore, but it needed additional financing to overcome the problems Hammond had left it. Several accidents in the mine shaft caused by poor timbering and a notorious compound made it difficult to get and keep African laborers. Besides funds to improve working conditions, capital was needed to mine the ore and install a 200-stamp mill. Less promising properties in the Goldfields's stable for which it would be impossible to raise capital should, Rudd thought, get first call on Goldfields's available reserves. But for the Robinson Deep local management, working closely with the London directors, proposed a debenture issue of £ 300,000 at 5½ percent to be offered at 98. Holders would have the right to convert their debentures at the rate of £ 9 per Robinson Deep share. Before the debentures were issued in April 1897, these shares had stood in the market as low as £ 6. Subscriptions were arranged months in advance and even before the mine's shareholders formally approved. Neumann subscribed for a third. Other Johannesburg promoters, including Henry Marshall and Abe Bailey, took up sizeable amounts. Rudd absorbed £ 50,000 on his own behalf and an additional £ 50,000 for two business firms in Cape Town. Other Goldfields's directors took up £ 8500 of £ 60,000 made available to Robinson Deep shareholders. What was left was to be acquired by Gold Fields Deep.[59] The mine's directors had the right to redeem all outstanding debentures after June 1899. But, significantly enough, they had all been exchanged for shares which, during 1899 when the company went into profitable production, reached a market high of £ 14.[60] Thus, Goldfields used debentures to attract capital from industry insiders.

59. For lists of individuals taking up Robinson Deep debentures see E. S. Birkenruth to J. C. Prinsep, 24 May and 23 August, 1897, CGFSA—LA.

60. Once the Robinson Deep started crushing on a large scale (100 stamps were in operation by March 1899), it was able to reconstruct and double its share capital to £ 900,000 and offer pro rata two new shares for each held in the old company.

In addition to earning interest at little risk and at very competitive rates, these insiders acquired shares at prices below market rates. There is little doubt they later speculated with these shares.

Meanwhile the small investor appeared to be about to get a break. The working costs on the mines the corporation controlled were going down as the new local management team proved very effective. Local government could be more helpful, but, reported Lord Harris, his company was "by no means ill disposed towards Kruger." The principle his government had enunciated of taxing declared net profits of the mining companies was not unfair. They were not "working under a crushing tyranny."[61] By 1899 the Simmer and Jack and the Robinson Deep were producing gold. Before the war halted mining, the two mines brought Goldfields dividends worth £ 415,000 and its shareholders had been swelled by 1300 new members. Though no dividend on ordinary shares was declared, Goldfields rang up a profit of £ 1 million.[62] Just as the war intervened, Goldfields was on the threshold of completing the transition from a speculative to a development oriented company, one able to award its shareholders large dividends from the profitable production of its subsidiaries. For it, as for the Corner House, the war came at a most inopportune time.

Although the mines were forced to lie idle for more than two years, they produced sufficient gold in 1902 to make Goldfields's directors optimistic enough to allot a 25 percent dividend on ordinary capital. The allotment would, of course, stir market interest. So would some of the mines Goldfields controlled. Between 1903 and 1913 the Simmer and Jack and the Robinson Deep returned £ 782,000 in dividends on an issued capital of £ 4 million. After 1907 Knights Deep proved similarly profitable. But other mines Goldfields managed were not. These included the Sub Nigel in the Heidelberg district, and the Jupiter and

61. Lord Harris to J. Chamberlain, 20 November 1898, quoted in R. V. Kubicek, *The Administration of Imperialism: Joseph Chamberlain at the Colonial Office* (Durham, N.C., 1969), p. 136, n. 56.

62. CGFSA, Report of Proceedings At Ordinary General Meeting, 14 November 1899, CGFSA—LA.

Simmer Deep on the central Rand. These three mines, whose issued capital stood in 1913 at £ 3,200,000 in £ 1 shares, of which Goldfields and the South African Gold Trust held about 850,000, had yielded only £ 145,000 in dividends. Between 1903–13 Goldfields ordinary shares earned an average of 11.73 percent and stood in the market on the eve of World War I at £ 2. They had been quoted as high as 10⅛ in 1902.[63]

Some of the factors accounting for the spotty performance of Goldfields's stable of mines were similar to those affecting the Corner House properties on the Rand. These included declining yields at depth, labor shortages and political uncertainties. An added difficulty in Goldfields's case was that some of its mining properties contained ore that faulting made very difficult to locate or which was very low grade.[64] Like the Corner House, Goldfields used available technology and mining techniques as well as cost-conscious management to meet these problems. Goldfields also exploited economies of scale through the amalgamation of adjoining properties. In 1906, for example, the Simmer Deep was formed from four existing mines, consisted of more than 1000 deep-level claims located south and southeast of the Simmer and Jack, and issued £ 1,750,000 in capital. Local management also joined in the move by the Chamber of Mines to reduce wages and ameliorate working conditions. To these measures of efficiency, consolidation, and exploitation Goldfields added retrenchment. In the three years to the end of 1910 it decreased its commitments in the Transvaal by more than £ 1,750,000.[65] It even offered to sell out its Rand interests to the Corner House.[66]

While cutting back in the Transvaal, Goldfields looked for new business outside southern Africa. As early as 1892 shares of an Australian mining company were among Goldfields's holdings, but it was not until Tarbutt interested his fellow directors in West African gold mining that Goldfields made significant in-

63. Market values and divided performances are from the *Mining Manual*, various years.

64. Cf. Cartwright, *Gold Paved*, pp. 111, 128–32.

65. L. Reyersbach to R. Schumacher, 13 January 1911, BRA.

66. Same to same, 9 August 1912, and L. Reyersbach to L. Phillips, 2 November 1913, *ibid.*

vestments outside the Rand. In 1900 Goldfields took a small interest in the Gold Coast Agency, a London-based exploration firm. By 1908 Goldfields and the South African Gold Trust had taken up shares in half a dozen Gold Coast mines. By 1911 these holdings included 400,000 shares of which the Trust held 280,000. In that year Goldfields altered its capital, the first increase since 1898, by the issue of 1,250,000 £ 1, 6 percent second preference shares. The fully subscribed issue enabled Goldfields to form a company to take over assets it had acquired during the previous three years in North and Central America. The new enterprise, Gold Fields American Development Company, had a capital of £ 2.5 million. Goldfields's vendor interest, represented by a million £ 1 shares, included holdings in alluvial gold fields and borax deposits in California, hydroelectric facilities on the Mississippi River, a power and coal company in Dawson City, and oil fields in Mexico. Other interests in the American hemisphere were held in an alluvial gold mining company in Colombia, a coal mining concern in western Canada and oil leases in Trinidad. During the period 1908–11, Goldfields also held 124,000 shares in Lena Goldfields of London which mined alluvial deposits in Siberia. It also held an interest for a short time in the Spassky Copper Mine which operated in the same region of Russia. A small amount of short-term foreign government securities and a sizable amount of British government stock completed Goldfields's investment portfolio.[67]

While Goldfields's investment program altered and its capital increased, several changes occurred in the makeup of its shareholders.[68] They increased, not only because of its new preference share issue, but also because some of its longstanding large subscribers reduced their holdings. The Arbuthnots, the Rothschilds and the Curries retained interests, but the amount of ordinary shares they held decreased. In 1898, for example, the Arbuthnots held almost 3000 ordinary shares; by 1904 they held none. The

67. See Appendix B. Central Mining beat out Goldfields for control of oil-bearing property in Trinidad. Cartwright, *Golden Age*, p. 70.

68. Derived from CGFSA, Summaries of Capital and Shares, 1898, 1904, 1914, BT, Register of Companies, File No. 36936.

Currie holdings, which were in excess of 5000 shares in 1898, had been extinguished by 1914, and the Rothschilds during that period cut their ordinary shareholdings from more than 13,000 to less than 7400. The Rothschilds also eschewed preference shares, and the Arbuthnots and Curries took up only first preference scrip. Although death and retirement may have partly accounted for these reduced holdings, another factor was also likely operative. These financial interests concluded that selling off ordinary shares at prices well above what they had cost and investing elsewhere was safer. Why entertain risk when dividends were modest? Even the 6 percent preference shares may have been considered no longer secure. It is instructive to note that Rudd, who continued to keep in close touch with the directors after his own retirement from the board, did not leave his capital in Goldfields. In 1898 he held 46,970 ordinary shares. By 1904 he had sold off all but 1075 and he took up no preference shares. He continued, nevertheless, to hold large blocks of shares in the few lucrative mines under Goldfields's control.[69] A general picture of the subscription in Goldfields's mines as of 1904 is given in Table 5.2.

Another feature of Goldfields's subscriber pattern was the decline in the holdings and activity of the mining market brokers who had featured prominently in the early years of the firm's existence. Henry Hirsch, who held 5735 ordinary shares in 1898, retained 705 in 1904 and none in 1914. Ludwig Neumann, brother of Sigismund and a member of the Hirsch firm, held 16,800 in 1898 and nil in 1904 and 1914. His preference shares decreased in these years from 24,400 to 15,000 to 1625. Only the Scottish interest maintained its large commitments. Three banks in particular, the British Linen Company, the Commercial Bank of Scotland and the National Bank of Scotland, invariably had several thousand ordinary and preference shares on hand and, as the equity summaries showed, had been involved each year in nu-

69. Apparently Rhodes also held on to shares in several gold mines. For his holdings, including vendor shares, in three properties see D. Chaplin to C. J. Rhodes, 13 February 1902, Rhodes Papers, MSS. Afr. S. 228: X.

Table 5.2. *Number of Shareholders and Their Holdings in Mines Controlled by Goldfields, 1904*

Name of company	Issued capital £	No. of share-holders	Average holding £ shares
Rose Deep	425,000	3,993	55
South Geldenhuis Deep	367,000	3,294	37
Simmer & Jack East	600,000	1,896	147
Nigel Deep	450,000	4,197	99
Simmer & Jack Proprietary	3,000,000	7,090	147
Robinson Deep	950,000	2,590	188

Note: These holdings exclude, of course, shares held by nominees for the parent companies, Goldfields and the South African Gold Trust.
Source: Report received by the intelligence department of CGFSA, 29 February 1904, CGFSA—LA.

merous share transactions.[70] The European shareholders had only been a small element among Goldfields investors in the early years, but if one assumes that most of its bearer shares were in French hands, then they became a much larger group after 1900. In 1898 only 167,000 ordinary shares were in the form of bearer warrants; but this number increased to 630,000 in 1904 and 837,000 or 42 percent in 1914. One might further safely conjecture that many of these bearer shares were held in small numbers by the small French investor.[71] Indeed, ordinary shares had been very widely dispersed. Apart from the blocks held by directors in the name of the company and its subsidiaries, only five people held more than 2000; only 32 held 2000 or more preference shares. Goldfields could earn the investor 6 percent; but knowledgeable financiers and market operators in selling off common stock to small investors indicated they believed it would not earn more or was too risky to keep.

By 1914 Goldfields, though it had become a better managed

70. This continued Scottish interest in gold shares may have been sustained by active local stock markets. Cf. W. A. Thomas, *The Provincial Stock Exchanges* (London, 1973), p. 311.
71. See chap. viii, this volume.

and more efficient corporation than it had been in the early 1890s, had disappointed its ordinary shareholders for a decade. It was not able through gold production to duplicate the profit performance of 1895–96 which had been responsible for over-inflating market values and investor expectations. Goldfields did seek to live up to these expectations, but not through its past commitments. Though it retained a small interest in moribund Rhodesian mining, its efforts in the decade after the Anglo-Boer War were less directed towards southern African, as its cutback on the Rand showed, and more to opportunities elsewhere, as its investments in North America indicated. These new investment strategies had, however, not paid off. Goldfields had become an international, one might say a multinational corporation, sustained significantly, but not very profitably, by three successful South African gold mines.

While Goldfields's investment policies underwent a radical alternation, its investor profile also substantially altered. From its inception Goldfields had a large clientele, but it was concentrated in and about the City and included a number of important financial groupings. These included important banking institutions such as the Arbuthnots and especially the Rothschilds. Several stockbrokers also held large blocks of shares. However, by the early 1900s these backers had significantly reduced their share holdings. Scotland and France and the rest of England took up some of the slack, but the small investors rather than large interests acquired shares. Thus, as Goldfields's capital increased and its investments became worldwide, its investors grew more numerous and dispersed.

• 6 •

The Houses of Ill Repute

The enterprises of three mining groups, the Barnato family, Joseph Robinson, and George Farrar and associates, accounted for about 20 percent or £ 15.8 million of the Rand's dividends in the period 1902–13.[1] At the same time these enterprises issued shares with a nominal value of about £ 18 million. If these figures are compared with those generated by the Corner House and Goldfields, a significant difference emerges. These three groups, in the aggregate, issued only £ 4 million share capital less than the Corner House and Goldfields combined, but yielded £ 31 million less in dividends. This discrepancy may in part be accounted for by the relative poor quality of the ore in the properties they acquired and by unsatisfactory mine management programs. However, a major contributing factor was their financial methods which may not have differed in kind, but certainly differed in degree, when compared to the techniques employed by the Corner House and Goldfields.

1. The Barnatos' Wizardry

Barney Barnato had been forced into a back seat in Kimberley through Wernher, Beit's support of Rhodes's amalgamation schemes. He also had been very behindhand in moving into the Rand. Yet by 1913, the Barnato group under the control of his cousin, Solomon Joel, surpassed both the Corner House and Goldfields. It became the leading force in the Diamond Syndi-

1. See Table 4.1.

cate and assumed a leadership role on the gold mines through its plunge into far-east Rand development. In the interval, cooperation between Wernher, Beit and Goldfields, on the one hand, and the Barnato group, on the other, had been minimal and acrimony common. What has been described as the "strongly divergent identities"[2] of South Africa's mining magnates no doubt helped account for this lack of cooperation. But contrasting business methods also minimized opportunities for joint enterprises.

For several years after Barnato began to invest in the Transvaal in December 1888, most of his gold mining company formation was directed toward booming shares outrageously. Later, after Joel assumed command, the group downgraded though never stopped this practice, and became more development oriented. Its early emphasis on share promotion is indicated by certain features in the performance of its subsidiaries. Between 1889 and 1913 the group floated and controlled more than 30 mines in the Transvaal. Something like 80 percent of the total of their issued share capital was offered before 1902, while about 80 percent of the dividends they generated were declared after that date.

One of Barnato's most notorious early flotations was the Eagle Gold Mining Company. Formed in February 1889, it acquired 400 acres of a farm seven miles southwest of Johannesburg. Though it was located far from the outcrops of the main reef series and deep-level possibilities had not yet been mooted, he capitalized the property at £ 350,000—all but £ 50,000 of which went to the vendors. (Goldfields was founded in 1887 with a nominal capital of only £ 250,000 and Rand Mines in 1893 with only £ 300,000 and on terms not so favorable to their vendors.) In the same month Barnato reconstructed the National Gold Mining Company with 35 claims on or immediately south of the main reef outcrop on the west Rand. All but 30,000 of its 170,000 shares went to the vendors. The share boom broke before too many shares of these two undertakings reached the public's portfolios, and they were reconstructed on somewhat more realistic terms in 1891. Though hardly adjoining concerns, the Eagle and the Na-

2. Roberts, *Diamond Magnates,* p. 306.

tional amalgamated as the Unified Main Reef Gold Mining Company with a capital of £ 55,000 of which £ 40,785 was issued to the shareholders in the old companies. Eighteen claims south of the reef and a twenty-stamp battery, the assets of the New Edinburgh Gold Mining Company, were then acquired for 45,000 shares. Additional mining ground adjacent to the outcrop property was purchased for 40,000 shares in 1893. By then, renamed the New Unified Gold Mining Company, it had an issued capital of £ 140,000 but little of this had been allotted for working capital, and it borrowed at 12 percent from Barnato's loan and investment company. The first substantial share issue for working capital was made during a further reconstruction in 1895. The vendor interest was scaled down, the old shareholders getting two new for five held or 56,000 shares; they were offered 28,000 at par, these guaranteed, and the guarantors were to take up or had options on the rest (66,000) at par. The Barnatos were the guarantors and, one assumes, holders of many of the old shares which they had effectively allotted themselves at rates much below par. Up to this time the properties had absorbed about £ 85,000 in working capital and produced only 28,626 ounces of gold valued at £ 103,815. The New Unified's shafts found broken ground and patchy reef. Indeed, milling operations had to be suspended during 1895. This performance, coupled with the fact that the latest capital arrangements came on the eve of the break in the mining share boom, prevented the market value of the shares rising above par. The mine continued a disappointment to its shareholders and did not resume milling until late 1898. In 1899, in the nine months before war was declared, it produced gold worth £ 56,836 at a loss of £ 1281. During the flurry of market activity at the close of the war, a pro rata issue of 100,000 shares was guaranteed by its parent financial house for a commission of 5 percent. With the proceeds from the new capital the old mill was replaced by new equipment, including a sixty-stamp battery, and a new program adopted to exploit knowledge gathered of the nature and course of the dykes and faults which broke up the reefs. Milling resumed in 1903. Despite labor problems the mine paid its first dividend in 1908, and by 1913 when it had produced almost £ 2 million worth of gold, it had returned 100 percent on its issued capital of £ 250,000. Its shares in the interim had reached market values as high as £ 2⅛.[3] Here then was an example of a highly watered flotation consisting of a marginal outcrop mine and 450 acres freehold far from the outcrop, being transformed by a reduction of its capital, an absorption of its debts by its parent financial house (at of course high interest) and, after long neglect, effective reorganization which produced gold at a profit.

An example of a financial undertaking which the Barnatos came to control but did little to transform, was a mine called Buffelsdoorn Estate in the Potchefstroom district 60 miles southwest of Johannesburg. The property, on which development began in 1889, was expanded by 1895 to include claims on several farms and covered 30,000 acres. Gold was extracted from the reefs on the property from 1890 and though by 1895 a total of 67,000 ounces had been produced, the mine steadily lost money. The largeness of the mining area and its possibilities had obtained for its developers, the Pullinger brothers, some financial backing from the Johannesburg entrepreneurs. However, the more knowledgeable among them, especially Eckstein's, learned from an early date that an immense dyke intersected the reef and would likely kill off any chances the low-grade mine had of making a profit from production. Whether the Barnatos knew of its limitations or not, they did reconstruct it on a large scale in 1895 to make the most of the share boom. Its capital was increased to £ 550,000 by the creation of 300,000 new shares of which the vendors were awarded 200,000 and who took up a further 50,000 at £ 2.10s. The remaining 50,000 were put into the market at £ 3. The Estate company also acquired over half the shares of the Buffelsdoorn A Gold Mining Company, floated the same year with an issued capital of £ 212,500 to which it had turned over 200 claims. Another distinct group of Johannesburg speculators

3. L. Cohen, *Reminiscences of Johannesburg and London* (London, 1924), p. 113; Dennis Edwards and Company, *The Gold Fields of South Africa* (Cape Town, 1890), p. 169; Goldmann, *Witwatersrand Companies*, pp. 162–63, 243; Goldmann, *South African Mines*, I, 302–4; Mabson, *Mines of the Transvaal*, various years.

also got in on the promotion. It floated the Buffelsdoorn Consolidated out of unworked ground adjoining the Barnato undertakings, awarded itself 175,000 shares, and issued another 100,000 at par, ostensibly for working capital. Thus, by the middle of 1895, these three companies generated more than one million shares, most of which their organizers could use for speculative purposes. Through Edgar Vincent and the Ottoman Bank, large numbers of the shares of the Barnato-controlled companies were placed in Paris. Buffelsdoorn Estate, which began in 1895 at £ 3.10s, reached £ 9 on the London market by the end of August. Buffelsdoorn Consolidated rose to 3⅛. These quotations tailed off sharply when the boom broke to about £ 3 and £ 1 respectively. Before the war they had dropped below par. All three companies were in liquidation by 1908. None ever declared a dividend.[4]

It is impossible to determine what amounts gullible investors or even professional speculators lost on these flotations. But they were considerable. Edgar Vincent, for example, was sufficiently out of pocket to threaten to make it so hot for Barnato in Paris that he would be unable to place his stocks outside of England if the Buffelsdoorn Estate's financial affairs were not reformed.[5] During improved market conditions in 1899, the Barnato group did guarantee a reconstruction of the company which liquidated an indebtedness of about £ 380,000 and lent it a further £ 10,000 at 8 percent.

While it indulged significantly in profiting from booming marginal mines, the Barnato group also acquired a few rich outcrop producers on the eastern edges of the central Rand which became essential mainstays of the group's performance. Three outcrops, the (New) Primrose, the Glencairn and the Ginsberg, accounted for 84 percent of the dividends declared by the Barnato gold mining enterprises before the Anglo-Boer War, and 47 percent between 1902 and 1913.

4. W. P. Taylor, *African Treasures* (London, 1932), pp. 107–12; Goldmann, *South African Mines,* II, 7–14; *Stock Exchange Official Year-Book,* 1899, pp. 2080–81; *Mining Manual,* various years.

5. E. Vincent to S. Evans, 22 August 1896, BRA.

Though these mining enterprises came under the aegis of Barnato's main investment trust, that financial institution was more concerned during its formative years with real estate. The Johannesburg Consolidated Investment Company was formed in the Transvaal in 1889 to own and manage two businesses. These included the Johannesburg Waterworks, Estate and Exploration Company which was in a state of near-bankruptcy when Barnato acquired it during the slump of 1889. It supplied the water-short city with much of what it used through an inadequate spring-fed system. The waterworks firm became a wholly owned subsidiary of JCI in 1895 and was acquired after the South African War by the municipality for about a £ 1 million. JCI also took over the assets of four estate companies that controlled a large tract of ground immediately northeast of the Johannesburg townsite. Through the Johannesburg Estate Company, one of the few concerns of the period in which he as well as Eckstein's were represented, Barnato and JCI were interested in residential development and commercial real estate. Though the evidence available does not allow a precise estimate, the Barnato group had by 1895 invested about £ 200,000 in real estate, had about £ 400,000 out in short-term loans, and had sunk £ 800,000 to £ 900,000 in mining property and shares.[6] The mining end of the business was expanded in that year by the creation of Barnato Consolidated Mines formed to hold gold shares and deep-level mining claims. It, JCI, and their subsidiaries created more than 5,000,000 shares, on the basis of an investment of about £ 1,500,000, during the 1894–95 boom. Some measure of the magnitude of the overvaluation of actual investments, as well as their potential, may be gained from an analysis of statements published by Barnato Consolidated. With the exception of one property in Lourenço Marques, its holdings were all in the Transvaal and mainly on the Rand. Its shareholders were told that the company's interests were "equivalent to about 2500 claims, some of which are situated in the immediate neighbour-

6. *The Story of 'Johnnies,' 1889–1964: A History of the Johannesburg Consolidated Investment Co. Ltd.* (Johannesburg, 1965); *Mining Manual,* various years.

hood of companies whose shares represent . . . a value of from £ 20,000 to £ 50,000 per claim," and some of which were "held in conjunction with" Goldfields, Rand Mines and "other leading firms and corporations." Since only 87 of the claims held were in the central Rand, while 700 were in the western and 1500 in the far-east Rand, very few of them were held in conjunction with either Goldfields or Rand Mines, which were primarily concentrated in the central and east-central Rand.[7] It is significant to note that the deep-level ground south of the New Primrose and Glencairn mines, rich Barnato-controlled outcrops, was held by either Rand Mines or Goldfields. Barnato Consolidated listed no holdings in it. Indeed, Goldfields and Rand Mines avoided joint undertakings with Barnato, especially when it came to the rich ground of the central Rand. At the same time many of the claims Barnato Consolidated listed as in its possession were either on the dip of marginal outcrops, or quite far removed from mining development. Thus very little of its mining ground was near that of companies who were valuing their claims for more than £ 20,000 apiece. Yet Barnato Consolidated on the strength of its holdings started life with an issued capital of £ 1 million, and contributed appreciably to the market glut which was an essential cause of the inevitable break which not only caught short a lot of its shareholders, but threatened Barnato's own fortune.[8]

The fate of two investment firms geared to Barnato's speculations is instructive. The Barnato Banking Company was formed during the boom with an issued capital of £ 2,500,000 to acquire gold and diamond shares for which it paid prices well above par, though somewhat lower than current inflated market quotations. When the panic struck, Barnato was forced to promise publicly to buy back these securities at the price which he sold them to the Bank. The Bank was liquidated in 1896 and JCI took over its assets, paying out 1,503,125 shares at the rate of 5 shares for 8 Bank shares. The London–Paris Financial and Mining Corporation, founded in 1895 and with which JCI divided its interests, also had to reduce its capital from £ 500,000 to

7. *Statist,* 23 November 1895, pp. 613–14.
8. Kubicek, *Journal of British Studies,* XI, 99–100.

£ 375,000. The source of all its shareholders' difficulties was "that in the time of the boom of 1895 they invested heavily in the stocks of a very speculative nature, in the main belonging to one group of South African mining securities."[9]

Barney Barnato's gaudy promotions and unstable temperament fostered the creation of highly speculative undertakings based mostly on marginal or undeveloped properties. Tempted by the share boom, his group used these undertakings to flood the market with a vast quantity of watered stock. Undermined by the torrent which was fed as well by his fellow magnates, especially Robinson and Farrar, the market collapsed, endangering his financial resources and impairing his health.

After Barney Barnato's death by suicide in 1897 and that of his cousin Woolf Joel, who was murdered in 1898, it must have taken the latter's brother Solly some time to reorganize and redirect the group's financial policies, a program interrupted by the outbreak of the South African war. Very little evidence exists even to chart the program, let alone to reveal Joel's capital sources. However, in 1905 JCI absorbed Barnato Consolidated Mines and the occasion required more public disclosure of the holdings of the two companies than usual. By this time Barnato Consolidated had converted a number of its claim holdings into shares and, following the pattern set by Goldfields and Rand Mines, extinguished in 1902 the founders' rights (25 percent of the profits after dividends of 100 percent had been paid), in this case by issuing 250,000 shares to the Barnatos. Since the company had not yet paid a dividend, the move was less a concession to existing shareholders and more an invitation to potential new ones whose capital would be needed to do something with more than 1400 undeveloped claims which it still retained. What claims it had converted into shares in mining flotations were largely located on the east Rand. The small number of claims it once held on the central Rand were absorbed for shares by the Ferreira Deep and Jumpers Deep, both controlled by Rand Mines. The Corner House even absorbed Barnato Consolidated

9. *Statist,* 18 March 1899, p. 438.

claims located below the New Unified mine when it floated the Main Reef West in 1899.[10]

JCI, before it absorbed Barnato Consolidated, claimed to have assets worth £ 5,154,000. Five percent of this amount (about £ 250,000) was represented by holdings in Barnato Consolidated, 10 to 20 percent (£ 500,000–£ 1,000,000) by shares in diamond companies, perhaps 20 percent by gold mining shares which included about £ 500,000 tied up in its two most productive mines, the New Primrose and the Glencairn. A substantial amount of its assets, more than £ 850,000, was also on loan to mining companies; of this amount 40 percent was out to the moribund Langlaagte Royal on the west-central Rand. JCI's real estate investments were valued at about £ 900,000 or 17 percent of its total assets. Another £ 400,000 was out in short-term, high-yield loans on the London and Johannesburg money markets. It had £ 230,000 in cash on hand. During the next decade JCI's assets were valued at between £ 5,700,000 and £ 4,000,000; the lower figures was for 1914. While its investments in real estate declined marginally, those in short-term loans increased slightly and loans to mining companies were extinguished. Though it was forced to depreciate or write off a substantial part of the assets it had acquired through the absorption of Barnato Consolidated Mines in 1905, its investments in stocks and shares increased over the period, reaching £ 3,200,000 or 80 percent of the total assets in 1914.

JCI acquired its large security holdings through two distinctive initiatives. It sold off mining ground and assets held on the central Rand to other houses bent on various amalgamation schemes. JCI, for example, liquidated at a profit its loan to Langlaagte Royal through selling it to Crown Mines which the Corner House put together in 1909. Its second initiative featured extensive development on the east and far-east Rand. While the Corner House and Goldfields either sought to curtail, consolidate, or avoid development, JCI plunged ahead. It beat them out in a deal to acquire mining ground from the government

10. *Ibid.*, 1 July 1905, p. 7; *South African Mining Journal*, 12 August 1905, p. 524, and 25 September 1905, p. 872; *Mines of the Transvaal*, various years.

and, on property thus acquired south of the Corner House's Modderfontein mines, formed in 1910 the Government Gold Mining Areas Company with a capital of £ 1,400,000, almost all of which Barnato Brothers took up at par. In addition to its flotation of Government Areas, and its retention of three outcrops (Ginsberg, Glencairn, and New Primrose) with a total issued capital of £ 1 million, JCI controlled three other mines: the Witwatersrand Gold Mining Company (a T-shaped property with claims both on and well below the outcrops capitalized at £ 425,000), the New Rietfontein located north of the main reef series (£ 610,084) and the Van Ryn Deep (£ 500,000), a deep-level on the far-east Rand just northwest of Government Areas which started production in 1913. All these east and far-east Rand undertakings had an issued capital of more than £ 5 million of which JCI may have held about 40 percent. By selling off shares it acquired in the central Rand amalgamations, by reaping profits from its outcrop producers, by limiting dividends to an average yield of 6 percent during 1902–13, and by doing well off its diamond interests, JCI managed to finance its east and far-east Rand undertakings without substantial capital increases (its share capital stood at £ 3,950,000 unchanged since 1905 when it absorbed Barnato Consolidated for 1,200,000 shares), and without drastically depreciating its stock values. Its shares hovered about par at the end of the period.

Solly Joel, meanwhile, augmented the Barnato wealth which had been depleted by the mining market crash of 1895–96 and the dislocations of war in South Africa. He used his own personal fortune to "gamble in almost any department of the Stock Exchange, including Americans" and as far as South Africa was concerned "concentrated almost entirely on Diamonds where" his holdings were estimated "at somewhere in the neighborhood of £ 4,000,000."[11] JCI's shareholders, whoever they might be,

11. L. Reyersbach to R. Schumacher, 27 March 1914, BRA; also H. Heim to J. Wernher, 9 October 1911, *ibid.*, which notes that Barnatos were consistent buyers of De Beers stock while Wernher, Beit were sellers. After the war Barnatos diversified extensively by going into the food business, real estate, and cotton production in England. S. Joel, *Ace of Diamonds, the Story of Solomon Barnato Joel* (London, 1958), pp. 142–44.

contributed less to this personal wealth than had the investors who plunged for Barney Barnato's speculations in the early 1890s. They also stood less chance of losing their capital, but could only expect modest returns. In contrast to the Corner House and Goldfields, the mining end of the Barnato group increased rather than reduced its commitments in the Transvaal. Moreover, the group's holdings in property remained extensive and its investment in sectors of the South African economy other than mining and property, larger and more venturesome than its rivals.[12]

2. Robinson's Chicanery

When the House of Lords in 1922 challenged the award of a peerage to Sir Joseph B. Robinson, Lord Harris, Goldfields's chairman, led the attack. He pointed to Robinson's sordid financial deals, revealed through litigation recently brought against him by Solly Joel, by which he had made extraordinary profits during 1906–9 at the expense of his companies' shareholders. These revelations, coupled with Robinson's known pro-Boer sympathies fueled public outrage. No doubt to the relief of Prime Minister David Lloyd George, the retired mining magnate declined the honor.[13] That two gold mining entrepreneurs should attack one of their own kind suggests Robinson's financial transactions had been much worse than many of their own questionable practices. However, his worst sin, as far as they were concerned, was his total disregard for the interests and sensibilities of his fellow Rand capitalists. Joel took him to court, not because Robinson had exploited the investing public, but because he had got the better of him in a business deal.[14]

12. *Mining Manual,* 1915, pp. 324–25.
13. *The Times,* 23 and 30 June 1922.
14. Joel discovered he had paid too much when he acquired Robinson's principal mining interests in 1916 for £ 4,500,000. Through the court action he recovered more than £ 500,000, *Cape Times,* 2 July 1920; and Robinson v. Randfontein Estate Gold Mining Company, *South African Law Reports, Decisions of the Supreme Court Appellate Division, 1920–21* (Cape Town, 1922), pp. 168–271.

Robinson, who was the first Kimberley magnate to arrive on the Rand in 1886, was also a man at this juncture of very limited financial means. Born in the Cape, a first-generation offspring of the 1820 settlers, he became a traveling wool merchant who bought the clip of Afrikaner farmers. An early arrival at the river diggings and later at the Kimberley pipe, he bought diamonds, acquired claims, then founded several companies. He became one of Kimberley's most important mining promoters. Self-made, egotistical, and quarrelsome in the extreme, he was quite unable to cooperate in business with anyone. He never learned, like most of his fellow magnates, to cultivate advantageous arrangements with competitors which did not restrict opportunities for independent initiatives. This inability to cooperate, coupled with serious landfalls in the Kimberley pipe which forced his most lucrative property to lie idle, pushed him by 1886 to the verge of bankruptcy.[15] These inhibiting difficulties also prevented him from taking a lead, or being a significant factor, in the amalgamative process which allowed the ascendancy of De Beers. He had been, however, party to an amalgamation proposal which involved an international consortium consisting of Brazilian diamond interests, a London-based exploration company and two French banks.[16] It was none of these contacts but, paradoxically enough, another diamond magnate, Alfred Beit (in league with Rhodes, whom Robinson hated) who lent him £ 20,000 or £ 25,000 which enabled Robinson to try his luck on the Rand.[17]

Using his fluent taal to good advantage, Robinson bargained

15. He had to place shares nominally worth £ 100,000 in two of his companies in the hands of the Cape of Good Hope Bank as collateral for loans to keep going. Roberts, *Diamond Magnates,* pp. 175–76.

16. The British firm was the London and South African Exploration Co., Gregory, *Oppenheimer,* p. 52; Roberts *Diamond Magnates,* p. 174; P. Lewsen (ed.), *Selections From the Correspondence of J. X. Merriman,* (Cape Town, 1960), pp. 199–200.

17. Many versions of this transaction exist, but most obscure the fact that Robinson, though strapped for capital, had assets. These were shares in diamond companies which, given Beit's own involvement in the amalgamative process in Kimberley, would have been useful had Robinson been unable to pay back the loan. Indeed, Beit "'arranged to take over Robinson's position from the Cape of Good Hope Bank.'" Percy FitzPatrick, quoted in Roberts, *Diamond Magnates,* p. 217.

assiduously with Boer owners for likely mining properties. His purchases led to the formation of the lucrative mine that bore his name on the farm Turffontein, which became part of the central Rand. Eckstein's bought him and his associate, Maurice Marcus, out of it in 1888 for £ 250,000.[18] Robinson also acquired properties further west on the neighboring farm Langlaagte, and on Randfontein (on what became the far-west Rand some 20 miles from Johannesburg), which formed the basis for the flotation of two mining clusters with, what was for the time, extremely large capital provisions. One cluster consisted of the Langlaagte Estate, formed in 1888 with a capital of £ 450,000, and the Block B Langlaagte, floated the following year at £ 632,500. The other began with the Randfontein Estates Gold Mining Company, formed in 1889 with a capital of £ 2 million out of very large holdings on eight farms the mining area of which amounted to almost 3000 claims or about 4.5 square miles. These three companies, though they had a total authorized capital of more than £ 3 million, provided only 423,500 £ 1 shares for issue as working capital. Some of these were issued at a premium and, along with 50,000 new shares added to the Langlaagte Estate's capital, had by 1895 generated £ 618,600 in working capital.[19] Meanwhile Randfontein failed to provide dividends, though Langlaagte Estate yielded £ 682,400, and the Block B £ 20,000. Any outside investors, tying their capital to Robinson's undertakings and waiting for dividends, were not turning much profit if at all. Had they made the most of the share boom of 1888–89, when Langlaagte Estate shares stood as high as £ 7,[20] they would have prospered exceedingly. Robinson no doubt took the opportunity to make large profits. If, for example, on a conservative estimate, his share of the vendor interest in Langlaagte Estate had been one quarter of the 400,000 vendor shares which cost him £ 10,000 (a very generous estimate), and he sold them for £ 2, rebought at £ 3, sold at £ 5 and retained his interest by buying again after the break, when they bottomed at £ 2, his profit

18. See chap. iv, p. 58, n. 8, this volume.
19. Goldmann, *South African Mines,* I, 23–30, 184–96, 333–45.
20. *Economist,* 28 November 1891, p. 1522.

would have been £ 190,000. If, as was likely, he sold, bought and resold several times on the rising market it would have been even greater.

Some of these super profits may have been lost in the short-lived depression before the second boom began in 1894. But by 1895 Robinson was able to extinguish the Corner House's interest in Randfontein which had been obtained through Beit's timely loan. He need not be dependent on the connection any longer, a consideration which no doubt pleased the Corner House as much as it satisfied Robinson.[21]

His intractable, fractious nature meant the relationship could not have been sustained for long, but the break likely came when it did because Robinson had found his own connections through which to tap Europe's capital. Exploiting these links and the euphoric market conditions of 1894–95, he executed an extraordinary set of flotations based on Randfontein's assets. Mining reports indicated considerable potential in well-defined, gold-bearing conglomerates on Randfontein property.[22] Though these reefs ran north-south, they were believed to be extensions of the main reef series. Despite favorable assessments by the experts, the company had, up to 1895, spent only about £ 100,000 on the development of its immense holdings, and much of it had been sloppy and haphazard. Nonetheless, the Estate company formed five subsidiaries on about half its mining ground. Only one of these had produced gold, and then not until 1895, but by September these subsidiaries had issued more than 2 million £ 1 shares of which 1,328,700 went to the parent company as its vendor interest. Robinson founded a bank the previous month and used its assets to purchase a large block of shares of the Estate Company and its subsidiaries. Named after its founder, The Robinson South African Banking Company issued 750,000 £ 4 shares which were run up to £ 11. Randfontein Estates' shares peaked at 4⅜.

21. Wernher, who was inclined to give most people's follies and foibles the benefit of the doubt, thought Robinson "a black hearted cur" and "too vicious and selfish" to boot. J. Wernher to L. Phillips, 1 September 1907 and 8 January 1908, BRA.

22. The reports are summarized in *Mines of the Transvaal,* various years.

A financial group featuring one of France's great credit banks, the Société Générale, provided the continental link. It likely enabled Robinson to do "an enormous business" in Paris with Randfontein shares.[23] Moreover, it supplied the necessary capital for the formation of Robinson's bank: £ 1.5 million in cash. Robinson, on the other hand, put up mostly overvalued Randfontein shares. When the break came, the Estate company's shares fell below £ 2. Investors or speculators who had purchased its scrip or bank stock at a premium would have lost considerably. Robinson and his Paris backers, however, were not out of pocket. When his bank went into liquidation in 1905, it returned £ 3 per share. It had, as well, paid out dividends of about £ 1.4 million.[24]

Some of Robinson's business tactics were known to his fellow Randlords and assorted promoters and brokers in Johannesburg. Insiders in the City likely knew; and the *Economist* certainly suspected. But his companies operated in great secrecy. Registered in the Transvaal, they avoided even the token scrutiny of shareholders resident in Johannesburg. General meetings were held outside the city without or at very short notice. On at least one occasion a meeting was presided over by a chairman whose relationship to Robinson "was one of subservient docility" and with a secretary the only other person in attendance. Robinson's large vendor interest coupled with "an adequate number of proxies" assured him total control. As the Transvaal supreme court justice who made these remarks concluded, Robinson abused the group system which involved "the management and direction of the policy and affairs of the various companies by some controlling authority through nominee directors."[25] But his company directors were not allowed to exercise independent judgment, or develop initiatives. Thus, Robinson's version of the group system was different from that developed by Goldfields and the Corner House which, sometimes to the regret of headquarters, allowed local directors considerable scope for action, political as well as financial.

23. Wernher, Beit & Co. to H. Eckstein & Co., 16 March 1895, BRA.
24. Same to same, 2 August 1895, *ibid.*
25. *South African Law Reports, Appellate Division, 1920–21*, pp. 184, 196.

Since his tactics were not given a public airing until years later, Robinson was able to mount another large speculation in 1899. Market conditions had improved; new reefs were discovered on the Randfontein properties. Hammond was hired to produce a glowing report. Six mining companies with a total of almost £ 3 million in issued capital, all of which was allotted to the parent company, were floated.[26] But the war intervened before Robinson could proceed with these flotations.

While the Langlaagte mines continued, after resumption, as prolific gold and dividend producers, the Randfontein Estate properties did not begin to produce appreciable yields until after 1905, and significant amounts until 1909. By then Robinson had reversed his prewar Balkanization program. Seven of the uneconomic mining units floated before 1900 for speculative purposes were formed into the Randfontein Central. It allotted £ 2 million in share capital to individual holders of scrip in the old companies, to Randfontein Estates, and to Waterval Trust, a subsidiary holding company, for additional claims and cash advances. Five other small units amalgamated to form a second large venture, the Randfontein South Gold Mining Company, which also allotted issued capital of £ 2 million. Shares in the old companies, the greater part held by Randfontein Estates, were exchanged for new ones on an average of less than half of their nominal value. At the same time Robinson, as Joel's litigation against him subsequently revealed, did not bother to inform the shareholders in the amalgamations that additional claims acquired were purchased from him at exorbitant prices. Through the Waterval Trust, he sold to the companies he controlled for cash or shares worth £ 572,250 mining property that cost him £ 105,000. He thus had used a common mining company flotation practice in an especially flagrant manner. Given the generally depressed state of the mining market at the time of these amal-

26. Up to 1902 the Randfontein Estate mines had yielded gold worth £ 1,264,570 and dividends of only £ 187,500 on an issued capital of £ 5,707,-500. Langlaagte Estate and the Block B Langlaagte, by contrast, produced gold worth £ 4,709,408 and dividends of £ 1,440,842 on an issued capital of £ 1,102,500. Chamber of Mines, *Annexure to the Report for 1902,* Exhibit 4; and *Mines of the Transvaal,* 1904–5, pp. 528–35.

gamations, Robinson had likely chosen to exploit his companies by vendor sale transactions rather than by stock deals in the share market. Cash for development meantime had to come from debenture issues. Randfontein Estates, for example, offered shareholders £ 2 million in 6 percent first mortgage debentures at par in 1909. The underwriters, which one assumes included Robinson, took up more than £ 1.3 million of the issue at 95. Thus, Robinson and any of his French backers who might still be party to his financial schemes got at least 6 percent for anything they spent on development. Randfontein Estates also came to hold almost £ 3 million in 6 percent debentures issued by Randfontein Central which in 1911 had, in another amalgamation move, absorbed Randfontein South, thereby effecting a complete consolidation of Robinson's enterprises on the far-west Rand.[27]

Even from the well-informed promagnate vantage point of the editorial offices of the *Statist* it was impossible to determine, because of Robinson's secretiveness, what advantages these amalgamation schemes provided for improved development. Dividend yields were meager, expenses charged against profits were not satisfactorily explained: "Year after year," the *Statist* later recalled, "smooth prophecies of the directors were pronounced, but their non-fruition became wearisome, and shareholders became very bitter, the more so as they were unable to effectively combat a species of stubborn passive resistance to demands for information."[28]

Only when Joel's experts had a close look at the Randfontein Central mine in 1917 was it revealed how badly the undertaking was run, and how little the opportunities for amalgamation were exploited. JCI's board complained that

> the underground workings have suffered through a minimum amount of development having been done, and more particularly through a constant effort to obtain the maximum gold without due regard for the future. . . . The shafts are expensive to maintain and poorly equipped. . . . It will also be advisable to put in hand as early as possible a central pumping scheme, as there are large quantities of

27. *Mining Manual,* 1915, pp. 545–48.
28. *Statist,* 17 March 1917, p. 444.

water to be dealt with. . . . In the past considerable items have been allocated to other accounts which should, strictly speaking, be charged to working costs.[29]

Though Robinson was forced to decline a peerage in 1922, he had accepted a baronetcy in 1908. He received the honor on the recommendation of the Transvaal's premier, Louis Botha, presumably for his support of Het Volk and for his efforts to repatriate Chinese miners in opposition to other Randlords who wanted to keep them as long as possible.[30] The honor, therefore, seemed to be partly in recognition of Robinson's opposition to a practice which both the Het Volk and Britain's Liberal Party deplored. It was, however, recognition of a gesture which obscured Robinson's own exploitation of Chinese workers. Indeed, given the mismanagement on his properties, it is not surprising that one of their infrequent riots against working conditions occurred on one of his mines.[31] He schemed as well to frustrate Chamber of Mines initiatives to monopsonize the recruitment and allocation of African labor, again one suspects because his own practices would have come under scrutiny of other members of the Chamber.[32]

In any event Robinson felt little commitment to either his workers or to South Africa. Although born in the Cape, he had after 1894 remained mostly abroad and chose to live in grotesque opulence in London's Mayfair.[33] Here he felt little responsibility toward the shareholders in his companies. He used them as he used his fellow entrepreneurs, his company directors, his mine laborers: as grist for his mill to provide fame and fortune. At the time he sold out to Joel, this maverick capitalist was worth about £ 5–6 million. Through him a sizable amount of French capital had been diverted from developing South Africa's gold mines to Britain, where it was siphoned into his immense personal fortune. We have no way of telling in what Robinson kept his wealth with the exception of London real estate and objets d'art. If an

29. Quoted in *ibid.*, p. 445.
30. Roberts, *Diamond Magnates,* pp. 296–97; Jeeves, *Journal of Southern African Studies,* II, 22; Mawby, *Historical Journal,* XVII, 390.
31. Denoon, *Journal of African History,* VII, 492.
32. Jeeves, *Journal of Southern African Studies,* II, 22–23.
33. Gutsche, *Florence Phillips,* pp. 129, 168, 173.

editorial which appeared at his death in the *Cape Times*[34] is any indication, English-speaking whites in South Africa were livid when they learned how little he was prepared to be a benefactor in his native land.

3. Farrar's Mismanagement

George Farrar became one of the foremost Rand entrpreneurs despite the fact he had not the Kimberley connection behind him. Indeed, he put together East Rand Proprietary Mines (ERPM), a company which controlled the largest single block of mining ground on the Rand. By 1914, however, mismanagement of the property, coupled with a well-entrenched disillusionment in its main body of shareholders, forced the Corner House, which had little enthusiasm for the chore, to assume control of its affairs.

From an upper middle-class English family of professionals and industrialists, Farrar, a trained engineer, went to the Cape in 1879 to assess the potential of the local market for agricultural machinery. Turning to the sale of mining equipment, and then to mining promotion in the Transvaal, by 1891 he was or had been on the boards of a colliery, a silver mine, a Lydenburg gold venture, an alluvial undertaking 35 miles west of Johannesburg, and nine Rand companies.[35] It is conceivable that capital for his initial forays into Rand company formation came from the resources of the Bedford engineering house of his uncles, Frederick and James Howard, which, after Fraser and Chalmers, was a major supplier of Rand machinery.[36] But his subsequent financial activity was fueled by London stockbrokers and Paris financiers through the Anglo-French Exploration Company. This firm, formed in December 1889 to exploit the first Rand mining boom, included on its board Ernest Mocatta, George Cawston, and Edward Wagg, all members of the London stock exchange. Cawston diverted his

34. *Cape Times,* 7 November 1929.
35. Goldmann, *Witwatersrand Companies, passim.* His brother Sidney also acted as consulting engineer to a number of the Rand companies.
36. de Launay, *Les Mines d'or,* p. 116.

attention to Rhodesia,[37] and Farrar soon joined the company as its managing director in South Africa. Its original capital of £ 150,300 was increased to £ 320,300 by 1895, and it acquired a large interest in Farrar's flotations on the east Rand. In these, and other deals, Farrar seems to have had no aversion to co-operating with the whole spectrum of mining entrepreneurs. He joined Carl Hanau, the Rand's most reckless speculator, John Henderson, a minor promoter who was a failure as a developer,[38] and partners in Eckstein's, the ablest and most important entrepreneurs. He also had dealings with Goldfields, the Barnatos, and Neumann. These associations, and the backing of Anglo-French, enabled him eventually to obtain control of several blocks of contiguous claims along a six-mile stretch of the main reef series nine miles east of Johannesburg. In 1892, with the help of Eckstein's, he and Hanau formed the H. F. Syndicate. It supplied £ 90,000 working capital to five mines in this area, floated another undertaking, and acquired water rights and large additional blocks of mining ground. By the end of 1892 its nominal capital stood at £ 70,000 divided into 700 shares with a par value of £ 100, but which were issued at from £ 200–£ 800. One of the allottees, Eckstein's, left a record of its participation. It took up and retained or distributed to Wernher, Beit in London and Jules Porges in Paris, about 30 percent of the issued shares, most of which cost £ 200. Anglo-French had a large share, increased by taking up scrip initially issued to Henderson, and Neumann had a small interest.[39] Eckstein's own holdings (which stood at 53 shares and which cost about £ 10,600), entitled it to almost 40,000 £ 1 shares in ERPM which Farrar formed in 1893 to acquire the syndicate's assets, obtain additional properties, and push on with adding deep-level ground to several mines it would control. The syndicate, as its vendor right, took up 420,000 of ERPM's original capital of £ 650,000; the balance was issued at about par to provide £ 240,000 in working capital. This cash went into the reconstruction and development of six subsidiary

37. Galbraith, *Crown and Charter*, p. 54.
38. See chap. vii, pp. 163–69, this volume.
39. Profit and Loss Statement on H. F. Company shares, 30 June 1896, BRA.

mines which, by mid-1895, had an issued capital of £ 995,500 of which the parent company held £ 552,065.

These financial arrangements generated a great deal of scrip which in the hands of Mocatta and Wagg could be used to advantage in the mining share boom of 1895. But they were quite inappropriate for the needs of ERPM's subsidiaries. They were located on ground where the reefs were broken through a dyke intrusion very close to where they outcropped and had not been as productive as the central Rand mines. To mid-1895 the subsidiaries produced gold worth only £ 11,200. To make the most of the reefs near the surface and develop their deep-levels, these mines, with a total area of almost 600 claims, needed far more working capital than was provided. At the same time it became clear that Farrar and his associates had no intention of diverting profits from stock sales to make up the difference. ERPM shares began 1895 at 2⅜, rose to a high of 12¾, plunged to 3¾ at the beginning of 1896; they rallied to 8⅞ midway through 1896 but declined steadily to 1⁷⁄₁₆ by May 1897. Meanwhile, Wernher, Beit sold out its large holdings at what Wernher thought was too cheap a price, and retained only its founders interest.[40] Farrar and his associates tried so many jobbing transactions they were "perhaps as much discredited in Paris as Barney" Barnato. Wernher also learned that Farrar was "lining his own pockets with capital raised for East Rand" Proprietary Mines through a £ 375,000 debenture issue.[41] Shortly before the South African war, three of ERPM's six subsidiaries began to produce sufficient gold to yield modest dividends, but not enough to allow the parent company to do so. Its issued capital was now £ 845,800, the increases representing vendor shares (about 100,000) for additional claims and the repayment of most of £ 600,000 in debentures.

ERPM, like the other houses, faced postwar labor shortages

40. Participants in the H. F. Syndicate were entitled to 25 percent of the profits after a 100 percent dividend was declared, later modified to a first payment to shareholders by way of dividends of £ 920,000 before founders. Cash dividends were not forthcoming for several years but the Corner House was to acquire shares in lieu of dividends through ground-floor participation in subsequent reconstructions, and the conversion of ERPM debentures.

41. J. Werhner to G. Rouliot, 18 December 1896 and 15 April 1897, BRA.

and George Farrar, a strong Milnerite, became the leading advocate among the Randlords for the introduction of Chinese labor. Like other houses the Farrar group also engaged in a flurry of capital rearrangements in 1902 and amalgamations in 1908–9. The net result was disastrous for its shareholders and cannot be simply accounted for by labor difficulties. Through claims it held to the south, ERPM extended the mining ground of its three producing companies (the Driefontein, Angelo, and Comet). It also used outcrop and deep-level claims, and a small nonproducer (the Agnes Munro) to construct a fourth large enterprise (Cason Gold Mines). It retained a controlling interest in two other properties (the Cinderella and New Blue Sky), and held a large block of claims to the south and east of these two undertakings. It also participated in new mines formed on ground south of these previously mentioned properties. To finance its subsidiaries and participations, ERPM increased its share capital to £ 1 million by offering 150,000 shares at £ 8 to its shareholders and the H. F. Company. Out of the profits of two of its mines (the Angelo and Driefontein Consolidated), ERPM started to pay dividends in 1903 which averaged 22 percent during the five-year period to 1907. Since many of its shares must have passed hands at a premium (during 1902–7 their market values did not go below £ 3),[42] and since no dividend had been declared during the company's first decade of operation, these dividends, expressed as a percentage of what outside investors actually paid for ERPM shares, were hardly impressive.

As of October 1903, 62 percent of its share capital, then standing at £ 990,000 issued, was held by British investors. What fraction of this figure was vendor or working capital shares held by its founders and directors is not known, but a conservative estimate, based on the H. F. Company's connections with ERPM, would be about one-third or about 20 percent of the total issue. Continental shareholders, led by France, held 26 percent; South Africa only 4 percent. The remaining 8 percent was outstanding.[43]

42. The market value of ERPM shares in 1902 ranged between $7\frac{5}{8}$ and $10\frac{5}{16}$.
43. H. P. Fraser, secretary of ERPM, to H. Eckstein & Co., 8 October 1903, BRA.

The Proprietary company, given its extensive commitments on the east Rand, could not show a meaningful profit on the basis of the performance of two smallish mines. This consideration, coupled with the amalgamative trend underway throughout the Rand, may well explain ERPM's next financial maneuver. In July 1908 its capital was increased to £ 2,500,000. The entire assets of the parent company's six subsidiaries were acquired through canceling shares held in them and issuing fully paid shares for outstanding scrip. In addition, the holdings of various mining interests in ground to the south and east of these subsidiaries were acquired. The most important of these acquisitions was the Hercules Company. Its financial history sheds light on the extent to which the Farrar group's priorities stressed speculative as opposed to development policies. It was originally formed in 1902 with a modest capital of £ 145,000 to acquire extensive tracts of deep-level ground, about 800 claims in all, on the east Rand. Eckstein's, Neumann, and Farrar, the chief vendors, acquired equal participations of about 45,000 shares each. Smaller allotments went to two small-time Johannesburg promoters and to Edgar Vincent, the chief director of the Ottoman bank. In 1904 the £ 1 shares were converted into 5 shilling scrip and the capital increased to £ 250,000 by creating an additional 420,000 5 shilling shares. The principal participants took up 100,000 of these latter shares at £ 2 for working capital. These and their vendor shares were pooled and managed by representatives of the principal participants. The pool was to sell 100,000 shares at the discretion of these managers, and a further 100,000 not under £ 2½, and to purchase back up to one-third, but only at prices at least 10 percent below the sale price. Sales to the public were to be carried out by the stockbroking firm in which Mocatta and Wagg, directors of Anglo-French, were partners.[44] Shaftsinking began in 1905, but was suspended in 1907, and it is doubtful that these brokers were able to place many shares with the public before the company was absorbed by ERPM in 1908 for 160,000 £ 1 shares. Besides acquiring the total assets of its subsidiaries

44. Hercules Co. (Syndicate), n.d., *ibid.*

and such deep-level undertakings as the Hercules Company, ERPM extinguished the H. F. Company's founders' right through issuing 333,333 shares. These transactions created the largest single block of mining ground on the Rand (some 3680 claims), enabled ERPM to announce the yield of its former subsidiaries in aggregate figures, and assign all their profits to ERPM for re-investment, depreciation, or dividends.

The amalgamation gave greater scope for efficient and careful mining, much needed because of extensive low-grade ore and underground water in the property. But it also provided its directors with cheap scrip for further speculation. Again, they chose to stress speculation at the expense of development. The company published deliberately misleading statements. Monthly production returns were inflated by adding in gold belonging properly to subsequent operations. Working costs were deflated by assigning certain costs to future development instead of current expenses. Too much unpayable ore was mined. Reduction equipment was run so inefficiently that thousands of ounces of gold were lost. Various departments of the huge undertaking were not well coordinated.[45] The coverup of limited yields and mismanagement enabled ERPM to skim off dividends which averaged 38 percent during 1908–11 and prevent ERPM's market price from plummeting sharply, though it declined steadily.

While skimming off profits, the Farrar group did little to arrest the decline. It refused to participate in the Corner House effort to sweeten the French press with subsidies.[46] More significant, however, was the withdrawal of its investment in ERPM. As early as 1906 Farrar and his brothers had been persistent sellers of gold shares. Anglo-French began to reduce its ERPM holdings in late 1910.[47] By 1912 the Farrars and Anglo-French were largely out of ERPM. The Corner House, meantime, though it had not participated in ERPM's management, retained the interest obtained through its original founders' participation and a seat on ERPM's board. With the withdrawal of Farrar, Anglo-French,

45. L. Reyersbach to L. Phillips, 6 October 1911, *ibid.*
46. See chap. iv, p. 82, this volume.
47. F. Eckstein to L. Phillips, 23 September 1906 and 1 October 1911, BRA.

and Neumann as well, the Corner House discovered somewhat to its surprise that it held the largest single block of shares in the company, slightly more than 140,000 of the almost 2,500,000 issued. Moreover, Wernher, Beit could command another 500,000 through proxies and were urged, particularly by Paris, to assume control. Though Farrar was allowed to stay on as chairman, the Corner House appointed ERPM's superintending engineer through whom it acquired technical control, and the unwelcome opportunity to reorganize the ramshackle organization.

Given the Corner House's lack of zeal, the difficulties inherent in the mine, the notorious reputation it had acquired among investors, South Africa's turbulent politics, and the Transvaal's labor problems, ERPM showed little evidence of recovery before 1914. Indeed, for years to come it was "touch and go as to whether mining should continue."[48]

Like the Corner House and Goldfields, the investment portfolio of Anglo-French Exploration revealed a distinct trend away from the Rand. Its share capital, increased to £ 1 million by 1902, featured half in 6 percent preference shares. Ordinary shares in the decade 1902–12 yielded an average of about 8 percent, but by 1913 both were quoted well below par. Though Anglo-French no longer retained ERPM scrip it held appreciable blocks of shares in 10 mines as well as 9000 shares in Rand Mines which had a total market value in 1913 of about £ 385,000. It also held shares in subsidiaries interested in real estate in Johannesburg and land, coal, and tin in the Transvaal, with a value of about £ 80,000. But investments elsewhere in Africa, including a Rhodesian explorations subsidiary, soda deposits in East Africa and banking in Egypt, were worth about £ 50,000. American railroad bonds made up most of the corporation's financial interests in the Americas which also included a Canadian gold mine and railways in Argentina and Mexico. These investments had a market value of about £ 150,000. A Spanish copper mine, mineral developments in Australia, an Indian railway, British Consols, and unclassified investments were worth about £ 135,000.[49] Thus,

48. Cartwright, *Golden Age,* p. 94.
49. *Mining Manual,* 1915, pp. 25–26.

by 1913 Anglo-French's interests outside the Union of South Africa accounted for some 40 percent of the market value of its investment portfolio of about £ 800,000.

Given his active career as a politician and soldier, and the ramshackle nature of ERPM's financial history, there is some doubt that George Farrar applied himself systematically to his business interests after about 1895. To the extent that he did engage in Transvaal mining, he was much more the promoter and less the developer. The withdrawal of his capital, that of the Anglo-French Exploration Company and, one suspects, that of disgruntled French financiers from ERPM can be accounted for by unwelcome trends in Transvaal politics[50] and labor problems. But ERPM's performance was also conditioned by its capital and mining strategies. These, geared to short-term stock market manipulations which lined the pockets of the Farrar brothers and London stockbrokers like Mocatta and Wagg, contributed significantly to ERPM's inability to be a significant or efficient gold producer.

50. To Farrar, a strong exponent of British political dominance, the victory of Botha and Smuts in 1907 was a severe setback.

• 7 •

The Minor Groups and the Rand's Capital Needs

In the literature on enterprises which concentrated on financing Rand gold mines before 1914, some groupings stand out. Others do not. The extent and importance of the operations and even the identity of several mine financing firms are obscure. Despite differences in size, function (in the degree to which they were promoters or developers), and organization (to the extent they typified the group system), five houses overshadowed the rest. These were the Wernher, Beit complex, Goldfields, the Barnato group, Robinson's enterprises, and the concerns of Farrar and his associates. Most Rand commentators, following Emden's classification for the mid-1890s, assume there were only five additional significant mining groups. These were George Albu or General Mining, A. Goerz and Company, S. Neumann and Company, the Lewis and Marks partnership, and the Abe Bailey interests. Together, the "Big Ten," Emden claimed, controlled the mines of the Rand and dominated stock market operations. He did, however, mention five additional "smaller" undertakings with financial interests in the mines.[1] Two of these latter concerns, along with the "Big Ten," were included in a list of 13 "great controlling groups" compiled by the informed editors of the *Statist* in 1905.[2] What follows not only attempts to clear up classificatory confusion but tries to set out more fully and precisely than the existing literature does the identity, activity, and impact on the Rand's capital structure of nine lesser financial

1. Emden, *Randlords,* pp. 207, 335–36. He ranked the various groups though he noted their relative importance was subject to constant change.
2. *Statist,* 26 August 1905, pp. 347–48.

undertakings. In addition to studying the five firms which rounded out Emden's "Big Ten," it examines concerns founded by Anton Dunkelsbuhler, John Crosbie Aitken Henderson, Ludwig Ehrlich, and Carl Hanau.[3] Much of what these nine enterprises did adversely affected the Rand's financial development, particularly during the post–Boer war years.

1. The German Connection

Substantial German capital was, as noted previously, funneled into the gold mines through the Wernher, Beit complex. In 1906, for example, the Corner House placed a value of £ 46 million on the Rand undertakings it controlled or in which it had significant investments. At least £ 1,250,000 or 2.7 percent of this amount was held in Germany.[4] In 1915, 4.4 percent of the shares of the Corner House's gold mining enterprises was held by German, Austrian, or Turkish shareholders.[5] But some other Rand entrepreneurs were much more dependent on German backing. A rough aggregate estimate of German capital in South African gold mining at the outbreak of World War I can be obtained from the records and statements of custodians of enemy property seized in Britain and South Africa. It was not less than £ 13

3. Three groupings mentioned by Emden or the *Statist* which are not treated are the Ochs brothers, the Berlein-Dettelbach group and the interests of Julius and Arnold Friedlander. While these various interests participated in some Rand promotions, their commitments were found to be so marginal or temporary and information about them so sparse that they are omitted. It seems clear, however, that their financial activities primarily centered either on Kimberley or, as in the case of the Ochs brothers, on south-central Africa.

4. About £ 14,130,000 was in bearer warrants and the Corner House could not accurately trace its ownership though it assumed these warrants were held on the continent. Most of them would have been in French hands but it is likely an appreciable amount was lodged in Germany. Shareholdings—France, Germany and Elsewhere, 31 December 1906, BRA.

5. Only a small fraction of this percentage was in Austrian or Turkish hands. Percentage of German, Austrian and Turkish Shareholdings in Relation to Issued Share Capital, received in H. Eckstein & Co. records department, 5 August 1915, *ibid.*

million, and it may have been as high as £ 21 million.[6] Three enterprises, financed largely through Germany's big joint stock banks, accounted for much of this investment. George Albu, who founded the General Mining and Finance Corporation in 1895; Adolf Goerz, whose interests were put into a company first registered in Germany in 1893 and reconstructed in 1897 in the Transvaal; and Anton Dunkelsbuhler, instrumental in the development of Consolidated Mines Selection formed in 1897, were the key entrepreneurs behind them. The mines these enterprises controlled accounted for 6 percent or £ 4,789,000 of the Rand's dividend yield and 10.5 percent or £ 31,589,000 of its production during 1902–13.[7] While these figures indicate these three enterprises were not insignificant factors in Rand development, they do not reflect the substantial amounts of capital they diverted to several mines on the west and far-east Rand which had not produced dividends or gold before 1914.

Albu followed a familiar pattern. He came to Johannesburg by way of Kimberley where he had arrived from Berlin in 1876. There he set up as a broker and later as a diamond company promoter. His first significant Rand venture began in 1888 when he became manager of the Meyer and Charlton, a poorly run outcrop property on the central Rand whose share capital was largely held in Kimberley. He turned the mine into a very successful dividend payer and ensured it a long life by enlarging its claim area. By 1895 the mine's share capital of £ 85,000, much

6. The maximum figure includes arbitrarily an amount of £ 6,500,000 or one-half the value assigned to unspecified securities held in Britain by branches of the German banks which had been heavy investors in Transvaal gold mines. It also includes the value realized on sales of seized securities made after the war by the South African government. The minimum figure takes the values of securities seized in South Africa as reported to the British government and was likely determined on nominal or depressed prewar market values. These figures exclude the investment of Germans domiciled in South Africa worth about £ 3,000,000. See: Enemy Debts Committee, Memorandum on Returns of Debts and Property, February 1918, PRO BT 8/12; Property Held or Managed on Behalf of Alien Enemies . . . [categories B, C, D], BT 8/17, BT 8/18, BT 8/19; Rand Mines, Dividend No. 23, Shareholders Resident in Germany, Austria and Turkey, document in author's possession; *Cape Times*, 17 August 1920 and 17 July 1922.

7. Derived from various reports of the Transvaal Chamber of Mines.

of which had been issued at a premium and which supplied over £ 100,000 in working capital, was distributed among 1234 shareholders. Only 182 were South African residents; the remainder lived in Europe, most of them in Germany.[8] Albu also acquired interests in other mining properties with which he probably speculated successfully during the boom of 1894–95. At its end, with the backing of the Dresdner Bank, he founded and became chairman of the General Mining and Finance Corporation which was registered in the Transvaal in December 1895. His brother, Leopold, became its managing director in London. Other board members included Eugen Gutmann and Martin Luebeck, directors respectively of the Dresdner Bank in Berlin (the head office) and London (a branch founded in 1895). A Berlin committee included representatives of another *Grossbank*, the Disconto-Gesellschaft, and one of Germany's largest private banks, S. Bleichröder. The Corporation's nominal capital of £ 1,250,000 included 1000 founders' shares allotted to the Albu brothers which entitled them to 25 percent of the profits after a 10 percent dividend had been paid. Initially the remaining issued shares were held privately by the Albus, the Dresdner, and other German banks.[9]

In 1902 General Mining made its first public issue and provided a breakdown of its assets. The Albus, the Dresdner, the Disconto-Gesellschaft, and S. Bleichröder, as holders of the original share issue, sold 300,000 shares to the public at £ 2.5 and, the following year, took up reserve shares at £ 2.15. In 1906 this syndicate, along with another Berlin *Grossbank*, the A. Schaaffhausen'scher Bankverein, took up the final increase of capital before 1914, 625,000 new shares at £ 1.5, and offered it for £ 1.10 pro rata to existing shareholders. These arrangements

8. Goldmann, *South African Mines*, I, 226–33; and annual reports for 1895 and 1896 of the Meyer and Charlton Gold Mining Company.

9. G. Nathan, a General Mining director, was described as the "watchdog" of the Dresdner Bank in the Albu concerns and was a brother of one of the bank's leading men. L. Reyersbach to L. Phillips, 25 July 1913, BRA. For the status and interests of the private bank, S. Bleichröder, see F. Stern, *Gold and Iron: Bismarck, Bleichröder, and the Building of the German Empire* (New York, 1977), pp. 542–46.

served to generate more than £ 2 million in working capital for an ambitious postwar development program. By then General Mining already managed nine mines whose total issued capital was almost £ 3 million in 1902 and more than £ 5 million by 1909. Three of these mines, including the Meyer and Charlton which continued to pay impressive dividends, were outcrop properties on the central Rand. Another, Cinderella Deep, floated just before the war and located on the east Rand south of the Farrar properties, was described as the most optimistic and expensive venture on the Rand in the new century.[10] On the far-east Rand, General Mining controlled the Van Ryn mine which was northwest of and adjacent to Wernher, Beit's Modderfontein. But the center of the General Mining's development program was the west Rand. As early as 1899 it had taken control of the Violet Consolidated away from a rival firm, Henderson's Transvaal Estates.[11] Out of this property, the adjoining West Rand Mines, and various claims held by numerous parties, including Neumann and the Goerz Company, it created West Rand Consolidated Mines in 1907. This undertaking was on 1785 claims located immediately east of Robinson's Randfontein and had an issued capital of £ 2 million and a debenture debt (as of 1909) of £ 500,000. Another mine on the west Rand which the Albus controlled, Roodepoort United Main Reef, an outcrop company with some noncontiguous deep-level claims, acquired adjacent properties in 1909 which more than tripled its claim holdings. To effect this amalgamation, Roodepoort United's issued capital was increased from 295,000 to 460,000 shares; General Mining purchased 113,000 shares of the new issue at a premium. To the west and south of its Roodepoort interests General Mining, through the New Steyn Estate Gold Mines, held 11½ square miles of freehold on which it retained control of sizable mynpachts and mining claim areas.[12] It was thus in a position to

10. Cartwright, *Gold Miners,* p. 150.
11. *Statist,* 4 March 1899, pp. 353–55.
12. It also had a 15 percent participation in West African Mines Ltd., the joint venture of Goldfields and the Corner House. F. Eckstein to L. Phillips, 10 December 1909, BRA.

fashion huge undertakings in the Roodepoort district through additions and consolidations.

But whatever its intentions for further development these had to be shelved because the corporation was in considerable difficulty. In the 12 year period 1902–13, it paid dividends on its ordinary shares only five times, and these averaged 5.6 percent. During that period many shares, as we have noted, were acquired or exchanged hands at a distinct premium so that actual interest earned for many holders, including the banks, was less than 5.6 percent. Not surprisingly these shares, which were quoted at £ 4 in 1902 showed a steady decline, dipped below par in 1911, and were quoted in 1913 as low as 8s 9d.

A number of factors, some general to the industry, some quite specific to General Mining, accounted for this performance which left General Mining's balance sheets in a "terrible" state and George Albu "terribly down-in-the-mouth." He and his brother held 350,000 or 18.6 percent of the corporation's shares. Their attempt to push on with development and, for example, find further money in Berlin for the Cinderella and Roodepoort United "failed absolutely."[13] At least 800,000 shares or 42.6 percent of General Mining's issued capital was by then likely held in Germany.[14] The corporation's properties had been plagued, like the whole Rand industry, by labor shortages. Moreover, the Transvaal Chamber of Mines, to which the Corporation's undertakings belonged, concentrated available labor on proven producers. The Meyer and Charlton, despite its impressive yields, could not offset the drain on capital and resources caused by the corporation's extensive development program which had been slowed by labor difficulties. General Mining had interests in a large colliery development on the east Rand, numerous shares in mining companies it did not control, sufficient real estate holdings to form a subsidiary to take them over, and some West African interests.[15]

13. L. Reyersbach to R. Schumacher, 30 May 1913, *ibid.*

14. Based on the fact that the corporation purchased 800,000 of its own shares from the custodian of enemy property in 1922. *Cape Times,* 13 June 1922.

15. *Mining Manual,* 1915.

But these were also either a drain or, if profitable, insufficiently so.

Adolf Goerz, a mining engineer, was evidently sent to the Rand in 1888 as an agent of German interests wanting not only to acquire gold properties but also to develop a market for mining machinery. Those interests were led by the Deutsche Bank and the Berliner Handels-Gesellschaft who acted upon encouraging reports of the Rand's potential provided by experts sent out to the Transvaal by the German government. Along with his principal clerk, Amandus Brakhan, he acquired interests on behalf of his backers in syndicates and companies already established on the central Rand.[16] His largest holdings were, however, on the yet to be developed far-east Rand on the farms Modderfontein and Geduld. These interests were put into a firm, A. Goerz and Company, established in Germany in 1893. It paid substantial dividends on the basis of profitable share dealing during the 1894–95 boom. Partly as a result of a decision to push ahead with far-east Rand development, and partly as a result of the advantages of operating out of Johannesburg, the company was reconstructed in late 1897 with an increased capital and registered in the Transvaal. Most of its £ 1 million issued ordinary share capital was allotted to the old company and the remainder (360,000 shares) absorbed at a small premium by a syndicate headed by the Deutsche Bank. Its directorship, though German dominated, contained British and French representation, a measure likely designed to attract investment from outside Germany and which perhaps facilitated the sale in 1898 of 200,000 vendor shares at 32s 6d. Its international character was clearly evident. "Though much of its capital was held in Germany it was a Transvaal concern, registered in the South African Republic. Yet it had a London office and its chairman was British and a peer of the Realm."[17]

16. For example, under an agreement of 30 December 1890, Eckstein's arranged for Goerz to take up shares in the Jumpers Gold Mining Company to which the Deutsche Bank was entitled through the purchase of a mortgage bond the mine had issued.

17. J. R. Shorten, *The Johannesburg Saga* (Cape Town, 1970), p. 546.

The company held shares in six producing outcrop mines of which it came to control three.[18] It had significant holdings in two developing mines on the west Rand (Lancaster West and Roodepoort Central Deep) and held a variety of interests in claims and syndicates in other Transvaal districts as well as Rhodesia. Given Goerz's engineering background, it is not surprising that it was a large shareholder in two companies ancillary, but nevertheless important, to the mining industry. These were the Rand Central Electric Works and the Rand Central Ore Reduction Company.[19] These firms, while providing a common service for several mines, were also outlets for German electrical and mining equipment.

Development work started in 1898 and culminated the following year with the flotation by the company of its far-east Rand holdings. Geduld Proprietary Mines had an initial issued capital of £ 400,000 and Modderfontein Deep Levels £ 90,000. Their development was disrupted by the war, but Goerz and Company used its reserves to pay dividends of about 10 percent every year from 1898 to 1902 with the exception of 1900. Thereafter it was unable to sustain this performance. It only paid dividends twice (15 percent in 1904 and 10 percent in 1908) during the ensuing decade. Its shares, which reached a market high of £ 4¼ in 1902 on expectations of successful resumption, declined below par in 1907, picked up as a consequence of the 1908–9 recovery, but fell well below par thereafter, reaching a low of less than 7s in 1913.

Though the development-oriented company's founder died in 1900, his loss was more than made up for by his successors: Brakhan, its managing director in Johannesburg who replaced Lord Battersea as chairman in 1904; and Henry Strakosch, an Austrian-born banker who had joined the Goerz enterprises in

18. It managed the Princess Estate, the Lancaster, and the May Consolidated; two of the other mines it was interested in were Albu ventures.

19. The former was to be absorbed into the Victoria Falls and Transvaal Power Company which came to be a major supplier of electrical power on the Rand. *Stock Exchange Official Year-Book*, 1913, p. 631. The latter, before it went into liquidation in 1903, treated or provided the machinery to treat mill tailings. Goldmann, *South African Mines*, II, 194.

1896 and who became managing director in London in 1902. It was not a lack of managerial skill and initiative which accounted for the company's difficulties.

Goerz and Company embarked on a diversification program during the war and explored mining possibilities in Australia, India, America, and Spain, as well as elsewhere in southern Africa. Through these initiatives it acquired an interest in the Otavi Mines and Railway Company (formed in 1901 to exploit copper, land, and railway concessions in Southwest Africa), and laid the groundwork for extending its operations beyond South Africa after 1906 when its development plans on the far-east Rand foundered. To execute these plans its issued capital was increased from £ 1,000,000 to £ 1,400,000, its founders shares extinguished, and £ 739,000 raised for working capital and reserves. The Deutsche Bank took a prominent part in these financial arrangements and absorbed at least 75,000 shares at £ 2.10s. The Geduld Proprietary, which under Goerz control issued more than £ 1 million shares, was plagued by flooding, did not produce gold in quantity until 1911, and provided no dividend until 1914. The Modder Deep, whose issued capital was increased to £ 263,000, absorbed more than £ 100,000 in development costs in the year 1911 alone and did not start crushing until December 1914. Another far-east Rand venture, Van Dyk Proprietary Mines, formed in 1904 with an issued capital of £ 500,000 all of which Goerz and Company held, suspended operations in 1910 owing its parent company £ 70,000. Meanwhile, only one of the three outcrops it controlled, the May Consolidated, was producing substantial profits, and it faced a short life.[20] The other two, the Princess Estate and Lancaster West, extended their lives by absorbing neighboring properties during 1909–11.

Another property in which Goerz and Company acquired extensive interests was a small deep-level proposition immediately east of and adjacent to Robinson's Randfontein Estates. South Randfontein Deep had been formed in 1895. By 1910 limited exploratory work had not revealed payable ore. Either the

20. It went into liquidation in 1917.

Goerz interests had larger designs on developing ground east of Robinson's holdings where a number of the houses together or separately held extensive mining ground, or they saw possibilities for a speculation. The parent firm and its officials held almost 28 percent of South Randfontein Deep's issued capital in 1910 which they obtained cheaply through a recent reconstruction.[21] But, as Table 7.1 indicates, some 1000 outsiders on the continent and in Britain were certainly out something (they had paid at least 5s on some 225,000 of the mine's 441,647 10s shares) when it went into liquidation a few years later.

While neither its speculative nor its development programs in the Transvaal proved to be money spinners, Goerz and Company activities elsewhere also proved disappointing before 1914. It had participated in a modest way along with Central Mining and Goldfields in West African mines. Prospecting in Mexico led it to float the La Fe Mining Company to work several small silver mines. This venture led to Goerz and Company obtaining control of San Francisco Mines of Mexico. Neither rewarded the parent company's shareholders.[22] Meanwhile German investors had lost so heavily over Goerz as well as General Mining stocks that they would not look at gold shares.[23]

The third financial organization through which German banks supplied capital to the Rand was not on Emden's "Big Ten" list. Consolidated Mines Selection was formed in London in 1897. It acquired the widely dispersed assets of two firms formed during the 1894–95 boom: African Metals Company and the Mines Selection Company. The board of the former was largely composed of German financiers headed by Mac Kempner. But a London-based mining engineer, Walter McDermott, was a director of both.[24] The Mines Selection Company was more in-

21. About one half of the issued shares had been allotted pro rata to holders of shares in a previous company of the same name.

22. Derived from various numbers of the *Mining Manual* and the *Stock Exchange Official Year-Book.*

23. F. Eckstein to L. Phillips, 6 June 1913, BRA.

24. Goldmann, *South African Mines,* II, 135, 150. McDermott and Duffield, mining engineers and metallurgists, had connections with Fraser and Chalmers, W. McDermott to J. Wernher, 20 August 1895, BRA.

Table 7.1. ***Geographic Distribution of Shareholders: South Randfontein Deep Ltd., 1910***

Geographical area	Number of share-holders	Amount held	%
Great Britain			
City of London			
Co. officials & A. Goerz & Co.	9	123,086	27.87
stockbrokers & jobbers	70	27,013	6.12
other	106	54,964	12.45
London (excluding the City)	128	37,942	8.59
England (excluding London & the City)	291	39,175	8.87
Scotland	37	5,410	1.22
Ireland	27	2,646	.60
Wales	2	200	.05
subtotal	670	290,436	65.77
Continent of Europe			
France	6	1,670	.38
Germany: Dresdner, Deutsche & Direction Disconto Banks	3	39,938	9.04
Germany: other shareholders	98	27,208	6.16
Other	8	2,170	.49
subtotal	115	70,986	16.07
Other			
South Africa: stock brokers and jobbers	48	23,341	5.28
South Africa: other shareholders	240	55,714	12.62
British Empire (excluding South Africa) and USA	6	770	.17
Unclassified	3	400	.09
subtotal	297	80,225	18.16
Total	1,082	441,647	100.00

Note: Authorized Capital: £ 400,000 in 800,000 10/– shares. Issued Capital: £ 220,823.10s in 441,647 shares.
Source: PRO BT 31/12954/105518.

terested in West Australian gold mining than Transvaal properties but the amalgamation was likely designed to pursue serious development of holdings on the far-east Rand. CMS also dabbled in mining promotions in North and Central America as well as Australia. It was paying substantial dividends on an issued capital of £ 300,000 when the Anglo-Boer war broke out. In anticipation of profitable resumption on the return of peace, its backers ordered a major reconstruction. In early 1903 the Darmstädter Bank guaranteed the issue of 200,000 new shares at a small premium and took up at least 50,000. In 1905 a London-based firm of diamond merchants, Anton Dunkelsbuhler and Company, turned over its assets on the Rand to Consolidated Mines Selection for 400,000 shares and control of its board.[25]

Dunkelsbuhler had started out as a diamond buyer at Kimberley in the 1870s. He had not been directly involved in company formation on the Rand but he had taken up shares in mines and houses formed by his Kimberley contemporaries. He also participated in syndicates which held claims for development and in debenture issues. His interests and contacts were thus valuable assets and may have accounted for increased German bank support. The Darmstädter guaranteed a £ 400,000 5 percent debenture issue. The three other big "D" banks, the Dresdner, the Deutsche Bank and the Disconto-Gesellschaft were also probably interested.[26] This backing enabled CMS to become involved in far-east Rand development. It controlled two gold mines, Brakpan and Springs, with an issued capital of £ 1,483,-500 and a successful colliery operation, the Transvaal Coal Trust, with an issued capital of £ 500,000. It had also participated in the consortium got up by the Corner House to obtain the government lease on Modderfontein which had been outbid by the Barnato group.[27] It held shares in 13 other mines from one end of the gold fields to the other, and in diamond mines in the Transvaal and Orange Free State. While its South African holdings represented 75 percent of its assets, it continued to try to profit from mining ventures elsewhere. It acquired interests in the West African mining activities of other Rand-based houses;

25. Dunkelsbuhler had been represented on the CMS board from its formation, Gregory, *Oppenheimer*, p. 81.

26. Cartwright, *Golden Age*, p. 90; comparison of company's directorate with the boards of several German banks.

27. Cartwright, *Golden Age*, pp. 24–25.

it participated in the formation of a Brazilian mineral firm, Itabira Iron Ore Company. And it retained its earlier interest in mining properties in Australia, the United States, and Canada.[28] Its West African and Brazilian participations, though they came to nought, were likely an attempt to hedge against disappointments on the Rand. From 1905 to 1912 Consolidated Mines Selections paid no dividends. Springs Mines, formed in 1909, absorbed about £ 500,000 before 1914 and would not yield its first dividend, payable in shares, until 1918. The Transvaal Coal Trust which paid dividends every year between 1903 and 1911 at an average of 6 percent seems to have been the parent company's single source of profits. Only when Brakpan Mines, formed in 1903 and having absorbed more than £ 800,000 before it began producing gold in 1910, paid its first dividend, a hefty 40 percent in 1912, did CMS begin to benefit from its far-east Rand development program. It declared 10 percent in 1912–13 and 5 percent in 1913–14, but this was on a share capital reduced by half in 1911 to £ 552,500. Much of its debenture debt was still outstanding as well.[29]

One particularly well-informed Rand commentator has argued "that by 1890 there was probably more German capital invested in South African gold mining shares than British."[30] Certainly German capital and expertise found an important place in the Rand's early development. Moreover, stabilized by appreciable German bank involvement, the financial commitment was not

28. The latter was in British Columbia.

29. Like other financial houses with continental bank connections, CMS was shorn of its German investors during the war. Even excluding share capital held directly by German banks, which must have been appreciable, about 25 percent of its capital at par value was in German hands. Calculated from BT 8/17, BT 8/18, BT 8/19. It failed in a bid to sell off its South African interests to the Corner House in 1915. But these interests, which included the Transvaal Coal Trust (renamed the Rand Selection Corporation in 1916), were absorbed in 1922 by the Anglo American Corporation through which American capital was for the first time to obtain a position in the Transvaal mining business. Cartwright, *Golden Age,* pp. 91–92; Gregory, *Oppenheimer,* pp. 82–90. Ernest Oppenheimer, who founded Anglo American in 1917, had started his business apprenticeship with Dunkelsbuhler.

30. [Cartwright] in Shorten, *Johannesburg Saga,* p. 545.

dislodged by war, turbulent politics or labor shortages. German expertise had concluded that not only the central Rand but also its eastward, and possibly its westward, extensions contained colossal amounts of payable ore. For almost a decade the Albu, Goerz, and Dunkelsbuhler enterprises largely avoided the temptations of speculation and persisted with ambitious development programs. When, after several years these programs had yielded meager results, German capitalists finally became disillusioned with the Rand. On the eve of World War I they were cutting back commitments and refusing the developers additional financing. And some of the developers were looking elsewhere for more profitable mining ventures.

2. The Fringe Operators

The eight financial organizations thus far examined (the Corner House, Goldfields, the three houses of ill repute, and the three enterprises backed by German banks) were extensively committed to financing Rand gold properties and, therefore, can be categorized as mining houses. But Robinson's organization and the Farrar interests were so ineffectually managed and so prone to speculation that it would not be appropriate to classify them as part of the group system. The features of this system, through which a parent company provided appreciable technical and administrative support as well as financial backing to the mines it controlled, were, however, clearly apparent in the operations of the three German-based houses as well as those of the Corner House, Goldfields and, in its later development, the Barnato group. At least six other business groupings, not easily classified as mining houses or participants in the group system, were, nevertheless, clearly evident in the Rand's financial development. Though individually they were dwarfed by bigger houses, their collective input was important. Because so much of the activity of the minor groupings was devoted to stock dealing, and because none sustained a large interest in mine development, they are also referred to in what follows as fringe operators or promoters.

Sigismund Neumann was the most important fringe operator. By 1895 he and his representatives held directorships in 37 mines with an issued capital of £ 7,400,000. In 1902 the Chamber of Mines listed 10 mines as members of a Neumann group. Eleven years later his private company was listed as controlling eight Rand properties with an issued capital of almost £ 5 million.[31] But his interests in these various undertakings were never very concentrated and they became quite unstable.

Two factors accounted for the dispersed and volatile nature of his mining commitments. First, he used contacts established in Kimberley, where he arrived from Bavaria in the early 1870s to set up as a diamond buyer, to participate in the enterprises of other capitalists. Indeed, he and his associates on the Rand specialized in ground floor participations in widely dispersed blocks of claims, options, and concessions which they sold for cash or vendor shares to the developers. He also snapped up properties adjacent to larger blocks of mining ground with the intention of exploiting their value as it increased through development work on the nearby undertakings. This practice prompted Ernest Rhodes to observe that Neumann worked "like a jackal and picks up what he can after the lions have fed themselves." Another Goldfields official complained that Neumann was "trying to lie on our backs as usual," in the running of Knight's Central, a mine jointly floated by the Corner House, Goldfields, and others.[32] Neumann frequently appeared as a participant in Corner House schemes. These included the original Porges–Kann gold syndicate, the Diamond Syndicate, the second-row deep-level program, the effort to stem the break in the 1895 boom,

31. Goldmann, *South African Mines,* I, *passim; Annexure to the Thirteenth Report of the Transvaal Chamber of Mines for the Year 1902* (Johannesburg, 1903), Exhibit 1; *Transvaal Chamber of Mines for the Year 1913,* p. 557.

32. E. Rhodes to H. E. M. Davies, 1894, quoted in "Notes on the History of 'The Gold Fields,'" typed MS, New Consolidated Gold Fields Intelligence Department, n.d., CGFSA—JA; and C. S. Stanhope to Lord Harris, 4 November 1898, *ibid.*

the subsidies for the French press, and the gamble in West African shares.[33] To a lesser extent he was involved with Goldfields,[34] and his interest in Farrar's undertakings obtained him a seat on the board of East Rand Proprietary Mines. Though he might acquire substantial interests in several companies which earned him or his representatives numerous directorships, Neumann was content to let others do much of the management and development work. But with the Wernher, Beit partnership withdrawing from Rand commitments he was left without a major source of support for his schemes.

A second factor which undermined his Rand commitments was his decision, in the face of the Rand's decline, to become a London-based merchant banker involved in varied ventures. In 1907 he took into partnership Martin Luebeck, who had been employed in Johannesburg by the Albus and who had later served as the chief manager of the London branch of the Dresdner bank. The new firm, styled S. Neumann, Luebeck and Company, started with a capital of £ 1 million. It made its first venture as an issuing house in 1910 when, along with Lloyds Bank, it guaranteed a £ 2 million 4 percent loan for the city of Budapest.[35] The contacts, as well as the profits, derived from his Rand ventures aided Neumann to set up as an international financier. For though he had once been dependent on the Corner House for some of his connections with western European capital sources, he developed his own clients. His brother Ludwig was a partner in Leopold Hirsch and Company, the most influential stockbroking firm engaged in the mining share market. In 1895 this company, acting for Neumann and another Rand promoter,

33. J. Porges & Co. to H. Eckstein & Co., 27 June 1889, BRA; G. Lenzen, *The History of Diamond Production and the Diamond Trade* (London, 1970), p. 166; A. Beit to L. Phillips, 1 February 1895, BRA; Wernher, Beit & Co. to H. Eckstein & Co., 19 October 1895, *ibid.;* F. Eckstein to L. Phillips, 17 November 1905 and 10 December 1909, *ibid.*

34. Agreement of 21 February 1893, BT. Register of Companies, File No. 36936; Notes on capital structure of Boksburg Gold Mining Syndicate, 31 December 1906; Knights Deep, 31 September 1906; Glen Deep, 31 July 1907; Booysens Estates, 20 November 1914; all in CGFSA—JA.

35. F. Eckstein to L. Phillips, 15 February 1907, BRA; T. Milner to L. Reyersbach, 15 February 1910, *ibid.* The issue was badly handled and the underwriters were stuck with 96.6 percent of it.

Henry B. Marshall, acquired the whole of the Vogelstruisfontein farm located on the west Rand.[36] It was obtained from Donald Currie, the shipping magnate, who likely had further dealings with Neumann. By 1895 Neumann was also tapping French capital sources through a trust company with a capital of £ 800,000. In 1904 he helped establish Association Minière, a Paris company with an issued capital of £ 600,000 chaired by a French financier, Fernand Robellaz, that specialized in South African mining shares.[37] The fortunes of the Association Minière, along with Neumann's, were hard hit by the Rand's poor postwar performance. This setback (Neumann was reported to be hopelessly depressed and "very despondent")[38] may have been a factor in his decision to set up in merchant banking, and there is little doubt that it led Neumann to withdraw what he could of his own capital from the Rand. Though he continued to hold gold shares and speculate occasionally and erratically on the mining market, by 1914 Neumann took little interest in the Rand.[39]

Emden ranked the "Abe Bailey group" as the least important among the "Big Ten" which controlled the mines on the Rand in the mid-90s. The *Dictionary of South African Biography* has further minimized his role, asserting that his "impatience prevented him from founding an established mining-house." He "left it to others to bring the mines to production stage." By contrast the *Statist* listed the Bailey organization in 1905 as one of the Rand's 13 "great controlling groups."[40] While Bailey was not development oriented, he was, nevertheless, a company promoter who was a significant factor in the capitalization of the industry, particularly in the years immediately after the Anglo-Boer War.

Though his early business career did not include the important

36. Characteristically enough Wernher, Beit participated in the development of a mining property on the farm, Vogelstruis Consolidated Deep Mines, and managed a pool of its shares. A. Beit to L. Phillips, 8 March 1895, and same to H. Eckstein & Co., 23 March 1895, *ibid.*

37. J. Wernher to H. Eckstein & Co., 2 February 1895, *ibid.*

38. F. Eckstein to L. Phillips, 5 January and 2 November 1906, *ibid.*

39. L. Reyersbach to R. Schumacher, 27 March 1914, *ibid.*

40. Emden, *Randlords,* p. 207; *Dictionary of South African Biography* (Cape Town, 1972), II, 18–20; *Statist,* 26 August 1905, pp. 347–48.

Kimberley connection, he was able to exploit the Rand's promotional potential. Like Robinson, he was born in the Cape. He was the son of a shopkeeper and worked for a time with a textile firm in England. But Bailey forsook trade and industry when he showed up at Barberton in 1886 as a company promoter. The following year he set up in Johannesburg as a stockbroker. He and his clients probably lost heavily in the panic of 1889–90,[41] but evidentally he was able to recover through the 1894–95 boom. By then his stock and claim holdings entitled him to seats on the boards of nine mining companies with an issued capital of £ 1,338,000.[42] His first corporate undertaking was modest by Rand standards. He formed South African Gold Mines in 1897 to deal in claims and shares with an authorized capital of just £ 40,000.[43] By 1899 it had only increased to £ 154,000 when even individual outcrop mines had larger capital structures. He may have wished to operate on a larger scale, but his backing for the most part at this juncture must have been local and, therefore, limited. While the ubiquitous Neumann took an interest, his chief backer was a local entrepreneur, Julius Jeppe. The Jeppe family had emigrated to South Africa from Germany in 1870 and had been active in business in Pretoria before investing in real estate in Johannesburg.[44]

Though the resources Bailey could command were limited he was adept at acquiring strategic shares and claims cheaply. These especially involved second-row, deep-level undertakings which the large developers, such as the Corner House and Goldfields, were slow to take up or let slip when the first-row, deep-level mines proved more expensive and took longer to bring into profitable production than originally expected. Promoters could make large profits if they were prepared to take up ground-floor interest in anticipation of subsequent development, able to get shares in and representation on boards of the companies acquiring these interests, and willing to exploit market conditions

41. Cartwright, *Corner House*, p. 101.
42. Derived from Goldmann, *South African Mines*, I, *passim*.
43. *Mining Manual*, 1915, p. 612.
44. *Dictionary of South African Biography*, II, 340–41.

with these shares and the information obtained through such representation. Bailey was just such a promoter. By 1904, for example, South African Gold Mines, despite its small capital which still stood at £ 154,000, had very substantial holdings. These included more than one million shares in 14 deep-level undertakings, three of which Bailey controlled, and another four in which he held directorships. His company also held 14 separate blocks of deep-level mining ground averaging 70 claims.[45]

Bailey supplemented his mining interests, as did a number of Rand promoters, with extensive real estate operations in Johannesburg and the Transvaal. In 1896 he formed a company to handle his Johannesburg interests. Called the Witwatersrand Township Estate and Finance Corporation, it acquired the Johannesburg assets and expertise of the Jeppes, and by 1910 its issued capital of £ 200,000 had generated £ 380,000 in dividends.

Profits from Bailey's real estate deals may have been diverted to mining promotion; if so the maneuver was not successful. By 1914 the £ 1 shares of South African Gold Mines, of which about 180,000 had been issued, were quoted as low as 7s 6d. Its debenture debt stood at about £ 70,000. Its only assets included a controlling share interest in two nonproducing second-row, deep-level mines, (the East Rand Deep and French Rand Deep) and some small claim holdings. With its capital depreciated, and its mining interests reduced, it was later absorbed by a finance corporation which had been formed out of Witwatersrand Townships.[46] Thus, Bailey not only contributed to the inflationary pressures which beset postwar, deep-level development through his dealings in shares and claims, but he also added to the deflationary pressures affecting share values by a reduction in his capital commitment to mining finance.

If Bailey was primarily a promoter with little regard for concerted development, the Lewis and Marks group combined

45. Derived from *Mines of the Transvaal,* various years.

46. This new enterprise was called the South African Townships Mining and Finance Corporation. Younger than most of his Rand contemporaries, Bailey became more important as a mining magnate and politician after 1914.

both functions in its varied financial, land, and industrial undertakings. The group was ranked ninth among Emden's "Big Ten" who controlled Rand gold mining in the mid-1890s. But Emden was quite mistaken. Neither Sammy Marks nor Isaac Lewis appear as directors of a single Rand property in 1895.[47] It was only after the Anglo-Boer War that the partnership, by then involved in manifold enterprises in South Africa, took up a significant interest in the Rand. Indeed, the range of its economic activity made it unique among the so-called groups.

The background and backing of the partnership was also unique among Rand entrepreneurs. Marks, the son of an itinerant pedlar, emigrated from Lithuania to South Africa by way of Sheffield in 1868. Along with Lewis, his second cousin and brother-in-law, he was among the thousands of Jews from eastern Europe who immigrated to South Africa in the late nineteenth century.[48] By either origin, education, social standing or economic status, these East European Jews had little in common with such members of their ethnic group as Porges and Beit or even, for that matter, the Barnatos and Joels. These disparities accounted for minimal cooperation and considerable competition in business, and different assessments of the local political situation. Marks, for example, avoided the Johannesburg conspiracy.[49] He started in South Africa as a pedlar of jewelry in the Western Cape. He and Lewis turned diamond buyers and, likely with family support, acquired substantial claim holdings in the Kimberley mine. These, along with the interests of Porges and Wernher, formed the basis upon which the French Diamond Company was floated. Squeezed out of the company, Lewis and Marks continued a Kimberley connection as suppliers for its fuel needs.[50] Later they joined the rush to Barberton. Here they

47. See Goldmann, *South African Mines,* I, *passim.* They did have a small interest in a Goldfields speculation on Rietfontein located north of the main outcrop. I. Lewis to E. H. Dunning, 20 October 1893, CGFSA—JA.

48. G. Saron and L. Hotz (eds.), *The Jews in South Africa: A History* (Cape Town, 1955), pp. 59–69. Marks was instrumental in inspiring a good deal of this migration.

49. Marais, *Kruger,* p. 63.

50. Roberts, *Diamond Magnates,* pp. 104–5.

gained control of the Sheba mine formed in 1887. It paid out enormous dividends when it started up.[51] Though it was subsequently never a large producer its shares were boomed when market conditions allowed.

Whatever profit Lewis and Marks made out of these ventures at Kimberley and Barberton, and it must have been considerable, they reinvested in a large number of varied enterprises: collieries, Johannesburg real estate, farming, and consumer-oriented secondary industries. The latter included a distillery, a brick works (in which Eckstein's at one time participated), a glass factory, a tannery, a boot factory, and food preserving plants. But much of their capital seems to have been tied up in land with mineral development potential. They owned outright or had interests in millions of acres of land in the Transvaal and Orange Free State, much of it acquired for 2s 6d or less per acre. Marks, for example, was for some years a director of the Transvaal Estates and Development Company, registered in 1889, which controlled almost two million acres, and of the Transvaal Consolidated Land and Exploration Company, formed by the Corner House in 1892, which owned more than three million acres.[52]

Much of the partnership's backing in its formative years likely came from savings of recently settled East European Jewish immigrants. Though relatively limited, this backing could be made to go a long way. The Boer republics were capital poor. Few of the entrepreneurs engaged on the Rand were prepared to bother much with other, less prepossessing, economic opportunities. Marks, on the other hand, struck up amicable relations with the Transvaal government. Kruger, though he found much to dislike and worry about in the *uitlanders* swarming into the republic, was willing to offer monopolies and concessions to some of them in order to fashion a program of economic nationalism.[53] Marks was thus able to profit in the prewar period from cooperating with and exploiting concessions granted by the Transvaal

51. Emden, *Randlords*, p. 282.
52. Cartwright, *Golden Age*, p. 268.
53. Gordon, *Boer Opposition*, p. 36.

government.[54] It was only after the war that Lewis and Marks competed significantly in the international mining share market for larger amounts of capital to develop mines on the far-east Rand.

Though continuing to engage in significant and more extensive economic development in South Africa, Lewis and Marks carried out their Rand mining program much in the manner of promoters like Bailey. In 1901 the partnership registered in London the East Rand Mining Estates Company with an issued capital of £ 400,000 of which 55 percent went to the vendors for interests in several undeveloped farms. The most promising, Grootvlei and Palmiektkuil, lay immediately east of the Goerz company's Geduld Proprietary Mines. Lewis and Marks became significant shareholders in this Goerz enterprise and controlled Grootvlei Proprietary, a mining undertaking formed in 1904 with an issued capital of £ 360,250 of which East Rand Mining Estates received or subscribed almost 75 percent. The partnership also displaced Goldfields as the controlling interest in the East Rand Extension Gold Mining Company. This company, whose main block of claims lay immediately east of Farrar's huge property, held numerous other claims and interests in the Boksburg area. Its authorized capital was about £ 300,000. The partnership's interests in these east and far-east Rand properties were put into a large holding company, the African and European Investment Company, registered in South Africa in 1904. Like the other enterprises the partnership floated it was heavily encumbered with vendor interests: £ 1,000,000 of its initial issued capital of £ 1,375,000 was in the form of vendor shares.[55] The interest these shares represented was much inflated. For example, the investment company took over the business and assets of the African and European Agency. It was formed in London in 1901 and by 1904 had issued 100,000 £ 1 shares on which 5s had been paid. Isaac Lewis, his brother Barnet, and other members of his

54. For information regarding the profits he made from the famous Dynamite concession, see A. P. Cartwright, *The Dynamite Company* (London, 1964), pp. 44, 48, 50.

55. The remainder were issued at 25s for working capital.

family were allotted 92,708 of these shares.[56] Possessing no appreciable assets, the agency was a paper company, to which, nevertheless, the African and European Investment Company assigned the £ 1 million of vendor shares. Besides taking up interests in gold mining ventures, the Investment Company acquired large holdings in subsidiary estate and exploration companies as well as freehold rights to 118 farms covering more than 700,000 acres in various districts of the Transvaal and Free State. It also acquired building lots in Johannesburg, an interest in the Sheba mine, participations in several Rhodesian gold mining enterprises, ownership of a further 133 farms (bringing its land interest by 1914 to 1,300,000 acres), and a Free State diamond mine. The partnership meanwhile had maintained interests in collieries, and in 1911 founded southern Africa's first steel company at Vereeniging. Neither the Investment Company with its diverse holdings, its subsidiary East Rand Mining Estates with varied mining properties, nor Grootvlei Proprietary had produced dividends by 1913. Their respective shares were all quoted below par. Thus the Lewis and Marks group had little to show investors from its postwar plunge into gold mines. While its other varied interests may have contributed significantly to South Africa's economic development, its heavily watered mining flotations seemed merely to add to the Rand's bloated capital structure.

A fringe operator who similarly affected the Rand's capital structure without contributing appreciably to development was John Crosbie Aitken Henderson. This Scottish-born entrepreneur was, like Farrar, diverted from business elsewhere in South Africa by the Rand's possibilities. He helped form several east Rand outcrop mines which provided him with a directorship in ERPM when it absorbed these enterprises on its formation in 1893. He also floated his own finance company, Henderson's Transvaal Estates, which was registered in London in 1894. The activities of this company have been virtually ignored in the literature on the Rand. Yet, despite appreciable interests held elsewhere in the Transvaal and later in Swaziland, it was as involved in

56. BT 31/9448/70183.

the gold fields as much as other fringe enterprises which have been given more attention. Moreover, its activities contributed to the Rand's postwar malaise not only through its own failures but by making difficulties for more able organizations.

One of the Estate company's worst features was an overload of vendor capital. For the holdings he put into it, Henderson allotted himself 250,000 of its authorized 300,000 £ 1 shares. These reached a high of £ 5 in the 1894–95 boom suggesting Henderson made ample profits from stock speculation, particularly because initial working capital was obtained through the issue of £ 50,000 in 6 percent debentures which were later exchanged for shares in the company. Though nominally a land-owning company, Henderson's firm was deeply involved on the Rand, but in a dispersed way. Most of its holdings consisted of gold and coal mining claims and shares on the borders of proven Rand properties. For example, it held 823 claims south of the second-row, deep-level claims of Goldfields's Simmer and Jack complex, almost 600 claims north of the main reef series on the central and west Rand, as well as numerous shares and claims in four coal-bearing properties on the east and far-east Rand. It also held a controlling interest in Henderson's Nigel, a mining property floated in 1895 in the Heidelberg district south of the far-east Rand. Its remaining assets were rights in several farms in five other districts of the Transvaal. By the turn of the century Henderson's Transvaal Estates had increased its capital to £ 2 million of which, by 1904, £ 1,730,000 were issued. Again much of this issue represented vendor capital which was used to speculate on the market. Its only dividend, 7.5 percent, was paid in 1902. A 6 percent debenture issue of £ 250,000 made in 1898 and which had been reduced to £ 127,000 by 1904 seems to have provided working capital. By then as well, Henderson's firm had enlarged its rights in land—in this case to interests in over 4,500,000 acres in the Transvaal and Swaziland. But it still retained its mining claim interests on the Rand and a number had been used to form actual companies.

These mines were marginal properties which competed for development capital. They did not fare well. Though Henderson had been ousted by General Mining from the management of one mine, Violet Consolidated, in 1899 his Estate company controlled three gold mines with an issued capital of £ 1,300,000.[57] Two of these, the Daggafontein Gold Mining Company (formed in 1902) and Henderson's Nigel, were on the far-east Rand. The third, Consolidated South Rand Mines Deep, was formed in 1902 to develop claims held south of the Simmer and Jack. There was a certain desperate quality about the choice of the cumbersome title for this central Rand second-row, deep-level property, crammed as it was with words evocative of the more successful houses. Before it went into voluntary liquidation in 1909, the Estate company relinquished control to the Abe Bailey interests. Up to 1910 Henderson's Nigel, though formed in 1895, spent only £ 11,500 in boring and shaftsinking. The Daggafontein proceeded very slowly with shaftsinking though boreholes had struck reef. Its £ 1 shares stood at 5s in 1913. While it is true much of the capital of these mines was in the form of moribund vendors shares, some of their scrip was in circulation and contributed, therefore, to the overload of gold shares in the mining market.

Henderson's entrepreneurial inabilities which had surfaced when he lost control of the Violet Consolidated, coupled with the Estate company's declining fortunes, allowed others to take control of it. They reregistered and reconstructed it in Rhodesia in 1908 and again in London in 1912. These maneuvers did not revive its fortunes. In 1913 its shares stood at par, but they had been devalued along the way and were worth only 5s. The small yearly surpluses on its balance sheets were derived from its holdings in a colliery in the Middleburg district of the Transvaal, land sales in Swaziland, and after 1910, when it bought into the Delegoa Bay Development Corporation, utility concessions in Lourenço Marques.[58]

The weaknesses in the Estate company's capital structure and

57. Actual financial control was accomplished through a wholly owned subsidiary called Henderson's Consolidated Corporation, or through the Daggafontein Prospecting Syndicate.

58. *Mining Manual,* 1915.

that of the mines it floated (all overweighted as they were with vendor capital), sloppy management, and unstructured development programs were factors as much to blame for their postwar performance as the marginal quality of ore and labor difficulties. These characteristics did not make Henderson's enterprises unique on the Rand. They simply possessed them in a more virulent form than did the ventures of most developers or other fringe promoters.

Henderson's Estate company did, however, possess one rather unique feature. Its capital sources were significantly different from most other speculative finance companies interested in mining promotion and operating on the Rand. It did not have the continental-Kimberley axis to exploit at its inception. Nor was it able, like Farrar, to establish a continental link. At the same time it did not benefit from local capital infusions as did Bailey's enterprises. By registering the company in London, Henderson was clearly seeking British finance capital. Though the company's development activities produced little actual profit, and though much of its share capital was retained for speculative purposes by Henderson, his relatives, his associates, and a coterie of stockbrokers specializing in mining shares, it acquired a host of clients, and by 1907 had more than 10,000 shareholders.[59] With but a few hundred of these, who held about 2 percent, located on the continent of Europe, and a smaller number of South African residents holding less than 0.2 percent, the overwhelming majority were concentrated in Britain.

The analysis in Table 7.2 of a pro rata allotment made in 1902 to holders of 65 percent of the Estate Company's issued capital gives some indication of how this British concentration was distributed. The allotment was taken up by some 2000 shareholders. About a dozen company officials and 30 London stockbrokers received 63 percent. Marginal amounts went to the continent and South Africa. The remaining 35 percent was absorbed in Britain. Close to a third of these shares were taken by investors with residential and business addresses in London. In Scotland

59. BT 31/5933/41750.

Table 7.2. ***Geographic Distribution of Shareholders: Henderson's Transvaal Estates, 1902***

Geographical area	*Number of shares*	*%*
Great Britain		
City of London		
stockbrokers	53,911	47.65
Estate Co. officials	17,696	15.65
other	7,551	6.67
London (excluding the City)	5,130	4.53
England (excluding London and the City)		
local stockbrokers	2,108	1.86
other	13,027	11.51
Scotland		
banks and stockbrokers	5,364	4.74
other	4,233	3.74
Ireland	1,012	.89
Wales	950	.84
Continent of Europe		
France	110	.10
Germany	990	.87
Other	214	.19
Other		
South Africa	33	.03
Miscellaneous and Unaccounted	822	.73
Total	113,151	100.00

Note: Authorized capital of Estate Company: £ 2,000,000. Issued capital: £ 1,729,341. Pro rata allotment made 24 June–24 August 1902; 1 share for 10 held: 113, 151.
Source: PRO BT 31/5933/4150.

several banks, led by a Glasgow branch of the Commercial Bank of Scotland, and a few stockbrokers, held almost 5 percent of the total allotment. Almost 2 percent was in the hands of local stockbrokers mostly located in England's northern industrial cities. The banks and local brokers were likely the vehicles through which the remaining some 17 percent of the allotment was distributed in England (11.5 percent), Scotland (3.7), Ireland (.9), and Wales (.8). Numerous shares held by the London and local stockbrokers as well as the Scottish banks would have been for unnamed clients. But even if these allotments could be discovered and included, it is unlikely they would fundamentally change the geographical distribution pattern of the Estate company's shares.

As previously noted, any analysis of the occupational pattern of shareholders based on available data must be used with extreme caution. The case of shareholders in Henderson's Transvaal Estates is no exception. The clerks who made up some of its share summaries for the register of companies were, however, more conscientious than most, and thus provided more occupational information. Still, as Table 7.3 illustrates, 45 percent of the 1902 allotment which was held by investors who were not company officials, stockbrokers or Scottish bank directors, was in the hands of "Gentlemen." Commerce and Industry accounted for 31 percent. Professionals, led by lawyers, held 16 percent. Whatever the occupations of the Estate Company's shareholders, and they ranged from 20 members of the working class who were mostly in domestic service, to 6 upper-class people with knighthoods or peerages, they did not make much profit. Indeed, most of them, unless they were well-informed or employed brokers who were knowledgeable about speculative mining market trends, would have lost much of what they put up.

Another marginal operator who contributed to inefficient competition for Rand development capital was Ludwig Ehrlich. His background, backing, and financial maneuvers were on the whole consistent with a number of patterns which have emerged in the analysis of the Rand promoter. A German banker who, like Neumann, came from Bavaria, he spent several years with the banking firm of Sulzbach Brothers, in Frankfurt and Paris, before arriving on the Rand in 1890.[60] Here he worked for Neumann before starting out on his own at the beginning of the 1894–95 boom. He participated, possibly with German capital obtained through his banking contacts, in such highly speculative ventures as the promotion of the Klipfontein Estate and Gold Mining Company. This company was formed in the midst of the

60. *Who's Who of Southern Africa, 1910.*

Table 7.3. *Shareholders' Occupation: Henderson's Transvaal Estates, 1902*

Occupation	*Number of share-holders*	*Amount held*	%
Commerce and Industry			
commercial employees	325	4,301	
merchants	153	3,039	
industry	86	1,681	
bankers (excluding Scottish)	24	423	
			31.04
Professionals			
lawyers	73	1,087	
medical	67	699	
clergy	40	642	
military	31	406	
miscellaneous	171	2,088	
			16.18
Other			
"gentlemen"	686	13,648	
women	198	1,779	
farmers	19	184	
titled	6	144	
working class	20	121	
no description	7	186	
			52.78
Total	1,906	30,428	100.00

Note: Authorized capital of Estate Company: £ 2,000,000. Issued capital: £ 1,729,341. Pro rata allotment made 24 June–24 August 1902; 1 share for 10 held: 113,151.

Source: PRO BT 31/5933/4150.

boom out of half a farm located north and east of Eckstein's Modderfontein mine on the far-east Rand. It acquired the assets of the Amatola Estate Gold Mining Company formed the previous year. Klipfontein retained 25,000 of its authorized 200,000 £ 1 shares in reserve and allotted a like number for working capital. Vendors and promoters got the rest. Ehrlich, one of Amatola's directors, obtained 50,000 of the new company's shares and £ 6250 in cash. Goldfields and three of its employees got 25,000 shares, as did the partners in Eckstein's and Wernher, Beit. Ehrlich's contribution to working capital was only £ 2068.[61] Not much was done with it. Operations on the Klipfontein property, which consisted only of borehole work, were suspended in August 1896, resumed in June 1899, and stopped again by the war.[62] Profits from such speculations enabled Ehrlich to set up in London in 1896 where his firm participated with the Exploration Company in the flotation of Consolidated Gold Fields of New Zealand.[63] Thus, at an early date, Ehrlich became involved in mining promotions outside South Africa. Other Rand-based promoters and developers later followed suit.

He was hardly a pacesetter, however, in floating a holding company to exploit his interests. In 1900 he took in Frederick Howard Hamilton as a partner. This Cambridge graduate, trained in the law, a former editor of the Johannesburg *Star*, and a member of the Reform Committee which plotted Kruger's overthrow, forsook his previous callings for the board rooms of the companies in which Ehrlich was involved. Chief among these was H. E. Proprietary. It was formed in 1901 with an authorized capital of £ 150,000. Almost a third of its shares went to the vendors, and half of these to Ehrlich and Hamilton. A Johannesburg solicitor, Charles Leonard, a South African prospector, Duncan Clark, and a Transvaal journalist and mining promoter, Francis Dormer, were also significant vendor participants. Over the next two years an additional 53,000 shares were issued for working capital and realized £ 85,000. Ehrlich acquired 18,000 of these at subpar prices. In fact, he and Hamilton awarded themselves more than 40,000 of 98,000 issued shares. By 1903 they reduced the holding by half. In the meantime the market value of the company's shares varied enormously, reach-

61. Notes on capital structure of Klipfontein Estate and Gold Mining Co. Ltd., n.d., with attached correspondence, CGFSA—JA.

62. In 1909 the property was fused with a neighboring company and came under the control of the Farrar group, though Ehrlich continued to maintain an interest in the new company called the Rand Klip. It produced no gold before 1913 and in 1916 was absorbed in the formation of the Modder East.

63. The Exploration Company was the creation of an American mining engineer, Hamilton Smith, who had decided that greener investment pastures lay outside South Africa.

ing a high of more than £ 10 in 1902 during the height of the short-lived postwar revival, and a low of £ 2⅜ in 1903 when the boomlet had passed. These market fluctuations were no doubt fostered by the partners' booming tactics, but a number of London stockbrokers were deeply involved. Some 280 speculators, most of whom were brokers or jobbers, had by 1903 sold off their holdings in H. E. Proprietary, leaving about 470 investors still on the company's books. William Sopper, a Throgmorton Street broker, operating on his own account or on behalf of the partners, was the most active tactician. He took up 10,000 shares on which £ 2 was payable in 1901 and placed all but 19 of these through nine transactions during 1902.[64]

These market maneuvers were backed by flimsy assets. They consisted mostly of gold claims located in the remote Murchison Range in the northeast Transvaal. What little prospecting the company undertook failed to reveal payable ore, and its shares soon fell below par.[65] While Ehrlich used the proprietary company to cash in on the Rand's fame, he still retained an interest there through holdings in other companies. He possessed a significant interest in Luipaard's Vlei Estate, a low-grade unprofitable outcrop mine on the far-west Rand, and in East Rand Deep, an underdeveloped mine near Boksburg south and east of Farrar's properties. The outcrop produced only £ 60,000 in dividends between 1888–1913 on an issued capital which topped £ 400,000, but its speculative potential in boom conditions was considerable. The deep-level undertaking, formed in 1902, issued 500,000 shares only 153,000 of which went for working capital. Abe Bailey took it over in 1908 when its capital was reduced to £ 60,000. Again, given the timing of its flotation and its overload of vendor capital, East Rand Deep also had speculative possibilities.

In sum, Ehrlich was one of the fringe promoters who used the Rand as a base for stock deals. Such promoters surfaced in boom

64. H. E. Proprietary Co., Summary of Capital and Shares, 12 January 1903, and statement of various allotments, 1901–1904, BT 31/16699/71157.

65. Its name and assets were later acquired by another of Ehrlich's companies which held mining interests in Russia and New Zealand and real estate in London. The merger was called H. E. Proprietary (New) Ltd.

years, like 1894–95 and 1902. They were prone to manipulate unprofitable or undeveloped Rand enterprises, and float ventures based on dubious assets located elsewhere in the Transvaal or even further afield in southern Africa to exploit the Rand's luster. In the end, however, they were instrumental in tarnishing it irreparably in the eyes of Europe's investors.

If any one fringe promoter was more responsible than others for undermining the Rand's reputation in the postwar years, that promoter was Carl Hanau. His venture was based on one of several Transvaal mineral finds which preoccupied Johannesburg's speculators and caused flurries in the mining share markets of Europe during 1902–5. Besides Ehrlich's dubious promotion in the Murchison Range, there was the formation of a diamond mine (the Premier), an abortive attempt to exploit a farm in the Klerksdorp district to the west of the Rand, and the booming of a tin find in the Bushveld which saw the shares of the company involved rise wildly.[66] Even representatives of the Corner House were among fortune seekers lured to Madagascar by promoters who it was discovered had salted ground with gold.[67] Only the Premier mine produced for a profit, while the market value of these other mineral promotions dropped by several million pounds.[68] Yet their collective effect on the Rand was not as significant as that made by Hanau's folly.

Hanau possessed many of the credentials of the archetypal Johannesburg promoter: extended residence in South Africa, European contacts, friendly relations with key men from Kimberley who developed the Rand. His father, a German trader, landed in South Africa in the early 1860s. After schooling in Germany he turned to business in South Africa. Ventures in Kimberley, Barberton and then on the Rand as a partner of Neumann followed. Like Neumann he acquired a host of ground-floor participations in properties developed by others. Unlike Neumann he seems to have had visions to be a developer in his own right. In 1902 he formed the Coronation Syndicate with an issued capi-

66. *Statist,* 1 September 1906, p. 541.
67. Cartwright, *Corner House,* pp. 232–33.
68. Cf. *South African Mining Journal,* 1 September 1906, pp. 541–42.

tal of £ 120,000 in £ 100 shares. The assets he put into it were freehold rights and options on several farms along a twenty-mile line running to the southeast from a point south of Heidelberg. Prospectors he employed had found gold-bearing reef in the area. He believed, or at least convinced others to believe, that he had found a southern extension of the main reef series developed on the central Rand, miles to the northwest. Boreholes were drilled, shafts sunk. In all perhaps £ 500,000 was expended on development. The Barnato group took an interest. Syndicate shares were boomed in Europe. By 1903 their market value reached £ 3000 which made the Syndicate's assets worth, at least on paper, £ 3,600,000. The following year, when the shares were fluctuating between £ 1600 and £ 1700, they were split into nominal £ 1 shares and a further 70,000 created, thus making the syndicate's issued capital £ 220,000 in £ 1 shares. These were quoted as high as £ 12¾. But Hanau had not discovered a second Rand, only a minor outcropping of little depth, a small patch of gold like many found elsewhere in southern Africa and which, on the basis of the Rand's reputation, raised enormous expectations. By 1906 the Syndicate's shares had dropped below 15s. The Barnatos had cut their losses and withdrawn. Hanau was broke. Many European plungers had lost heavily. When Hanau's bubble burst, several even more speculative ventures with "Coronation" somewhere in their title went into liquidation. A. P. Cartwright has concluded that "the Coronation crash had a disastrous effect on most of the prospecting ventures of the day. It became extremely difficult to persuade shareholders that the reefs might be found to the east or the west."[69] But Hanau's debacle not only made it hard to obtain backing to prospect for payable reef in the outlying districts. It added further to the Rand's unsavory reputation and drastically limited its attractiveness for both speculative and investment capital.

The minor financing groups were as remarkable for their diversity as for what they had in common. Certain similarities

69. Cartwright, *Gold Miners,* p. 154; also see, *Mines of the Transvaal,* 1904–5, pp. 147–51 and 1909–10, pp. 152–54; and the *Economist,* 19 November 1904, p. 1854; *South African Mining Journal,* 21 March 1903, pp. 25–26.

featured prominently in the business background of the entrepreneurs behind them. For example, several were the sons of small businessmen and had the advantage of the Kimberley connection. Yet their birth places, ethnic origins, and cultural experiences varied considerably. Though Abe Bailey and Samuel Marks were both Jews, there was little they had in common, and not even this would have been shared with John Henderson. Neither the latter nor Bailey had been at Kimberley. Although Marks had been there, his experience would not have encouraged him to exploit this connection—in contrast, for instance, to the use Neumann made of it. Thus, it is not surprising to discover that the business style and capital sources of the men behind the minor groups also varied significantly. A development-oriented Albu backed by German banks contrasted sharply with a speculative-prone Henderson who sought to fleece a cross section of Britain's investing public.

Whatever their background or business style these men behind the minor groups did manage one thing in common. They badly used and thus alienated their capital sources. The developers among them used capital lavishly when political uncertainty, labor difficulties, and the unproven nature of the ground they worked seemed to require more economical and cautious expenditures. The promoters, taking advantage of the Rand's reputation and the vast expectations associated with postwar recovery, floated companies bloated with vendor shares with which to boom the market. Almost without exception the enterprises formed by these developers and promoters after 1902 were poor dividend producers. Ironically enough, in several cases, they eroded or wiped out the fortunes of their creators as well as depleting or at least redistributing the capital of Europe's investing public.

• 8 •

The French Connection

The very important contribution French capital made to gold mining finance has been alluded to in the analysis of the South African houses. Although the Corner House operated out of London and its senior partners were German or English, the shareholders in its companies were mostly French. Farrar and his associates, the Barnatos, and Robinson all had extensive dealings in Paris. Goldfields, though predominantly a British-financed enterprise, also marketed substantial numbers of shares in France. What follows is an attempt to add some quantitative and qualitative dimensions to the French connection. In other words, how much French capital was attracted to mine finance, from what sources, and through which mechanisms? Some attempt is also made to describe a particular capital flow pattern fostered by mine finance practice, but which, ironically enough, bypassed the mines hungry for funds.

During the late nineteenth century, French investment in transferable securities increased enormously, but the number of Frenchmen who held stocks and bonds did not increase in the same proportion. Falling prices, increasing salaries, and stable monetary and fiscal arrangements favored the French social classes with substantial means. This minority, the upper middle classes and the financial elite, accumulated large savings. With agriculture depressed and land prices falling, these well-to-do groups put their savings in shares and debentures. By 1911 such transferable securities represented more than a third of the national wealth. Their value may have almost doubled from £ 2.6 billion in 1885 to £ 4.6 billion in 1913. Four out of every five of 10 million French households may have had savings invested in them. The average investors, making up about half the total number, with securities worth between £ 200 and £ 4000, held 45 percent. But a financial elite of only 2 percent, based on calculations for 1908, possessed about 50 percent of the value of transferable securities held in France.[1]

Foreign securities became an increasingly important part of these investments. Indeed, the French contribution to European investment abroad was very substantial. Investors attached little stigma to most foreign securities. They yielded more than home investment opportunities which, in any event, were not particularly plentiful. After 1892 the French government borrowed little on the financial market. Apart from the city of Paris, local authorities issued few loans. In the private sector, new companies and new issues were not numerous. What expansion that did occur in this sector was predominantly financed through earnings. Stock markets, public banks, and private financial institutions, the trend setters in the capital market, were inclined to push foreign rather than domestic securities in dealings with their clients. These domestic constraints and investment preferences fostered a huge absorption of foreign securities. They represented £ 700 million or 26 percent of the value of securities held by Frenchmen in 1885 and £ 1.8 billion or 40 percent in 1913. This proportion was, significantly enough, greater than in Britain in the same period.[2]

Only about 25 percent of the value of foreign securities in any one year appears to have been in equity stock. Moreover, this was mostly in railways and base metal mining and smelting enterprises, and largely issued by firms operating in Russia. Indeed, most French foreign investment was in Europe and not overseas. Nevertheless available evidence suggests that large amounts of francs went to purchase Transvaal gold shares. In 1895 two well-

1. Estimates are from Goffin, *Questions financières,* p. 99. He also estimates that 80 percent of 10 million French incomes were less than £ 100, 15 percent were £ 100 to £ 200; and only 5 percent amounted to more than £ 200. However, the latter 5 percent accounted for 25 percent of the national income. *Ibid.,* p. 105.

2. *Ibid.,* p. 135; Cameron, *France and Europe,* pp. 485–501; and C. P. Kindleberger, *Economic Growth in France and Britain, 1851–1950* (Cambridge, Mass., 1964), pp. 39–59.

placed Paris financiers claimed that the French had invested £ 30 million in gold scrip.[3] This amount represented 13 percent of the value of variable yield stocks held by French nationals which amounted to some £ 220 million.[4] By 1899, the well-informed *Statist* calculated that the French may have had £ 60 million in Rand gold shares which would have represented 25 percent of foreign stocks.[5] This calculation may seem a gross overestimate for it was much more than the total amount of capital invested in the mines.[6] However, there was a vast discrepancy between what was invested in gold shares and what was allotted the mines for working capital.

1. Paris Financiers and Gold Shares

Soon after mining started up on the Rand, its entrepreneurs, exploiting the speculative market surge of 1888–89, placed small numbers of gold shares in France. For example, shares in the Robinson mine were introduced in the *coulisse*, the unofficial Paris stock exchange, for a Porges-Kann syndicate by the Banque Russe et Française in October 1889. By 1893 close to half the Robinson mine's shareholders, or 913 out of 2055, were French.[7]

3. R. Kann to J. Wernher, 6 October 1895, BRA; and J. de Gunzburg to J. Wernher, 6 November 1895, *ibid.*

4. The figure of £ 220 million is from Goffin, *Questions financières,* p. 99.

5. *Statist,* 7 October 1899, p. 542; *L'Économiste français,* 22 October 1899, pp. 569–71. *Le Rentier* estimated £ 60 million of French capital was invested in the Transvaal (see *Economist,* 4 November 1899, pp. 1561–62), and the Cologne *Zeitung* £ 15 million of German capital (*ibid.,* pp. 1563–64). The best account of the stock market operations and swindles which fostered French investment in gold shares is in the Paris letters of the *Mining Journal.* See especially *ibid.,* 24 August 1895, p. 1007, and 7 September 1895, pp. 1080–82.

6. About £ 15 million from equity stock had been invested in the mines up to about the end of 1895. Kubicek, *Journal of British Studies,* XI, 85–86, n. 5. However, the market value of shares for mines with an issued capital of £ 34 million quoted in London was almost £ 152 million. *Economist,* 14 September 1895, pp. 1205–6.

7. J. Porges & Co. to H. Eckstein & Co., 15 October 1889, BRA; and notes made by E. Rosenthal, *ibid.* As of 6 July 1893, between 150,000 and 194,000 of the Robinson mine's issued shares were distributed in France. Almost 300,000 were in Britain, but most of these would have been held by the Corner House, and 52,000 were in South Africa. Notes from a legal brief got up for H. Eckstein & Co., n.d., *ibid.*

Although pushed at high prices during the boom, Robinson shares stood up well during the ensuing panic as the mine yielded immense dividends. So this first sampling by French investors of Rand offerings proved very palatable and no doubt helped to create an appetite for gold shares. Most of the several other companies in which the French acquired shares were also solid dividend payers and, therefore, relatively immune from the sharp depreciation characteristic of the scrip of many Rand undertakings in the postboom slump. The only company developed with French capital by French expertise in the industry's formative years was the Champ d'Or French Gold Mining Company formed in 1890 on ground located on the far-west Rand. Neither its capital structure nor its development proved sound. By the end of 1893 it was £ 30,000 in debt, partly because its first backer, the Banque Générale des Chemins de Fer et de l'Industrie, failed, and partly because of an overly ambitious mining program. Nonetheless, by early 1895 it had paid out £ 35,000 in dividends on an issued capital of £ 133,000.[8] Thus, even in this instance, Paris had been well treated. It was, therefore, well disposed towards the Rand when the second boom began in 1894.

Indeed, Paris was largely responsible for the boom. During 1894–95 France sank up to £ 32 million in Rand stock.[9] A number of factors in addition to previous satisfaction stimulated this outlay. First, Rand developers were able to call upon established financial contacts and make new arrangements through which to plant lucrative shares with French investors. Second, the Rand's most blatant speculators also formed alliances with some of Paris's notorious promoters, as well as some of its more solid financiers, to ensure that their worthless or vastly inflated paper was boomed successfully. Third, representatives of France's financial elite encouraged stock market excesses through their own speculation. Fourth, booming operations were facilitated by the opportunities to coordinate stock deals on the Paris market with jobbing in London and Johannesburg. Finally, cheap borrowing rates, the large concentration of savings available, and limited or apparently

8. Goldmann, *South African Mines,* I, 201–8.
9. J. de Gunzburg to J. Wernher, 6 November 1895, BRA.

less lucrative alternate outlets for surplus capital, also combined to create an extraordinarily favorable environment in which gold mining finance could become an immensely luxuriant if ultimately fragile growth.

The Corner House developed a varied array of arrangements to exploit the favorable environment. The group renewed the syndicates that its founding partners had constructed in the 1880s. Although Porges had retired from the partnership, he was living in Paris and became active in these syndicates. Into one he drew Michel Ephrussi, a reckless but well-connected financier. Rodolphe Kann, who had been involved in diamond financing in the 1880s, and who was connected with the private bank of A. J. Stern et Compagnie, took an active part in managing the Paris end of another syndicate. He often corresponded with Wernher in London, frequented the Bourse, and studied the Paris financial press and mining company reports. The Porges-Ephrussi and the Porges-Kann syndicates operated with shares in the personal portfolios of the Wernher, Beit partnership, the members of Eckstein's and their close associates. These men held large blocks of shares in the companies they controlled. Therefore, the Porges-Kann syndicate, for example, had at its disposal several hundred thousand marketable shares with a book value in excess of £ 700,000. To facilitate operations on the *coulisse*, the Corner House used the services of certain Paris brokers, V. MacSwiney et Compagnie, for example.[10] Wernher, who effectively controlled the syndicates and instructed cooperative Paris brokers, made a point of getting rid of shares in doubtful propositions. At the same time, he held onto shares in promising ventures. Even when sold they were usually reclaimed to boost rising prices or to stabilize a jittery or falling market. Thus the Corner House, its associates, and its holding companies (such as Rand Mines), always retained very large blocks of shares in the productive companies. These blocks, along with shares gradually absorbed and firmly re-

10. The arrangements with Porges, Kann, and MacSwiney et Cie. are from a voluminous correspondence in the BRA, much of it in French and German. See especially R. Kann to A. Beit, 28 February 1894; J. Porges to Wernher, Beit & Co., 20 July 1894; and R. Kann to J. Wernher, 5 August 1895.

tained by investors, particularly French investors, left relatively few of the shares of Corner House companies available for market operators.

In addition to pooling arrangements among partners and associates and working relationships with *coulissiers,* the Corner House cooperated with several French banks and certain *agents de change,* or stockbrokers, who were members of the *paraquet,* the official securities market in Paris. Among the private *banques d'affaires* with which the Corner House had dealings was the Paris branch of the Rothschilds. However, while its partners had made a connection with the branch in the 1880s during the diamond mine amalgamations, they had not cultivated it. Some of the Rothschild family operated in the Paris market as significant speculators in a manner Wernher thought ill-advised.[11] In any event, in the mid-1890s the Paris Rothschilds seemed more involved with securities out of the stable of Goldfields and the Chartered Company. Wernher, Beit, meanwhile, counted a number of other private bankers as their associates. These included Mirabuad et Compagnie from among the "upper reaches of French banking"[12] and founded by a Swiss family which had long been interested in transactions in gold. A. J. Stern et Compagnie participated in the Porges-Kann syndicate. Goudchaux et Compagnie often corresponded with the Corner House on gold share finance. Others, like Cahen d'Anvers et Cie. would take up allotments in Central Mining.

The public *banque d'affaires* with which the Corner House had extensive dealings was founded for the specific purpose of specializing in gold shares. The Compagnie Française de Mines d'Or de L'Afrique du Sud (Corfrador) was established in February 1895 with a capital of £ 400,000. Its backers included the Anglo-French Exploration Company of London, the American mining engineer Hamilton Smith, and the Banque Internationale de Paris.[13] This trust company did not confine its holdings to Corner

11. Wernher, Beit & Co. to H. Eckstein & Co., 19 April 1895, *ibid.;* and J. Wernher to G. Rouliot, 21 May 1897, *ibid.*

12. McKay, *Pioneers for Profit,* pp. 67–68.

13. R. Kann to J. Wernher, 6 January 1895, BRA. It was originally called the Cie. Française de Mines d'Or Exploration.

House stocks. Connected with the Farrar brothers through Anglo-French, it absorbed or marketed a lot of unpromising watered stock.

A more ambitious and much sounder firm launched late in 1895 was the Banque Française de L'Afrique du Sud with a capital of £ 2 million.[14] The Banque Française was formed primarily to stabilize the market and prevent a decline in the value of better quality shares. It is not surprising that some of Paris's more important financiers were involved. What is perhaps surprising was their broad connections. Baron Jacques de Gunzburg, its main inspiration and one of its directors, was head of a substantial private bank involved in numerous foreign enterprises. Among important government ministers of the day with whom he had dealings was Maurice Rouvier, a financier as well as politician. Gunzburg also had influential associates among members of the *paraquet* who lobbied the government for permission to introduce shares of small denomination on the official exchange.[15] The president of the Banque Française was Jacques Siegfried. A respected member of the French financial elite, he was a director of Five-Lille, one of France's largest metallurgical firms. Founding directors of the Banque Française also included two other industrialists, E. Duval and Firmin Rainbeaux; two *agents de change*, Charles Chalput and Charles Herbault, who resigned as president of the Syndicat de Agents de Change to take the post: and a well-known private banker, Hubert Henrotte of Hoskiers and Henrotte, a firm which agreed to serve as an agency in France for the gold share bank. The resources and talents of the French bank were sufficiently impressive to cause Wernher to contemplate that it take over Wernher, Beit's business on the Rand.[16]

Besides connections with Corfrador and the Banque Française, the Corner House had arrangements with a less specialized but

14. *Annuaire français des mines d'or*, 4 vols. (Paris, 1896–99), I, 68–73; J. de Gunzburg to J. Wernher, 6 November 1895, BRA; and *Economist*, 2 November 1895, p. 1434.

15. Most Rand stock was in £ 1 or 25 franc denominations while the minimum amount for shares eligible to be quoted on the *paraquet* was 100 francs. For Gunzburg's lobbying see his letter to J. Wernher, 11 June 1895, BRA.

16. J. Wernher to G. Rouliot, 8 February and 8 May 1896, *ibid.*

more important institution. This was the Banque de Paris et des Pays-Bas (Paribas) which "devoted by far the greater part of its resources to foreign operations."[17] It obtained the Paris agency business in 1894 for Goldfields's productive Simmer and Jack mine. It also was involved with Corfrador, the Banque Internationale, and French expertise in an effort to develop mines on the far-west Rand. In addition, the Paribas joined in 1895 with Stern et Compagnie in an expanded version of the Porges-Kann syndicate.[18]

During the 1894–95 boom at least one of France's great corporate banks, the Crédit Lyonnais, put capital into gold mine shares. Two of its directors, Henri Germain, who was also its president, and Georges Brolemann, were in contact with Kann and Wernher. Kann reported that they began very cautiously and invested on behalf of clients rather than using funds out of deposits. Anticipating the boom could not last, Germain spoke out against speculative excesses and in advance of the collapse called in loans to creditors speculating in gold shares.[19] For several years thereafter the Crédit Lyonnais was viewed by the Corner House as an institution hostile to gold shares.

Although the market in gold shares was made by *coulissiers* because foreign shares with low nominal values were not allowed a quotation on the *paraquet, agents de change* did operate on the unofficial market for their clients. In addition, some of them pressed for the introduction of the better class of gold share on the official market. The first to be thus admitted were the shares of Rand Mines in 1896.[20]

While the Corner House was directly or indirectly linked with numerous influential banks and stock market facilities through which it did a large share business in France, other Rand houses

17. Cameron, *France and Europe*, pp. 197–98.

18. A. Beit to L. Phillips, 15 December 1894, BRA; Wernher, Beit & Co. to H. Eckstein & Co., 15 February 1895, *ibid.;* and R. Kann to J. Wernher, 13 March 1895, *ibid.*

19. J. Porges to A. Beit, 13 December 1894, *ibid.;* and R. Kann to J. Wernher, 3 and 10 October 1895, *ibid.*

20. For a useful description of the regulations governing Bourse membership and operations and of the business practices of the *agents de change* see E. Kaufmann, *La Banque en France* (Paris, 1914), pp. 86–104.

also hooked up with the same or similar mechanisms. In 1896 Goldfields established the Trust Français to represent it in Paris and through which to offer French investors access to the share issues of the mines it controlled. The Trust's investment portfolios in October 1898 contained more than 200,000 gold shares, about half of which were shares in Goldfields itself.[21] Early in 1895 Sigismund Neumann arranged through Gunzburg the establishment of a syndicate operating with assets worth £ 600,000 to £ 800,000. This syndicate included participations by 25 *agents de change* and the most important gold share *coulissier,* the Paris branch of Leopold Hirsch and Company, one of London's top mining market operators. The Neumann-Gunzburg syndicate was supported by the Banque Internationale de Paris, one of whose directors, Jacques Kulp, was prominent in the development of the French Rand Deep mine on the far-west Rand and in the foundation of Corfrador.[22] Some idea of the dubious activity in which this syndicate engaged may be derived from the fact that it circulated a printed list of its backers which contained Wernher, Beit's name. This claim was false. Though the Corner House usually kept its complaints about other mining groups to itself, Kann felt he should deny in French financial circles that it was connected with the syndicate.[23] The Corner House was not interested for good reason. Neumann's holdings and options were diverse and fragmented and contained a lot of worthless stock.

An even more questionable syndicate was put together by Michel Ephrussi, again quite independently from and without the blessing of the Corner House. Ephrussi used shares obtained through two of Johannesburg's most freewheeling promoters, Barney Barnato and Abe Bailey. Two Paris-based directors of the Ottoman Bank, Comte Pillet-Will and Michel Heine, were also involved in the syndicate. The Vienna Landesbank branch in Paris and officials of the Comptoir D'Escompte were similarly interested. Backing from this coterie of financiers, particularly those

21. *Annuaire français des mines d'or,* I, 414–17.

22. R. Kann to J. Wernher, 31 January 1895, BRA; J. Porges to J. Wernher, 9 February 1895, *ibid.;* and R. Kann to J. Wernher, 10 February 1895, *ibid.*

23. R. Kann to J. Wernher, 6 January 1895, *ibid.*

from the Ottoman Bank, permitted Barnato to launch his own bank which helped to inundate the market with large quantities of watered stock in the latter part of 1895. Edgar Vincent of the Ottoman Bank was reported by Kann in October to be operating as a bull in the *coulisse* with stock valued at more than £ 1 million.[24]

Joseph Robinson's entry into the Paris market was apparently arranged through the Paribas. It, for example, in 1894 took up substantially more than 10,000 Randfontein shares. Its directors also bought shares for their personal account.[25] They, in addition, had to suffer Robinson's abrasive and devious ways. Perhaps this experience was sufficient to discourage them from being involved in later deals with Robinson. But he obtained support from even more prestigious financial quarters. Baron O. Hély d'Oisel, vice-president of the Société Générale, served on the board of Robinson's bank.[26] The Société Générale, like the Crédit Lyonnais and the Comptoir d'Escompte, was a first-rank corporate bank which combined "the deposit and discount functions . . . with . . . promotional and investment" services. The Société Générale "played a large role in foreign as well as domestic finance, underwriting government loans, financing railways and industrial enterprises, and participating in banks and credit companies."[27] Such an institution was, of course, in a position to introduce a host of Frenchmen to Robinson stock.

When the inevitable crash came, the Bourse, in the words of Jules Porges, "bled heavily."[28] The severe setback was caused in part by the sudden glut of shares that Farrar, Barnato, & Robinson, and their Paris associates had inflicted upon the market. The effect of this inundation was all the more traumatic because the Corner House had kept it starved of quality stock. The crash was

24. J. Porges to J. Wernher, 21 February 1895, *ibid.;* and R. Kann to J. Wernher, 13 March and 18 October 1895, *ibid.*

25. V. MacSwiney et Cie. to A. Beit, 5 March 1894, *ibid.;* and same to J. Wernher, 26 May 1894, *ibid.*

26. Skinner, *London Banks,* 1899, p. 117.

27. Cameron, *France and Europe,* p. 174.

28. J. Porges to J. Wernher, 8 November 1895, BRA.

also forced by the realization of the corporate banks that the market had been overloaded. They cut credit lines at a time when there was a sharp reduction in a ready and cheap money supply. As Kann observed, the Crédit Lyonnais and the Société Générale would lend no money at all, not even for good "shares. . . . It is also possible that the government, which will have to grant a big loan sooner or later in order to consolidate the floating debts, is advising the banks to keep money in short supply. . . . Money for the Stock Exchange is expensive both in Berlin and in Vienna, 6 to 8%."[29] The squeeze caught many clients of the *coulisiers* holding large blocks of vastly inflated shares or intending to make good on stock options with borrowed money. When they dumped shares, failed to pick up options or, in several instances, simply defaulted on bargains, the panic was on. The growing realization that most gold shares were enormously overpriced and the notoriety of the Jameson Raid further depressed the market. Wernher, Beit learned that the Paris Rothschilds took over the obligations of Jacques Lebaudy, one of the market's most erratic plungers, whose commitments may have amounted to several hundred thousand pounds.[30] This action, along with efforts by the Corner House and the Banque Française, brought some stability to the market and insured that the better stocks did not suffer large depreciations. But Barnato, Robinson, and Farrar shares dropped sharply.

The break seems to have come before the dubious shares held by speculators were passed in substantial numbers to the small French investor. For the glut had come suddenly in the latter part of 1895 just before the market broke. Moreover, gold shares were still distributed among very few investors. For example, in early 1896 the average number of French shareholders in 29 Rand mining companies was 397.[31] As Wernher observed, the large public in France (he meant the clientele of the *agents de*

29. R. Kann to J. Wernher, 14 October 1895, translated from the German, *ibid.*
30. Wernher, Beit & Co. to H. Eckstein & Co., 25 October 1895, *ibid.*
31. From memo by M. Herbanes, Cies. de mines d'or et d'autres enterprises Sud Africaine, 7 February 1896, Ministère des Finances, Série F. 30/298/4.

change), had hardly any gold shares yet. There was, he thought, "still a great opening."[32] Thus, losses at this juncture were largely confined to marginal financiers prone to speculation, their ill-advised creditors, and wealthy clients of the large banks who, along with investment bankers like the Rothschilds, could afford a market gamble.

2. The Losses of The Small Investor

During the next several years, Transvaal gold shares in large numbers were widely dispersed in France. This dispersal stemmed from three flurries in mining market activity. The first occurred during 1899 when, somewhat belatedly, deep-level mines began to show their potential for impressive dividend yields. It was cut short by the South African War. The second burst occurred in 1902–3 when the resumption of mining development held out the promise of impressive profits. The third recovery, moving in sympathy with general upward market trends, the introduction of Responsible Government in the Transvaal (a political development which was popular in pro-Boer France), and the amalgamation programs of the big mining houses, occurred in 1908–9. Thereafter French speculators and investors could not be enticed. Indeed, if anything, their experience during the previous decade or so made them strongly averse to Rand stock.

During the first flurry just before the war, the Banque Française took a lead in introducing the French to deep-level shares. The Corner House, which had taken up £ 100,000 of its issued capital of £ 2 million when the French bank had been founded in 1895, now increased its interest and sold the bank blocks of shares. Moreover, it was also the Banque Française which had introduced the shares of Rand Mines to the *paraquet*. Despite some bad advice from its Johannesburg representatives, it was able to

32. J. Wernher to G. Rouliot, 26 December 1895, BRA.

declare its first dividend, 4 percent, in 1898. And it no doubt was the leader in the placement process which prompted Wernher to observe early in 1899 that the bulk of the best gold shares would soon be in French hands.[33]

However, Paris's ability to discriminate between promising and worthless scrip was impaired when the Banque Française got into difficulty. The war had, of course, a debilitating effect on its investments. In addition, the Banque made several bad stock deals through poor advice from its Johannesburg representatives. It also was hurt by the loss of its able president, Jacques Siegfried. In protest against the war and his colleagues' decision to observe a neutral position and in keeping with his pro-Boer sympathies, he resigned.[34] The directors who remained, especially Gunzburg, were bent on diversifying the bank's holdings.

In 1901 the bank was reconstructed. Its interests were amalgamated with those of the Banque Internationale de Paris. The new institution, styled the Banque Française pour le Commerce et l'Industrie, took a substantial interest in Corfrador, which in turn took over the new bank's position in South Africa. Maurice Rouvier was appointed its president. Indeed, it was familiarly called the Banque Rouvier. However, in its first year of operation Rouvier left to return to government office and did not return to its presidency until 1906. Though he was certainly an important asset to the bank, he does not seem to have been a dominant force in its investment programs. Its vice-president, Ernest May, who had been with the Banque Internationale, was, along with Gunzburg likely more active than Rouvier in the management of the new bank. At the same time representatives of the Paribas, the Comptoir D'Escompte, and the Société Générale joined its board when these great banks took up part of the new institution's share capital. Rather than assume a leadership role in Transvaal mining finance, however, the Banque Rouvier was active in developing French-German economic cooperation and in par-

33. Same to same, 24 February 1899, BRA; and same to same, 13 April 1899, *ibid.*
34. Same to same, 17 November 1899, *ibid.*

ticipating in banking consortiums got up to issue and guarantee Turkish, South American, and other foreign bond issues.[35]

With no Paris financial institution providing restraint, Johannesburg operators were able to inflict a mass of paper on unsuspecting investors during 1902–3. Some Frenchmen had been soured by setbacks on the Russian investment scene. Yet thousands of French investors, like their British counterparts, sought more investments abroad than ever before. The publicity which the war gave to South Africa made it a far more familiar place, but the notoriety of the Randlords, while familiar in Britain, was not yet commonplace in France. Prospects for profits on the resumption of Transvaal gold mining seemed good. Thousands of ill-informed small investors sought gold shares while hundreds of Paris speculators boomed old stocks. Both lost heavily in the ensuing crash.

The Corner House, it will be recalled, founded the Central Mining and Investment Corporation to bring some stability to the depressed gold share market. French investors who had acquired a substantial interest in the industry had been among those urging the Corner House to take a lead. Just who these investors were and what they represented are revealed in Central Mining's shareholder lists. Given its £ 20 shares it was not set up to cater to the small investor; but the upper middle class and financial elite were well represented. Of Central Mining's 300,000 £ 20 shares, 146,650 or 48.9 percent were held in France. Of these 146,560 shares, 41,400 or 28.2 percent were corporate holdings and almost entirely lodged with *banque d'affaires.* The first-rank deposit banks (i.e. the Crédit Lyonnais, the Comptoir D'Escompte, and the Société Générale) took up only 3500 shares among them. The Paribas, on the other hand, held almost 9000, and the Banque Rouvier 2800. Corfrador, in which the Banque Rouvier held an interest, possessed 18,700. The remaining 105,250 shares not held by public banks were lodged with 1248 individuals. Conspicuous among them in terms of occupation and status

35. Same to same, 1 June 1901, *ibid.;* Kaufmann, *Banque en France,* pp. 135–38; and R. Poidevin, *Les Relations économiques et financières entre la France et l'Allemagne de 1899 à 1914* (Paris, 1969), pp. 206–7, 413–14.

were private bankers (246 holding 37,800) and stockbrokers (112 holding 21,000). *Propriétaires* and *rentiers*, 262 of whom held 12,730, were also much in evidence; but 119 professionals, including a handful of government officials, held only 3900, and 77 merchants and industrialists 5200. In each case the overwhelming majority were resident in Paris.[36]

While the Corner House established a corporation to assume responsibilities, it once hoped the Banque Française would take up, it also tried to manipulate the financial environment in which the shares of companies it controlled were traded. Wernher, through talks he had in Paris with financiers and politicians, including Rouvier, was convinced that the French journals must be bribed.[37] "Working up the French press in favour of our gold shares" was especially required because in late 1903, at least, buying power in France and Germany was far greater than in London where the City "was almost devoid of money."[38] When it came to company promotion the venality of editors and reporters was commonplace and widespread.[39] The Corner House had been in the habit in the 1890s of giving stock options to a few friendly French journals. This time, however, the manipulation was to be carried out on a very large scale. Working through Gunzburg, the Corner House gave "options to twenty-two of the most important French papers on the understanding that they must write first of all in favour of the importation of unskilled Asiatic labour being allowed in the Transvaal . . . [and] more or less in favour of the Witwatersrand generally."[40] The options which the Corner House and other mining groups gave were on 50,000 shares. In addition, the Corner House, the Albus, Goldfields, and Neumann provided a direct subsidy of about £ 2000 per month for a year. Though these stock options and subsidies

36. Derived from Returns of Allotments, 1905, Central Mining and Investment Corporation, BT, Register of Companies, File No. 84511. Socioeconomic categories from Daumard, *Les Fortunes françaises*.

37. F. Eckstein to L. Phillips, 11 November 1905, BRA.

38. Wernher, Beit & Co. to H. Eckstein & Co., 4 December 1903, *ibid.*

39. McKay, *Pioneers for Profit*, pp. 223–35; H. D. White, *The French International Accounts, 1880–1913* (Cambridge, Mass., 1933), pp. 280–81.

40. Wernher, Beit & Co. to H. Eckstein & Co., 4 December 1903, BRA.

did not lead to a restoration of confidence sufficient to attract substantial new capital, it was later conceded that "Gunzburg's arrangements with the Paris Papers [were] of incalculable value" in preventing investors from dumping large quantities of shares and thereby further depressing prices.[41]

The establishment of Central Mining and the press campaign slowed market declines during 1903–6, and made it possible for a modest revival in 1908–9. The Crédit Lyonnais, for example, considered the arch enemy of gold shares, was buying small amounts for its clients late in 1908. By late 1909 a large business in Corner House shares was being done in Paris. One of its senior partners expected France would gradually absorb all of its good dividend payers.[42] That trend, as noted previously, had been underway for some time. As early as December 1906, as Corner House calculations suggest, it was very well established. Twenty-seven gold mining companies, including Rand Mines, the holding company for deep-level operations in which Wernher, Beit and Central Mining had large interests, had an issued share capital of almost £ 14 million with a market value of £ 46 million. Controlling firms, that is Wernher, Beit, Central Mining, and Rand Mines, held 42 percent of this amount. (Rand Mines's holdings in the industry were valued at £ 10 million or 22 percent of the whole.) While less than 17 percent of the £ 46 million was held in Britain and less than 3 percent in South Africa, almost 39 percent was retained in France and Germany.[43] Most of the shares held on the Continent were bearer warrants and the Corner House was not able to determine in what amounts they were domiciled in each country. But, if one assumes these continental shares were distributed similarly to Central Mining's capital, than about 30 percent of the £ 46 million or almost £ 14 million was held in France. Taking into account that about one-half of Central Mining capital and one-third of Rand Mines's were lodged in France, it can be estimated that a third of the market value of the issued capital of the Corner House complex was in French hands.

41. F. Eckstein to L. Phillips, 16 March 1906, *ibid.*
42. Same to same, 16 October 1908 and 10 December 1909, *ibid.*
43. Shareholdings—France, Germany and Elsewhere, 13 December 1906, *ibid.*

Given the very large amount of vendor capital still retained by the private partnerships, that is, by Wernher, Beit and by Eckstein's, it is evident that Frenchmen held the majority of the Corner House shares that had been taken up by the investing public. It might also be suggested, on the basis of Corner House figures of 37,000 registered shareholders in its companies holding, on average, 393 shares,[44] that betwen 10,000 and 15,000 Frenchmen held its shares. Given the French partiality for bearer shares and the large numbers of these taken up, one might safely conjecture that the number of French investors was even higher.

But France had absorbed more than substantial amounts of the share capital of the productive mines in the Corner House stable. By 1908 it had acquired a good deal of rubbish, most of it at inflated prices. With market values on the decline, losses from investment in worthless and marginal stock were immense. Some indication of the kind and amount of shares the French acquired and the losses they suffered may be obtained from the contemporary estimates of Alfred Neymarck.

Neymarck isolated 35 Transvaal gold mines and seven mining houses whose shares were quoted in 1908 on the *coulisse*.[45] They had issued 32,184,000 shares with a total nominal value of £ 33 million. The issue price of these shares in aggregate was, however, £ 182 million and, taken at their highest quotation in the period 1901–8, their value was £ 190 million. By 1908 they had depreciated in value by £ 90 million in comparison to their issue price and £ 97 million on side their highest quotation. Further substantial depreciation occurred over the next few years. Neymarck's list did not contain many companies whose shares were dropped from *coulisse* quotations. Nor did it include companies unlisted in Paris whose shares were dealt in extensively by Frenchmen on the London market. Thus, one has no way of estimating French involvement in such speculative mania as the Coronation bubble.[46] Nevertheless, Neymarck's estimates are sug-

44. L. Reyersbach, 21 March 1906, Rand Mines, *Annual Report for 1905*.
45. A. Neymarck, *Finances contemporaines*, VI, *L'Épargne française et les valeurs mobilières, 1872–1910*, Pt. I (Paris, 1911), 486–87.
46. See chap. vii, p. 173, this volume.

gestive. If it is assumed that French investors took up about the same aggregate percentage of shares in these listed undertakings as they had acquired in the Corner House companies, then they held 30 percent or £ 10 million. At issue price these shares were worth £ 55 million and at highest quotation £ 57 million. Thus, the real and paper loss could, with some measure of confidence, be put at £ 25–30 million. Given the decline in gold share values after Neymarck made his estimates and the absence from his list of a number of moribund or liquidated ventures, one might suggest losses as high as £ 30–35 million.

Whatever the amount of the loss sustained it is unlikely that it was spread evenly through a cross section of the French investing public. The small investor was by the end of our period the "backbone" of the gold share market.[47] His gullibility could be exploited by a kept press. It was likely he could be dazzled by the dividend yields of some of the mines, and he "only realized very late, too late, at the moment when paper began to crumble that the dividend was fixed on the nominal rate of 25 francs [i.e. £ 1] at which the shares had been created."[48] Paris financiers and speculators had years of experience with South African mining shares and were unlikely to labor under such elementary misapprehensions. Indeed, as we have seen, many had been involved with the mining houses in elaborate market operations.

Having contributed to the financial squall in which many small French investors were caught, the financiers and speculators did little to improve the situation. By early 1911 continuous selling in Paris had, in the words of Friedrich Eckstein, put the gold share market in a "wretched state." Georges Rouliot who joined Corfrador when he retired from the Corner House, reported from Paris that for years past people had experienced nothing but deceptions. Now new losses had been "enormous" and "further losses" were predicted.[49] Two former employees of the liquidated Banque Française de l'Afrique du Sud, seeing an advantage in

47. F. Eckstein to L. Phillips, 29 March 1912, BRA.
48. Neymarck, *Finances contemporaines,* VI, Pt. I, 389.
49. F. Eckstein to L. Phillips, 17 March 1911, BRA; and G. Rouliot to F. Eckstein, 20 November 1911, *ibid.*

operating as bears, published the most gloomy predictions about the Rand's performance. Speculators like Albert Kahn, who had long been active in the gold share market, also sought personal advantage with no regard for market stability.[50] The Rothschilds were conspicuous by their absence. Lesser financiers such as Gustav Fleurquin, a former strong gold share advocate, withdrew from the business.[51] Gunzburg was much more active in pushing other offerings on the foreign securities market.

Financial leadership in the gold share market became so weak and the public outcry against losses so intense, that the government made enquiries in London to ascertain the financial strength of Central Mining and of Gold Mines Investment Company, a subsidiary of Goldfields, when they sought a quotation on the *paraquet*.[52] Neymarck, and other informed critics, disturbed by the losses on gold shares and the flow of capital abroad, demanded that 25 franc (£ 1) shares not be given quotations on the *coulisse*.[53] The Association Nationale de Porteurs Français de Valeurs Étrangères, similar in function to Britain's Council of Foreign Bondholders, intervened to force changes in the management at East Rand Proprietary Mines when its dividends and share values slipped sharply.[54]

Given the withdrawal of market leadership by the big financiers and the mounting losses of the average French investors which, in turn, caused them to lose interest in gold shares, annual increases in South African gold production and sustained dividend yields by many of the mines were insufficient to rekindle confidence. Two French members of the board of Central Mining

50. F. Eckstein to L. Phillips, 25 May and 6 July 1906, *ibid.;* and same to same, 3 January 1908, *ibid.*

51. J. Wernher to L. Phillips, 18 November 1909, *ibid.*

52. P. Cambon, French ambassador in London, to M. Rouvier, French prime minister, 13 July 1905, Ministère des Finances, Série F 30/296/105. Though Cambon thought the companies in question were sound enough, he thought many other less reputable firms were quoted on the *coulisse.* He noted that he had complained to his government ever since 1901 of "les graves inconvénients qui résulteraient pour nos petits capitalists de l'introduction en France des valeurs Sud Africaines." *Ibid.*

53. Neymarck, *Finances contemporaines,* VI, Pt. I, 388–89.

54. L. Reyersbach to L. Phillips, 22 December 1911, BRA; and same to E. A. Wallers, 2 February 1912, ibid.

warned the Corner House that if working costs which cut into dividends were not reduced, it would lose the French market altogether.[55] Such alarms and the "wretched state" of the market were likely instrumental in management squeezing labor, effecting new mining efficiencies, and cutting back on development. But given the exceedingly inefficient and inappropriate capital structure that the mining groups fastened on the industry, such measures were, at best, partial solutions. The basic problem was that dividend-yielding shares had been sold to the public at far too high a price and that large amounts of inflated marginal and worthless stock had been unloaded as well. As Gunzburg put it to Eckstein in 1911, the Corner House had for a decade been holding out for too high a figure when doing a big deal in Paris. He was, thought Eckstein, probably right. We must, he admitted, change our policy and let people make some money.[56] This change of heart coming as it did in 1911 was, to say the least, a bit belated.

55. F. Eckstein to L. Phillips, 16 February 1912, *ibid.*
56. Same to same, 31 March 1911, *ibid.*

·9·

Conclusion

As a first and fundamental step in developing an explanation of the interaction between European capitalism and South African developments, it is essential to clarify the role of the mines' controllers. Several labels and categories employed in studies of these magnates are misleading or unhelpful. To begin with they were not a homogeneous lot, but differences of nationality (some were not British), or ethnicity (many were Jews), or personality (witness Joseph B. Robinson's feuds with other magnates), while of some significance, were not of fundamental importance. The same may be said for the dichotomy perceived to exist between outcroppers and deep-levelers. The crucial distinctions were: (1) the different strategies employed by the controllers to profit from the claims and the shares they held in the mines and (2) the various mechanisms and sources they used to raise capital. Some, and preeminently the Corner House organization, were development oriented. Others, especially Goldfields before 1895 and the houses of ill repute throughout, combined a development function with very extensive speculative operations. Still others, fringe operators like John Henderson, Abe Bailey, and Carl Hanau, were pure and simple speculators with actual gold production playing little part in their financial plans. All sought capital through the stock markets and from banks but again there were appreciable differences. Goldfields was mostly dependent upon the London market while Goerz and Company and General Mining were dominated by large German banks. The Corner House, given its own substantial resources and the prestige it commanded, was less sensitive to market shifts or bank policy changes.

If the controllers were not homogeneous because they differed in their business strategies and relied upon rather different capital sources, is there a further important distinction to be made? Some of the magnates acted as if they were local entrepreneurs, able to control capital from the metropolitan area. The most outstanding of these regional entrepreneurs was Cecil Rhodes. We still lack a thorough study of Rhodes as financier, and this work, to the extent it does examine him in this role, is limited to his venture into Transvaal gold rather than Cape diamonds or Rhodesian mines and land. Here he has been shown to be as indifferent to the demands and sensibilities of City operators as he was to those of Westminster politicians or Whitehall civil servants. Goldfields's City-based financiers were, in Rhodes's words, an "ungrateful crew" who had "behaved disgracefully." Neither they nor British officialdom could control him, at least not until he failed ignominiously in his attempt to overthrow the Transvaal government.

But if Rhodes's financial activities were motivated by strong regional or local objectives, it is difficult to discover other controllers with such priorities. Certainly after his downfall local entrepreneurial aggression was sharply reduced. Thereafter, entrepreneurs resident in South Africa had to endure local government or cooperate with the imperial factor, and accept business strategies enunciated in London, or Paris, or Berlin. Despite long experience in South Africa, many of the controllers, either resident in the Transvaal or Britain, cultivated life styles and business practices far removed from or indifferent to the local scene. Though Percy FitzPatrick might pursue a political career in the Transvaal and maintain his roots, he was not really a typical mining magnate. James B. Taylor and Robinson were much more representative. They were South African born but took their fortunes to Britain. Lionel Phillips and George Farrar, though born in Britain, were active in local affairs, yet Phillips was forced by circumstances rather than moved by preference to return to South Africa, and Farrar allowed his City associates to fashion East Rand Proprietary Mines into a monument to speculation. The most important controller of the mines, Julius Wernher, the financial genius behind the Corner House, was of course an international entrepreneur who directly controlled local capital allocation and development tactics from his vantage point in the City. Both he and most of the other mining magnates sought funds from all of western Europe's primary and secondary markets. Through stock market operations, the entrepreneurs siphoned large amounts of capital into their personal fortunes. Much of what they did not spend on conspicuous consumption was redirected into safe government stocks or new extractive ventures outside South Africa. In the case of the Corner House this practice was well underway as early as 1895. In the case of Goldfields it began after the Anglo-Boer War. Thus, the strategies of these two mining houses served to amass significant amounts of wealth through gold mining finance which were then invested, neither in the gold mining industry nor in South Africa, but elsewhere in the world. Not only did the entrepreneurs' investment plans have an increasingly international bias but, interestingly enough, the experts they employed were drawn from several national backgrounds. Though the mines' controllers may be variously labelled, it was their function as international developers and speculators which was fundamental to the evolution of the industry.

The various business strategies of these international entrepreneurs had three very important effects upon the sources and volume of the capital which flowed into the gold mines. First, these strategies prevented the industry from developing its full potential as a steady provider of substantial dividends. Far too many of the controllers stressed market operations rather than gold production. Therefore, the ability of the industry to draw and hold investment as distinct from its dependence upon speculative capital was impaired. Second, these strategies led the developers and speculators controlling the mines to engage in self-defeating competition for capital. Ultimately even speculative stock exchange booms bypassed the "Kaffir market." Wernher's complaints about market dealings by other magnates which were clearly disruptive and which he could not prevent are instructive. So too was the fact that at the end of our period Solly Joel's Johannesburg Consolidated Investments could move ahead of two more powerful groups, the Corner House and Goldfields.

For the gold mines' controllers it was the competitive experience of their days on the Kimberley diggings rather than the monoply of diamond production which was the more conditioning influence. Eventually this persistent competition for capital prevented or dissuaded any single controlling group among the controllers from monopolizing production or finance. It also discouraged other interested groups from moving into the industry. A number of large amalgamations occurred in the post-Boer War period, but these featured properties within the groups. The size and number of the groups themselves, remained largely unchanged. It would not be until 1916–17 when the Barnatos absorbed Robinson's far-west Rand interests and Ernest Oppenheimer founded the Anglo American Corporation that the group picture in place in the mid-1890s significantly altered.

A third result of the entrepreneurs' strategies was extremely important. Their financial practices prevented or discouraged Europe's financial power houses, its corporate and merchant banks, from taking a firm grip on the mines' capital structure. Germany's big banks showed an inclination in the mid-1890s to move into the gold mines in a significant way. They backed General Mining, Adolf Goerz and Company, and Consolidated Mines Selection, all launched between 1893 and 1897. The establishment in 1895 of the Banque Française de L'Afrique du Sud, an institution which Wernher hoped would take over the Corner House's position on the Rand, also indicated that French finance capitalists were prepared to acquire concentrated holdings in and direct control of Rand gold mines. Yet neither German nor French bankers followed up on these beginnings. Indeed, by 1914 both were beating a retreat. The Banque Française had long since been absorbed by another financial institution with new and different investment priorities in which the gold mines played little part. Though the German banks supported a renewal of mining activity and expansion after the South African War, they also soon lost interest. Goldfields, the chief instrument of British capital on the Rand, was also cutting back on its South African position. This withdrawal of interest by such major institutions of finance capital as German and French banks and a British mining trust was, of course, partly explained by local political crises and war, and partly by labor and production problems. However, the volatile "Kaffir market," infested with irresponsible operators and the gross overvaluation of shares of sound producers, convinced Berlin and Paris that the Rand's profits, though substantial, could not offset the ravages of speculation.

The controllers of the industry had so mismanaged its capitalization that not only concentrated direct investment of banks and trusts, but even dispersed portfolio investment came to ignore the industry. When the big backers lost interest, the small-scale investors did take up some of the slack. Goldfields was a case in point. Its important investors, who included the Rothschilds, reduced or sold out their shares while the number of shareholders on Goldfields's books increased. But with the Rand's insiders holding on to large blocks of vendor capital in the best mines, these small-scale investors had to be content with modest yields of overpriced shares or suffer losses from watered stock in unpromising ventures. Such results led also to the belated revulsion of the French investors who had taken up large numbers of gold shares after the South African War. Thus, disaffection among the investors of western Europe, both big and small, in the decade before 1914, caused the South African gold mining industry to miss out on the opportunities to make the most out of the surge of foreign and colonial investment and the tendency of "finance capital" to concentrate and monopolize production. In contrast to the magnates' ability to pull capital out of Europe during the euphoric mining boom of 1894–95, they were unable to compete effectively for the surge of European capital after 1902–3.

When it comes to assessing the relationship between the entrepreneurs and government, one is struck not by the forcefulness but rather by the restraint with which the magnates used their economic power, at least after 1895. When the conspiracy mounted by Rhodes failed, it not only occasioned his downfall but chastened his coconspirators. They, and other magnates, would complain about but nonetheless accept the dynamite monopoly of Kruger's government. Apparent cooperation between that government and *uitlander* commercial interests was sufficient to make several of them willing to follow Milner's lead before the war. After it they wanted to be seen to be his supporters. They felt powerless to do anything when the newly elected Liberal government stopped the importation of Chinese labor and granted the Transvaal Responsible Government. Neither that local government nor the Union government after 1910 were ones the industry felt it could intimidate. On the contrary the men of the Corner House, the strongest and most successful of the mining groups, wrote and acted as if they felt themselves to be exceedingly vulnerable to government action. Why?

The answer, in part, lies with the business strategies of the mines' controllers. Several of their financial habits helped make them indifferent or unsure of themselves in dealings with various levels of government. Their growing notoriety, which gave government a certain advantage, was partly the result of their stock market dealings which, as we have noted, left investors with grievances against the industry. At the same time, their reluctance or inability to cooperate in the pursuit of capital for the mines helped to prevent them from uniting in other common causes. Because several of the magnates were absentee controllers who had amassed vast personal fortunes under the status quo and who had little regard for the interests of shareholders, they lacked the incentive actively to press government. Finally, the international dimensions of the business strategies of the more responsible controllers were incompatible with the priorities and perceptions of either the metropolitan government or local government. Goldfields's deliberate withdrawal of capital from South Africa and its investments outside the empire are instructive. So too was Wernher's expressed wish that the Transvaal be open to all nations.

How then does this study of gold mining finance square with the theories of economic imperialism introduced in Chapter 1? Hobson was right in noting the international scope of the controllers' activities. His often overlooked remark about the "great capitalist proletariat," that is, small and middling investors who were taken advantage of by the financial system, was also perceptive. However, it needs to be qualified. In the years before the Anglo-Boer War, South African gold mining shares were not widely distributed. Even when they became more dispersed in the new century, the small investor who took them up was from the very small part of the population which possessed the great majority of western Europe's wealth. At the same time throughout the period 1886–1914, much of the capital raised by the industry's strategies was speculative capital. If it is assumed that one reason why so many small-scale investors could be duped by market operators and mining promoters is that they could easily afford to take risks, and if it is also assumed that speculative capital movements based on mining shares indicated the existence of substantial amounts of capital which a financial elite could afford to gamble with, then mining finance does seem to reveal that there was "surplus" capital about, or as other economists might put it, that the supply of savings for investment purposes was more than sufficient.

Whether that "surplus" capital was a compelling impetus in Britain's involvement in South Africa, or whether it was drawn off to the detriment of domestic development in Europe are quite different matters and difficult to establish. While very substantial amounts of capital were allocated to the industry, and its financing arrangements attracted additional significant amounts some of which were used for other overseas purposes, it also fostered economic development in Europe. For example, capital intensive industry used European manufacture. Some of the super profits its controllers made were invested in European securities and real estate. Presumably gold production facilitated currency exchange and hence trade and commerce. While the assessment must remain impressionistic, it seems more likely that gold mining finance was a symptom rather than a cause of the economic inequalities in the advanced economies of Europe. That is, it reflected the general availability of huge amounts of savings held by relatively small numbers of people rather than representing a crucial overseas outlet for capital which would have otherwise been sunk into domestic production.

Adherents of the Hilferding-Lenin notion of "monopoly finance capital" will also not find this study wholly supportive of their contentions. To be sure, evidence of "bank capital" and evidence of attempts at concentration and monopoly are apparent in this study. However, these were incipient manifestations which, rather than gathering influence after 1900, declined in importance at least before 1914. And, to the extent monopoly finance capital was operative, it seemed that armed conflict was out of phase with or contrary to its immediate needs. Interestingly enough Kautsky's notion that finance capital could take on international as opposed to national dimensions and minimize rather than foster imperial rivalries and conflict has an element of relevance in the light of gold mining finance. However, in this case the fragmentary and chaotic character of finance capital curtailed its ability to promote such developments.

We are left with the peripheralist argument to reconsider. This study suggests that the emphasis given to economic elements presented in that argument needs to be revised. The gold mining entrepreneurs were very much of Europe's economy. Their business strategies, with the exception of Rhodes's, were an outgrowth of their association with the primary and secondary capital markets of Europe. While they could manipulate these markets, at least before the turn of the century, manipulation was hardly done with local objectives or priorities in mind. Whatever their background, whatever their length of residence in South Africa, the magnates as a group were primarily absentee controllers.

But if these magnates and their mining groups were extensions of Europe's capital markets, they also were exporters of Europe's machine and chemical technology. Recently developed devices to win the gold from the conglomerates were fundamental to the timing and evolution of the South African economic juggernaut. This juggernaut acted less to foster a growing disparity in the power relationship between Europe's nations and local states, as Fieldhouse's model assumes; rather, the development of the gold mining industry, a by-product of European capital formation and technological breakthroughs, allowed a local state to challenge Britain's hegemony. The ensuing confrontation inadvertently discouraged direct German and French investment, and was ultimately resolved by a reduction in British influence, even though imperial forces won the war.

Not surprisingly the business strategies of the internationally oriented controllers of South Africa's gold mines were out of step with the imperial priorities of a single nation. The controllers, on the other hand, used surprisingly little of the economic power they had amassed to make government more responsive to their wishes. The fragmentary nature of the capital structure of the gold mining industry was partly responsible for the relative lack of manipulation of government by the entrepreneurs. At the same time the impact of such elements in European economic activity as the monopoly of production and the concentration of capital was also dissipated by the diverse and divergent business strategies of the industry.

Finally we ask the question: what catalysts of the "new imperialism," Europe's rapid and vast thrusts abroad in the late nineteenth century, does our admittedly economically oriented study find to be important? Obviously capitalism was important, but not a capitalism featuring pronounced monopolistic trends; rather, there was a well-developed competition apparent in the scramble for claims which followed the first discovery of gold, a competition which was still visible, despite the development of the group system, in the successful efforts of Johannesburg Consolidated Investments to move ahead of the Corner House and Goldfields at the end of our period. Though there was considerable effort to monopsonize labor in South Africa, in Europe the industry's controllers engaged in a self-defeating competition for speculative and development capital.

It can also be argued that capitalism was in competition if not in conflict with imperialism and nationalism. Corner House financiers featured prominently in local politics. British strategists wanted the industry's development to foster the imperial connection. Although Boer generals lost the war, they perceived that the gold mines could paradoxically help them win the peace. However local political developments and British imperial priorities, both a function of defensive or aggressive nationalisms and very much conditioned by the industry's evolution, invariably operated against the needs and demands of the internationally oriented financial mechanisms and institutions which capitalized the industry. The last thing the capitalists wanted or needed in 1899 was a war, certainly not one instigated and won by Britain when the capitalist mechanisms and institutions most engaged in the industry were continental, that is French or German. If anything the war had the effect, at least in the short run, to assert a British presence which Europe's financiers found distinctly unwelcome. One recalls in this respect the history of the Banque Française de L'Afrique du Sud poised to take a leading role in gold mine finance only to be put off by the war. International capitalism, British imperialism, and Afrikaner nationalism did to some extent coexist. But these forces, all well entrenched in South Africa before 1914, were fundamentally at cross purposes. South African developments, consequently, should be seen basically as a function of clashing priorities and the inability of any one or combination of these forces to achieve supremacy.

Selected Bibliography

1. A Note on Sources

The key archival source used in this work are the papers left by Wernher, Beit and Company. I consulted these before they had been fully cataloged, but what I have cited can be located through a helpful guide recently published by Barlow Rand Limited and compiled by M. Fraser: *Inventory of the Archives of H. Eckstein & Co., 1887–1910* (Johannesburg, 1975). This inventory should be used in conjunction with the published works of A. P. Cartwright, and with the correspondence of one the most important Randlords published as this work went to press: M. Fraser and A. Jeeves (eds.), *All That Glittered: The Selected Correspondence of Lionel Phillips 1890–1924* (Cape Town, 1977). See especially Alan Jeeves's illuminating editorial introduction.

There has been indiscriminate weeding of the BT 31 series and it is a fact that most Rand gold mining concerns registered in the Transvaal instead of London have left lacunae in shareholding records. But the allotment lists for Goldfields and for Central Mining retained by the Register of Companies, London, proved very helpful.

Goldmann's *South African Mines,* Mabson's *Mines of the Transvaal,* and Skinner's *Mining Manual* are essential published sources for the purposes of tracing the formation, reconstruction, and liquidation of mining companies as well as for estimating issued capital and determining market values.

I have not cited all the many works on foreign and colonial investment which proved useful or which have been superseded. These can be easily found in the bibliographies and footnotes of works cited below. Essential references in this regard are A. I. Bloomfield, *Patterns of Fluctuation in International Investment Before 1914* (Princeton, 1968), and P. L. Cottrell, *British Overseas Investment in the Nineteenth Century* (London, 1975). These two works read in conjunction with E. J. R. Owen and R. B. Sutcliffe (eds.), *Studies in the Theory of Imperialism* (London, 1972), would serve as a starting point for other case studies along the lines of this book.

2. Archives

Barlow Rand Limited. Johannesburg.
Wernher, Beit and Company Papers.
Charter Consolidated Services Limited. London.
Miscellaneous share allotment records.
Consolidated Gold Fields of South Africa. Johannesburg.
Correspondence, general and miscellaneous, Files G, J, and K.
———. London.
Annual reports, minute books, Robinson Deep file, and Simmer and Jack file.
Ministère des Finances. Paris.
Série F. 30, 296 à 300.
Oxford University. Oxford.
Rhodes Papers, Rhodes House: MSS Afr. S. 228: IX, Finance; X, Gold Fields; XXIII, Transvaal; XXIV, Wernher, Beit & Co.
Public Record Office. London.
Series BT 8: Enemy debts committee.
Series BT 31: Registered companies liquidated or wound up.
Register of Companies. London.
Consolidated Gold Fields of South Africa, File No. 36936.
Central Mining and Investment Corporation, File No. 84511.

3. Newspapers and Periodicals

Cape Times.
Economist.
L'Économiste français.
Mining Journal.
Mining Manual.
Mines of the Transvaal.
South African Mining Journal.
Statist.
Stock Exchange Official Year-Book.
The Times.

4. Published Private Papers and Memoirs

Cohen, L. *Reminiscences of Johannesburg and London.* London, 1924.
FitzPatrick, J. P. *South African Memories.* London, 1932.

———. *The Transvaal From Within.* London, 1899.

Fraser, M. and A. Jeeves, eds. *All That Glittered: The Selected Correspondence of Lional Phillips, 1890–1924.* Cape Town, 1977.

Hammond, J. H. *The Autobiography of John Hays Hammond.* New York, 1935.

Lewsen, P., ed. *Selections From the Correspondence of J. X. Merriman.* Cape Town, 1960.

Phillips, L. *Some Reminiscences.* London, 1924.

Taylor, J. B. *A Pioneer Looks Back.* London, 1939.

Taylor, W. P. *African Treasures.* London, 1932.

5. Contemporary Works

Bassett, H. H. *Men of Note in Finance and Commerce.* London, 1900–1901.

Edwards, D. *The Gold Fields of South Africa.* Cape Town, 1890.

Fieldhouse, D. K., ed. *The Theory of Capitalist Imperialism.* London, 1967.

Goldmann, C. S. *The Financial, Statistical, and General History of the Gold and Other Companies of Witwatersrand, South Africa.* London, 1892.

———. *South African Mines; Their Position, Results, & Developments . . . and Kindred Concerns.* 3 vols. London, 1895–96.

Hatch, F. H., and J. A. Chalmers. *The Gold Mines of the Rand.* London, 1895.

Hobson, J. A. *The War in South Africa, Its Causes and Effects.* London, 1900.

———. *Imperialism: A Study.* London, 1902; 3rd ed., 1938.

———. *The Evolution of Modern Capitalism.* London, 2nd ed., 1906.

Kaufmann, E. *La Banque en France.* Paris, 1914.

Lamy, C., ed. *Annuaire français des mines d'or.* 4 vols. Paris, 1896–99.

Launay, L. de. *Les Mines d'or du Transvaal.* Paris, 1896.

———. O. C. Williams, trans. *The World's Gold.* London, 1908.

Lenin, V. I. *Imperialism, the Highest Stage of Capitalism.* Petrograd, 1917; Moscow, 11th impression, n.d.

Neymarck, A. *Finances contemporaines, VI, l'épargne française et les valeurs mobilières, 1872–1910.* Paris, 1911.

Rand Mines. *Annual Reports.* Johannesburg, 1894–1906.

Riesser, J. *The German Great Banks and Their Concentration.* Washington, 1911.

Skinner, T. *The London Banks, and Kindred Companies.* London, 1899.

South African Law Reports. *Decisions of the Supreme Court Appellate Division, 1920–21*. Cape Town, 1922.
Transvaal Chamber of Mines. *Annual Reports*. Johannesburg, 1898–1914.
Transvaal Government. *Report and Minutes of Evidence of the Transvaal Mining Industry Commission.* Pretoria, 1908.
Truscott, S. J. *The Witwatersrand Goldfields: Banket and Mining Practice*. London, 2nd ed., 1902.
Williams, G. F. *The Diamond Mines of South Africa.* 2 vols. New York, 1906.
Withers, H. *Stocks and Shares*. London, 2nd ed., 1917.

6. Secondary Sources

Books

Adam, H. *Modernizing Racial Domination, South Africa's Political Dynamics*. Berkeley, 1971.
Adamson, R. J., ed. *Gold Metallurgy in South Africa.* Johannesburg, 1972.
Adler, D. R.; M. E. Hidy, ed. *British Investment in American Railways, 1834–1898*. Charlottesville, Va., 1970.
Barkin, K. D. *The Controversy Over German Industrialization, 1890–1902*. Chicago, 1970.
Barraclough, G. *An Introduction to Contemporary History*. Harmondsworth, Middlesex; 2nd ed., 1967.
Bloomfield, A. I. *Patterns of Fluctuation in International Investment Before 1914*. Princeton, 1968.
Cairncross, A. K. *Home and Foreign Investment, 1870–1913; Studies in Capital Accumulation.* Cambridge, 1953.
Cameron, R. E. *France and the Economic Development of Europe, 1800–1914*. Princeton, 1961.
Cartwright, A. P. *The Gold Miners,* Johannesburg, 1962.
———. *The Dynamite Company; The Story of African Explosives and Chemical Industries Limited.* Cape Town, 1964.
———. *The Corner House; The Early History of Johannesburg*. Cape Town, 1965.
———. *Gold Paved the Way; The Story of the Gold Fields Group of Companies*. London, 1967.
———. *Golden Age; The Story of the Industrialization of South Africa and . . . the Corner House Group of Companies, 1910–1967*. Cape Town, 1968.
Cecco, M. de. *Money and Empire: The International Gold Standard 1890–1914,* Oxford, 1974.

Chilvers, H. A. *The Story of De Beers.* London, 1939.
Consolidated Gold Fields of South Africa. *The Gold Fields, 1887–1937.* London, 1937.
Cottrell, P. L. *British Overseas Investment in the Nineteenth Century.* London, 1975.
Daumard, A., *et al. Les Fortunes françaises au XIXe siècle.* Paris, 1973.
De Kock, W. J., and D. W. Kruger, eds. *Dictionary of South African Biography.* 2 vols. Cape Town, 1968–72.
Denoon, D. J. N. *A Grand Illusion; The Failure of Imperial Policy in the Transvaal Colony During the Period of Reconstruction, 1900–1905.* London, 1973.
Emden, P. H. *Randlords.* London, 1935.
Fieldhouse, D. K. *Economics and Empire, 1830–1914.* London, 1973.
Flint, J. E. *Cecil Rhodes.* Boston, 1974.
Ford, A. G. *The Gold Standard, 1880–1914: Britain and Argentina.* Oxford, 1962.
Frankel, S. H. *Capital Investment in Africa, Its Course and Effects.* London, 1938.
———. *Investment and the Return to Equity Capital in the South African Gold Mining Industry, 1887–1965.* Oxford, 1967.
Galbraith, J. S. *Crown and Charter: The Early Years of the British South Africa Company.* Berkeley, 1974.
Goodhart, C. A. E. *The Business of Banking, 1891–1914.* London, 1972.
Gordon, C. T. *The Growth of Boer Opposition to Kruger, 1890–1895.* Cape Town, 1970.
Gregory, T. *Ernest Oppenheimer and the Economic Development of Southern Africa.* Cape Town, 1962.
Gutsche, T. *No Ordinary Woman, The Life and Times of Florence Phillips.* Cape Town, 1966.
Hall, A. R. *The London Capital Market and Australia, 1870–1914.* Canberra, 1963.
Henderson, W. O. *The Rise of German Industrial Power.* Berkeley, 1975.
Hoffmann, W. G. *Das Wachstum der Deutschen Wirtschaft seit der Mitte des 19. Jahrhunderts.* Berlin, 1965.
Joel, S. *Ace of Diamonds, The Story of Solomon Barnato Joel.* London, 1958.
Johannesburg Consolidated Investment Company. *The Story of 'Johnnies,' 1889–1964: A History of the Johannesburg Consolidated Investment Company Limited.* Johannesburg, 1965.
Johnstone, F. A. *Class, Race and Gold: A Study of Class Relations and Racial Discrimination in South Africa.* London, 1976.
Kindleberger, C. P. *Economic Growth in France and Britain, 1851–1950.* Cambridge, Mass., 1964.

Kubicek, R. V. *The Administration of Imperialism: Joseph Chamberlain at the Colonial Office*. Durham, N.C., 1969.
Landes, D. S. *The Unbound Prometheus: Technological Change and Industrial Development in Western Europe From 1750 to the Present*. Cambridge, 1969.
Lenzen, G.; F. Bradley, trans. *The History of Diamond Production and the Diamond Trade*. London, 1970.
Letcher, O. *The Gold Mines of Southern Africa*. London, 1936.
Lichtheim, G. *Imperialism*. New York, 1971.
Lockhart, J. G., and C. M. Woodhouse. *Cecil Rhodes: The Colossus of Southern Africa*. New York, 1963.
Louis, W. R., ed. *Imperialism: The Robinson and Gallagher Controversy*. New York, 1976.
McKay, J. P. *Pioneers for Profit, Foreign Entrepreneurship and Russian Industrialization, 1885–1913*. Chicago, 1970.
McNeill, W. H. *The Rise of the West*. Chicago, 1963.
Marais, J. S. *The Fall of Kruger's Republic*. Oxford, 1961.
Morgan, E. V., and W. A. Thomas. *The Stock Exchange: Its History and Functions*. London, 1962.
Morgenstern, O. *The Validity of International Gold Movement Statistics*. Princeton, 1955.
———. *International Financial Transactions and Business Cycles*. Princeton, 1959.
Owen, E. R. J., and R. B. Sutcliffe, eds. *Studies in the Theory of Imperialism*. London, 1972.
Paterson, D. G. *British Direct Investment in Canada, 1890–1914*. Toronto, 1976.
Poidevin, R. *Les Relations économiques et financières entre la France et l'Allemagne de 1899 à 1914*. Paris, 1969.
Pollard, S., and D. W. Crossley. *The Wealth of Britain, 1085–1966*. London, 1968.
Roberts, B. *The Diamond Magnates*. London, 1972.
Robinson, R., and J. Gallagher. *Africa and the Victorians: The Climax of Imperialism in the Dark Continent*. London, 1961.
Saron, G., and L. Hotz, eds. *The Jews in South Africa; A History*. Cape Town, 1955.
Sayers, R. S. *Bank of England Operations, 1890–1914*. London, 1936.
Shorten, J. R. *The Johannesburg Saga*. Johannesburg, 1970.
Spence, C. C. *British Investments and the American Mining Frontier, 1860–1901*. Ithaca, N.Y., 1958.
Stern, F. *Gold and Iron: Bismarck, Bleichröder, and the Building of the German Empire*. New York, 1977.
Stolper, G., *et al.*; T. Stolper, trans. *The German Economy, 1870 to the Present*. New York, 1967.

Supple, B. E. *The Royal Exchange Assurance; A History of British Insurance, 1720–1970*. Cambridge, 1970.
Thomas, W. A. *The Provincial Stock Exchanges*. London, 1973.
Van der Horst, S. T. *Native Labour in South Africa*. London, 1942.
Van der Poel, J. *The Jameson Raid*. Cape Town, 1951.
Wareham, W. S., ed. *Register of Defunct and Other Companies Removed From The Stock Exchange Official Year-Book*. London, 1967.
Whale, P. B. *Joint Stock Banking in Germany*. London, 1930.
White, H. D. *The French International Accounts, 1880–1913*. Cambridge, Mass., 1933.
Wilson, F. *Labour in the South African Gold Mines, 1911–1969*. Cambridge, 1972.

Articles

Atmore, A., and S. Marks. "The Imperial Factor in South Africa in the Nineteenth Century: Towards a Reassessment," *Journal of Imperial and Commonwealth History*, III (1974), 105–39.
Baran, P. A., and P. M. Sweezy, "Notes on the Theory of Imperialism," *Monthly Review*, XVII (1966), 15–31.
Blainey, G. "Lost Causes of the Jameson Raid," *Economic History Review*, 2nd ser., XVIII (1965), 350–66.
Denoon, D. J. N. " 'Capitalist Influence' and the Transvaal Government During the Crown Colony Period, 1900–1906," *Historical Journal*, XI (1968), 301–31.
———. "The Transvaal Labour Crisis, 1901–6," *Journal of African History*, VII (1967), 481–94.
Drabble, J. H., and P. J. Drake. "More on the Financing of Malayan Rubber, 1905–23," *Economic History Review*, 2nd ser., XXVII (1974), 108–20.
Fieldhouse, D.K. " 'Imperialism': An Historiographical Revision," *Economic History Review*, 2nd ser., XIV (1961), 187–209.
Frankel, S. H. "Return to Capital Invested in the Witwatersrand Gold-Mining Industry, 1887–1932," *Economic Journal* (1935), 68–76.
Goffin, R. "Les Valeurs mobilières en France à la fin du XIXe et au début du XXe siècle, 1873–1913," in C. Morrisson and R. Goffin, *Questions financières aux XVIIIe et XIXe siècles* (1967), 91–148.
Hopkins, A. G. "Imperial Business in Africa, Part I: Sources," *Journal of African History*, XVII (1976), 29–48.
———. "Imperial Business in Africa, Part II: Interpretations," *Journal of African History*, XVII (1976), 267–90.
Irving, R. J. "British Railway Investment and Innovation, 1900–1914," *Business History*, XIII (1971), 39–63.
Jeeves, A. H. "The Rand Capitalists and the Coming of the South

African War, 1896–1899," *Canadian Historical Association Papers* (1973), 61–83.
———. "The Control of Migratory Labour on the South African Gold Mines in the Era of Kruger and Milner," *Journal of Southern African Studies*, II (1975), 3–29.
Kubicek, R. V. "Finance Capital and South African Goldmining, 1886–1914," *Journal of Imperial and Commonwealth History*, III (1975), 386–95.
———. "The Randlords in 1895: A Reassessment," *Journal of British Studies*, XI (1972), 84–103.
Landes, D. "Some Thoughts on the Nature of Economic Imperialism," *Journal of Economic History*, XXI (1961), 496–512.
———. "Japan and Europe: Contrasts in Industrialization," in W. W. Lockwood, ed. *The State and Economic Enterprise in Japan* (1965), 93–182.
Lemoine, R. J. "The Banking System of France," in H. P. Willis and B. H. Beckhart, eds. *Foreign Banking Systems* (1929), 522–626.
Lenman, B. and K. Donaldson. "Partners' Incomes, Investment and Diversification in the Scottish Linen Area, 1850–1921," *Business History*, XIII (1971), 1–18.
Mawby, A. A. "Capital, Government and Politics in the Transvaal, 1900–1907: A Revision and a Reversion," *Historical Journal*, XVII (1974), 387–415.
Mommsen, W. J. "Europäischer Finanzimperialismus Vor 1914: Ein Beitrag Zu Einer Pluralistischen Theorie Des Imperialismus," *Historische Zeitschrift*, CCXXIV (1977), 2–81.
Neuburger, H., and H. H. Stokes. "German Banks and German Growth, 1883–1913: an Empirical View," *Journal of Economic History*, XXXIV (1974), 710–31.
Paish, F. W. "The London New Issue Market," *Economica*, XVIII (1951), 1–17.
Paterson, D. G. "European Financial Capital and British Columbia: An Essay on the Role of the Regional Entrepreneur," *B.C. Studies*, (1974), 33–47.
Perrings, C. "The Production Process, Industrial Labour Strategies and Worker Responses in the Southern African Gold Mining Industry," *Journal of African History*, XVIII (1977), 129–35.
Phimister, I. R. "Rhodes, Rhodesia and the Rand," *Journal of Southern African Studies*, I (1974), 74–90.
Porter, A. N. "Sir Alfred Milner and the Press, 1897–1899," *Historical Journal*, XVI (1973), 323–39.
Quittner, P. "The Banking System of Germany," in H. P. Willis and B. H. Beckhart, eds. *Foreign Banking Systems* (1929), 627–722.
Richardson, P. "The Recruiting of Chinese Indentured Labour for the

South African Gold-Mines, 1903–1908," *Journal of African History*, XVIII (1977), 85–108.

Robinson, R. "Non-European Foundations of European Imperialism: Sketch for a Theory of Collaboration," in E. R. J. Owen and R. B. Sutcliffe, eds. *Studies in the Theory of Imperialism* (1972), 117–42.

Simon, M. "The Pattern of New British Portfolio Foreign Investment, 1865–1914," in J. H. Adler, ed. *Capital Movements and Economic Development* (1967), 33–60.

Stillson, R. T. "The Financing of Malayan Rubber, 1905–1923," *Economic History Review*, 2nd ser., XXIV (1971), 589–98.

Stokes, E. "Late Nineteenth-Century Colonial Expansion and the Attack on the Theory of Economic Imperialism: A Case of Mistaken Identity?" *Historical Journal*, XII (1969), 285–301.

W., E. L. "Profile of A Gold Mine," *Optima*, XXIII (1973), 78–83.

Appendix A. Share and Debenture Holdings of the Corner House Group, 1911–12

Data for the tables in this appendix was compiled from the following sources: Agreement between Wernher, Beit and Central Mining, 2 May 1911, BT, Register of Companies, File No. 84511; *Mining Manual; Mines of the Transvaal; Stock Exchange Year-Book; Moody's Manual of Railroads and Corporation Securities.*

Table A.1. *Share and Debenture Holdings of the Corner House in Transvaal Gold Mines, 1911–12*

Mining Company	Issued capital £	Holdings of RM £1 shares	Holdings of CMI £1 shares	Holdings of WB and Eckstein's[d] £1 shares	Total holdings of CH	Market value of CH holdings £[e]
Bantjes Cons'd	502306	81444	23826		105270	131600
CMI	5100000			117488[a]	117488	1204250
City Deep	1250000	206437	44897		251334	722585
City and Suburban	1360000		9725[b]		9725[a]	22490
Cons'd Main Reef	924364		600		600	540
Crown Mines	940106	852277	77536		929813	6392464
Durban Roodepoort Deep	440000	127017	85475		212492	212492
ERPM	2405897	55198	86000		141198	315700
" (5% debs)	1500000	£ 34000	£ 69000	£ 50000	£ 153000	145350
Ferreira Deep	910000	338450			338450	1359575
French Rand	514000		39724		39724	4965
Geldenhuis Deep	585753	282593	52868		335461	503000
Jupiter Gold Mining Co.	1014200	115558	102045		217603	136000
Knight's Deep	643526		1000		1000	2375
Luipaard's Vlei Estate	471812		7132		7132	4279
" " (5½% debs)	103920			£ 6120	£ 6102	5300
Main Reef West	491188	39782			39782	39782
" " " (6% debs)	300000			£ 34104	£ 34104	33300

Modderfontein 'B'	605000		191540		191540	622505
Modderfontein (Gov't Areas)	1400000	47500	47500		95000	100313
New Heriot	115000		3740		3740	14960
New Modderfontein	1400000	23670[b]			23670[b]	284040
Nourse Mines	827821	387583	29577		417160	808247
Randfontein Estates (6% debs)	1996760		£ 74380		£ 74380	68430
RM	531500		36600[c]	291000[c]	327600[c]	2047500
Robinson Gold Mining Co.	2750000		7885[d]		7885[d]	26612
Rose Deep	695000	269224	44598		313822	902238
South Deeps	125000	24463	21906		46369	46369
Transvaal Gold Mining Estate	604225		14578		14578	41000
" " " (5% debs)	124000		£ 9800	£ 24200	£ 34000	34000
Village Deep	1060671	114990	57125		172115	354987
Village Main Reef	472000	45347	437		45784	108737
" " " (5% debs)	n.a.		£ 5200		£ 5200	5200
Wolhuter Gold Mines	860000		14236	23720	37956	37956
9 Other Companies	2838792		17129		17129	16485
2 " " (5 –6% debs)	265790		£ 350	£ 1430	£ 1780	1780
	36128631					16757406

a. £12 shares.
b. £4 shares.
c. 5s shares.
d. £5 shares.
e. In some cases par or book values have been used.
d. WB is Wernher, Beit & Co.

Table A.2. *Share and Debenture Holdings of the Corner House in the Union of South Africa, 1911–12 (Excluding Transvaal Gold Mines)*

Company	Issued capital £	Holdings of RM	Holdings of CMI	Holdings of WB and Eckstein's	Total holdings of CH	Market value of CH holdings
Argus Printing	97377		25816		25816	97377
Brick & Potteries	65000		8332		8332	8332
British S.A. Transport			413		413	413
Booysens Estate	35698	5222	4684		9906	9906
Cape Times	200000		44007		44007	44007
Cape Electric Tramways	491222			40731	40731	20350
" " (6% debs)	219700			£ 11800	£ 11800	11800
" " (5% debs)	243300			£ 66400	£ 66400	61580
Cape Town Cons'd Tramways	300000			63804	63804	3190
" " " (5% debs)	450000			116100	116100	116100
Cape Asbestos (ordy.)	71500			3135	3135	160
" " (pfce)	60000			34158	34158	20048
Central Rand Freehold	10000		312		312	3530

Cons'd Bultfontein	721500		5500		5500	6880
De Beers Cons'd				7000	7000	119000
Diamond Syndicate			262190	524380	786570	786570
General Estates	225000	82125		82125	164250	164250
Johannesburg Estates	200000		1500		1500	560
Marais Molyneaux Synd.	30000		730		730	730
National Bank of S.A.	1100000		300		300	5600
Pretoria Portland Cement	150000	5758	5085		10843	10843
S. African Real Estate	150000		18957		18957	18957
Smartt Syndicate				13794	13794	13794
" " (debs)				£ 12000	£ 12000	12000
" " (loan)				£ 5250	£ 5250	5250
Transvaal Cons'd Land	971214		6094		6094	8380
Transvaal Hydraulic			1000		1000	1000
Transvaal Lands & Mines	47250		422648[a]		422648[a]	31698
Turffontein Estates	50000	4230	3774		8004	8004
Voorspoed Diamond M	372964		793		793	793
Victoria Falls & Transvaal Power	2708000	12000			12000	12000
						1603102

a. 1s. 6d. shares.

Table A.3. *Share and Debenture Holdings of the Corner House in Africa, 1911–12 (Excluding the Union of South Africa)*

Company	Issued capital	Holdings of RM	Holdings of CMI (shares)	Holdings of WB and Eckstein's (shares)	Total Holdings of CH (shares)	Market value of CH holdings
Southern Africa						
British Central Africa (5% debs)	650000		£ 8000		£ 8000	£ 8000
" " " (loan)	15000		£ 6200		£ 6200	£ 6200
Companhia do Nyassa	436530		10840		10840	10840
copper interests			£ 29398		£ 29398	£ 29398
Lourenco Marques Forwarding			3139		3139	3139
Otavi Exploring Synd.	63000		10000		10000	10000
Premier Tati	225747		2395		2395	2395
Rhodesia Broken Hill	500000		3636		3636	3636
Rhodesia Copper	416000		22733		22733	22733
South-West Africa	1750000			14823	14823	14823
Swaziland Tin	82000		27382		27382	27382
Toweli S.A. Estates			73000		73000	73000
Town Properties	140000		85000		85000	85000
Misc. Companies			23677		23677	23677

West Africa					
Appantoo Cons'd.	250000	58599		58599	58599
Abosso Gold Mines	349509	4102		4102	3845
Fanti Consolidated	597256	166847[a]		166847[a]	133100
Presta Block 'A'	496639	170144		170144	212680
West African Mines	100200	15290		15290	15290
W.A. Properties	1793604	414982		414982	414982
" " " (loans)		£ 6062		£ 6062	6062
North Africa					
Agricultural Bank of Egypt	1250000		1000	1000	8750
Sudan Plantations Synd.	135000	5000	5000	10000	15000
" " (3½ debs)	58000		£ 16700	£ 16700	15030
General					
African Ore Concentration (5% debs)		£ 1100		£ 1100	£ 1100
African Transcontinental Tel.	226850	2937		2937	2937
African & General Explr'n.		365		365	365
Trans-African Railway Synd		1100		1100	1100

a. 10s shares.

Table A.4. *Share and Debenture Holdings of the Corner House in Britain, 1911–12*

Company or government	Issued capital	Holdings of RM	Holdings of CMI	Holdings of WB and Eckstein's	Total holdings of CH	Market value of CH holdings £
Barrow Haematite Steel (5% debs)	317300			£ 11750	£ 11750	11750
British Aluminium	600620			33503	33503	5030
" " (6% pfce)	299570			24065	24065	6050
" " (5% debs)	720398			£ 25241	£ 25241	19190
" " (prior lien)	800000			64600	64600	58140
Consols (2½%)			£ 500000		£ 500000	411250
Charles Butters	50000		5815[a]		5815[a]	2908
Fraser & Chalmers	378000			25350[b]	25350[b]	50700
" " " (7½% pfce)	63000			2292[b]	2292[b]	9453
Irish Loan	10604422		£ 100000		£ 100000	83000
London Aluminium				396[c]	396[c]	20
London Wall Estate	20000			12348	12348	12348
" " " (5% pfce)	200000			134500	134500	134500
" " " (4% debs)	400000			£ 269000	£ 269000	269000
Medway Coal Exploration Synd.			500		500	500
Ore Concentration (1905)	224544		20731		20731	20731
Port of London			50000		50000	40500
Siemens Brothers (4½% debs)	150000			2950[d]	2950[d]	2660
Union Bank of London				330	330	n.a.
						1137730

a. 10s shares.
b. £3 shares.
c. 5s shares.
d. £5 shares.

Table A.5. *Share and Debenture Holdings of the Corner House in Europe, 1911–12*

Company or government		*Issued capital*	*Holdings of RM*	*Holdings of CMI*	*Holdings of WB and Eckstein's*	*Total holdings of CH*	*Market value of CH holdings £*
Austria							
Austrion Treasury Bonds	(4% debs)			Kr. 1000000		Kr. 1000000	41335
France							
Cie Francaise del'Amiante					1282	1282	60
" " "	(debs)				Frs. 17500	Frs. 17500	15750
Germany							
City of Berlin Bonds	(4%)			M. 990000		M. 990000	48500
Deutsche Kap Abestwerke					M. 240000	M. 240000	11740
Deutsche Uebersee Elektr.					550	550	990
German Gov't	(3½%)			M. 1000000		M. 1000000	46000
" " (1908)	(4%)			M. 1000000		M. 1000000	48530
" " (1909)	(4%)			M. 1000000		M. 1000000	50020
Internatle Kolenbergwerks				M. 320000		M. 320000	16000
Gibeon-Schnerf & Land				M. 25000		M. 25000	1250
Prussian Loan	(3½%)			M. 1000000		M. 1000000	46000
" "	(4%)			M. 4000000		M. 4000000	194120
" "	(4%)			M. 1000000		M. 1000000	50020
" Treasury Bonds	(4%)			M. 2000000		M. 2000000	97400
Vereiniste Glanzstoff Fabriken				M. 50000		M. 50000	2500
Portugal							
Lisbon	(5%)				£ 78600	£ 78600	76740
Lisbon Electric Tramways					15682	15682	16470
" " "	(6% pfce)				95674	95674	107930
Russia							
International Maikop		67312		1750		1750	60
Maikop Areas		450000		12100		12100	2400
							873815

Table A.6. *Share and Debenture Holdings of the Corner House in the Americas, 1911–12*

Company or government	Issued capital	Holdings of RM	Holdings of CMI	Holdings of WB and Eckstein's	Total holdings of CH	Market value of CH holdings £
North America						
Alaska Goldfields	250000		1865		1865	1865
Alaska Juneau Gold Mines			146850		146850	146850
British Canadian Lumber	3850000		£ 10224		£ 10224	10000
Butte Coalition	3000000		1144		1144	1020
Bertha Gold Mines			1188		1188	1188
Chicago Great Western Rwy	4600000			795	795	13560
Maritime Oilfields	99050		18300		18300	18300
Sacremento Gold Mining			1782		1782	1782
South Utah Mines	640000		£ 675		£ 675	413
Central America						
Costa Rica Light	177100			2422	2422	120
Costa Rica (5% debs)	2000000			£ 8450	£ 8450	6340
El Oro Mining & Railway	1150000			5749	5749	6280
Exploration	750000		7007		7007	5855
Ferrocarriles (6% debs)				£ 16320	£ 16320	15960
Mexico (5% debs)	22700000			£ 19600	19600	19600
South America						
Chilean Electric (5% debs)	418000			£ 155800	£ 155800	155800
Colombia Synd.			75		75	1500
						406433

Table A.7. *Market Value of Share and Debenture Holdings of the Corner House, 1911–12*

		£	£
Africa			
Transvaal Gold Mines		16757406	
Union of South Africa		1603102[a]	
Southern Africa		160000[b]	
West Africa		844558	
North Africa		38780	
General		5502	
	Subtotal	19409348	19409348
Britain	Subtotal	1137730	1137730
Europe			
Austria		41335	
France		15810	
Germany		613070	
Portugal		201140	
Russia		2460	
	Subtotal	873815	873815
Americas			
North America		194978	
Central America		54155	
South America		157300	
	Subtotal	406433	406433
TOTAL			21827326

a. A number of the market values for securities under this head were not available so par values were substituted. Since a number of the companies concerned were viable and active, this estimate is probably below market value.

b. Market values for securities under this head were not available so values 50 percent of par were substituted. Since a number of the companies concerned were inactive or their vendor shares were overvalued, this estimate is probably above market value.

Appendix B. Share and Debenture Holdings of the Goldfields Group

Data for the tables in this appendix was compiled from the following sources: *Mines of the Transvaal; Mining Manual; Stock Exchange Year-Book;* and *Moody's Manual of Railroads and Corporation Securities.*

Table B.1. *Share and Debenture Holdings of the Goldfields Group in Transvaal Gold Mines, 1913*

Company	Issued capital £	Holdings of CGFSA	Holdings of SAGT	Holdings of GMI	Total holdings	Market value of holdings £
Afrikaner Proprietary	280000	43333			43333	32499
East Rand Extension	293000	2[illegible]68			29968	5993
Jupiter	1014200	214688			214688	134180
Knights Deep	643526	401862		49057	450919	901838
Nourse Mines	827821	19865			19865	38488
Robinson Deep	1000000	404483	39236	16758	460477	1036073
Simmer & Jack Proprietary	3000000	1356974	206248	50951	1614173	1614173
Simmer & Jack East (5½ debs)			£ 52540		£ 52540	52540
Simmer Deep	1650000	327686	77138		404824	89960
" " (5½ debs)			£ 22700		£ 22700	22700
" " (5 debs)	269000	£ 82400	£ 108500		£ 190900	190900
South Deeps	130000	78031			78031	78031
Sub Nigel	431580	116549	110484	19152	246185	92319
						4289694

Table B.2. *Share and Debenture Holdings of the Goldfields Group in Africa, 1913 (Excluding Transvaal Gold Mines)*

Company	*Issued capital*	*Holdings of CGFSA*	*Holdings of SAGT*	*Holdings of GMI*	*Total holdings*	*Market value of holdings*
Union of South Africa						
African City Properties	220000		17925		17925	13444
African Land & Investment	300000	88320	48025		136345	136345
Booysens Estate	35698	18035			18035	18035
East Rietfontein Synd.	25000	6951			6951	6951
Elandsfontein Estate	30000	11753			11753	11753
Turffontein Estates	50000	23751			23751	23751
Victoria Falls & Transvaal Power	100000	58785	10000		68785	68785
" " " (pfce)	200000		51317	38627	89944	89944
Misc. Interests		£ 164731			£ 164731	164731
Southern Africa						
Bell Reef Development	181338	41955	7734		49689	49689
Cam-Motor Gold Mine	467500	42923	11604		54527	95422
Falcon Mines	400000		17542		17542	20831
" " (debs)	250000	£ 25328	£ 12270		£ 12270	12270

Gold Fields Rhodesian	2513887	647484	73533	49652	770669	818836
La Rochelle Synd.		11700			11700	11700
Lonely Reef Gold Mine	271007	10325			10325	10325
Mayo (Rhodesia)	152007		7913		7913	7913
Rhodesia Gold Mining & Investment	300000		8616		8616	6462
Shamva Mines	500000	12402	5267	4857	22526	70394
United Rhodesia (6% debs)	69400		£ 4100		£ 4100	4100
West Africa						
Abbontiakoom	623577	42119	22404		64523	21508
Cinnamon Bippo	252595	23994	38102		62096	7762
Fanti Cons'd	597256	17763[a]			17763[a]	22204
Fanti Mines	447991		124019[b]		124019[b]	31005
Gold Coast Amalgamated	434282	37675	26797	8414	72886	68331
Presta Block A	496639		19808		19808	16094
Ropp Tin	30000		1300		1300	2925
West African Mines	100200	10300	3400	6400	20100	25125
						1836635

a. 10 shilling shares.
b. 5 shilling shares.

Table B.3. *Share and Debenture Holdings of the Goldfields Group in the Americas, 1913*

Company or government	Issued capital £	Holdings of CGFSA	Holdings of SAGT	Holdings of GMI	Total holdings	Par value of holdings £
North America						
American Trona (7% pfce)	613000		$72100		$72100	1451
Central Petroleum			$30398	$30399	$60797	12433
General Motors		$125000			$125000	25562
Gold Fields American	2000000	1800000	200000		2000000	1500000
Granville Mining	1380000		20995	20995	41990	31493
" " (6% debs)	900000		£ 18194	£ 18194	£ 36388	36388
Mississippi River Power	3272000		$147700	$110800	$258500	52863
" " (pfce)	1227000	$249900			$249900	51104
" " (bonds)	716000	$212100			$212100	43374
Natomas Cons'd	3102000		$25000		$25000	5112
" " (6% bonds)	2515000		$99200	$49600	$148800	30430
Northern Light & Power	613000		$82400		$82400	16850
" " (5% bonds)	409000		$96900		$96900	19816
Oroville Dredging	562098		69270	41060	110330	91942
Western Dominion Collieries	100000		£ 8600		£ 8600	8600
Yuba Cons'd Gold Fields			33520	9580	43100	43100
Central America						
General Petroleum		19555			19555	19555
Oro Grande Mines		$20000			$20000	4090
Trinidad Leaseholds	750000		15300		15300	15300
Vera Cruz Mexico Oil			8000	29827	37827	37827
" " " (notes)				£ 11300	£ 11300	11300
South America						
Anglo-Colombian Devp't	250000	40636	16000	16000	56636	56636
Brazil Gov't (5%)			£ 9400		£ 9400	9400
Electric Light of Cochabamba (6%)	300000		£ 17400		£ 17400	17400
						2142026

Table B.4. *Share and Debenture Holdings of the Goldfields Group in Miscellaneous Securities, 1913*

Company or government	*Issued capital*	*Holdings of CGFSA*	*Holdings of SAGT*	*Holdings of GMI*	*Total holdings*	*Market value of holdings £*
British Cyanides (6% pfce)			18749		18749	7083
British Gov't Securities		£ 400739			£ 400739	400739
Maikop Combine (6%)			£ 6670	£ 6670	£ 13340	13340
Singapore Electric			17375		17375	17375
CGFSA (ordy)			5051		5051	5051
" (1st pfce)			18821		18821	18821
" (2nd pfce)			60097		60097	60097
GMI	500000	113559	39050		152609	104547
Misc debs & shares		£ 302256	£ 15305	£ 43000	360561	335561
						962614

Table B.5. ***Market Value of Share and Debenture Holdings of the Goldfields Group, 1913***

Africa	£	£
Transvaal Gold Mines	4289694	
Union of South Africa	533739	
Southern Africa	1107942	
West Africa	194954	
Subtotal		6126329
Americas		
North America	1970518	
Central America	88072	
South America	83436	
Subtotal		2142026
Other Investments		
Britain	407822	
Other	554792	
Subtotal		962614
Total		9230969

Index